IMMIGRATION, NATIONALITY AND CITIZENSHIP

SATVINDER S. JUSS

**With a Foreword by
The Hon. Mr Justice Stephen Sedley**

MANSELL

To My Parents

First published 1993 by
Mansell Publishing Limited. A Cassell Imprint
Villiers House, 41/47 Strand, London WC2N 5JE, England
387 Park Avenue South, New York, New York 10016–8810, USA

© Satvinder S. Juss 1993

Reprinted in paperback 1994

British Library Cataloguing in Publication Data
Juss, Satvinder S.
    Immigration, Nationality and
    Citizenship. – (Citizenship & the Law Series)
    I. Title II. Series
    344.10282

    ISBN 0–7201–2149–3 (Hardback)
    ISBN 0–7201–2212–0 (Paperback)

Library of Congress Cataloging-in-Publication Data
Juss, Satvinder S. (Satvinder Singh)
    Immigration, nationality and citizenship/Satvinder S. Juss.
        p.   cm. – (Citizenship and the law series)
    Includes bibliographical references and index.
    ISBN 0–7201–2149–3 (Hardback)
    ISBN 0–7201–2212–0 (Paperback)
        1. Emigration and immigration law – Great Britain.   2. Citizenship –
    Great Britain.   3. Aliens – Great Britain.   I. Title.   II. Series.
    KD4134.J87   1993
    342.41′082 – dc20
    [344.10282]   93–13688
                                                                                      CIP

Printed and bound in Great Britain by
Biddles Ltd, Guildford and King's Lynn

CITIZENSHIP AND THE LAW
SERIES

General Editor
ROBERT BLACKBURN

King's College, University of London

Contents

'In other words we have established one of the less liberal and one of the most arbitrary systems of immigration law in the world – in the civilised world at any rate.'

Lord Chancellor, Lord Hailsham
(HC Deb., col. 150, 8 March 1971)

Foreword

Societies have to define themselves, for they are simultaneously inclu-
ive and exclusive. They define themselves politically by constituting
comprehensive systems of lawful authority, geographically by setting
and defending their frontiers, and demographically by determining
who is to have the right to live within the frontiers.

That nineteenth-century artefact, the nation-state, has attempted
by its mere name to conflate two of these essentially distinct things
and to treat as a natural unity the population of a country (the nation)
and its polity (the state). In fact the pressures of economics, politics,
climate and inhumanity have kept human communities fragmenting
and re-forming since time began. States too have come and gone, but
until recent times the percolation or migration of individuals or
populations across their frontiers has been perennial. Such migrations
have not necessarily been unsolicited or informal, as the Statue of
Liberty still anachronistically reminds the world. Britain itself, as this
book reminds us, has historically been open to a wide variety of
visitors, if less so to settlers. But the territoriality of nationhood has
now reached a point where the price of systematic inclusion is
systematic exclusion. It is for this reason that the member states of the
European Community have had to lower their frontiers to each other's
citizens in order to give effect to Article 48 of the Treaty of Rome and
to permit the free movement of workers within the Community; while
their external frontiers have been correspondingly reinforced.

Nevertheless, the spectre at every nation-state's feast is the imper-
manence of much of what is publicly taken for granted. At any point
of history the state silently assumes the fixity of its territorial and
demographic composition (save exceptionally where territorial ambi-
tions or ethnic cleansing policies are openly articulated), and against

these it measures what accessions to its population it can tolerate. In much the same way, as recent historiography has shown, societies invent their own traditions, recreating the past in the image of the present. Yet national identity and consciousness, multi-faceted as they are, change constantly and sometimes dramatically. Professor Eric Hobsbawm in his important volume *Nations and Nationalism since 1870* remarks on this fact and comments that this is the area of national studies in which thinking and research are most urgently needed today. He points out that at the very time when the principle of nationality seems to have achieved hegemony in the world, it is ceasing to be a major vector of historical development. The economic unit which the nation-state was designed to be is increasingly non-viable, and nationalism has consequently become an increasingly negative and divisive phenomenon as the demands of the world economy for a new international division of labour maginalize its usefulness. The case in favour of 'ethno-political' groupings advanced by Tom Nairn and others is a difficult one which accepts a sometimes unpalatable contemporary reality at the cost of economic viability, and often of much more.

Yet a fundamental imperative keeps nation-states attempting to regenerate and preserve themselves, and to recreate their own history, in their current self-image. It is an endeavour which inevitably stresses uniformity at the expense of diversity. In the United Kingdom the paradox is particularly acute, for the state's very name draws attention to the fact that it is composed of several nations, unified only at the level of the state. It is this political unity, however, which has impressed the outside world. As a distinguished Kenyan Asian lawyer has remarked, the British are known to much of the world's population as energetic visitors, and visitors who did not historically take kindly to hosts who failed to welcome them; yet they now show a remarkable measure of diffidence when their former hosts try to visit them.

The society which identifies itself by exclusion in this way is, however, enormously diverse, and diverse in ways which defy categorization. The black soldier or police officer who, in uniform, represents the British state, to many white people still represents the stranger within the gates. (So does the Northumbrian to the Geordie or the Arsenal supporter to the Spurs supporter.) He or she may support the West Indies at cricket without forfeiting his or her role as a representative of the state; or support England without being able to earn acceptance as 'one of us'. The same individual on the city streets may be a Grenadian when speaking to a Jamaican. Their children will probably not know the difference, and will speak the same English dialect as the other children on their street, but they will never in our lifetime be allowed to shed the consciousness of being black. They are the visible minorities who cannot melt into the crowd.

This is the backdrop against which modern governments have been called upon to make provision for immigration control. It is almost 90 years now since control was first introduced at ports of entry, using the single criterion of 'desirability'. The wave of immigrants to which the Aliens Act 1905 responded was from the Jewish populations of eastern Europe, but since then endless upheavals have brought fresh waves of people to the United Kingdom seeking safety, work and shelter. Satvinder Juss's important thesis is that each wave has been met with a legislative response, but that none has been preceded by or has resulted in a worked-out policy derived more from fact and principle than from perceptions of short-term advantages and difficulties. In this respect the United Kingdom's immigration laws contrast strikingly with its race relations legislation.

For Commonwealth citizens the door remained open until 1962, since when the imperial sense of obligation has had to yield to the perceived need for universal controls. But what are the true nature and extent of this need? A welcome visitor is not a burden; but if today's stranger at the gates is perceived as tomorrow's stranger within, his or her arrival will be unwelcome. In this and other ways immigration control is tightly bound up with race relations. But how they interact is the subject of more rhetoric than science, of eloquent silences, excessive protestations and redolent denials. It is readily assumed, and not only by the white population, that more than minimal coloured immigration (which is what the politics of immigration control are principally about) will exacerbate already poor race relations. It is less easy to face the possibility that poor race relations and racially restrictive immigration rules are two manifestations of a third and more fundamental problem: a response to visible minorities which has never been reasoned out and articulated as a medium- or long-term national policy. Dr Juss argues that fears have been allowed to be substituted for a proper appraisal both of the United Kingdom's needs and, equally important, of its obligations.

To undertake such an exercise would mean asking what fears are real and which are night-terrors in an unstable world. It would mean wondering whether the round-dance of racial prejudice and racial discrimination could be broken, and at what point. It would mean asking whether patriality was a means rather than an end, and whether umbilical connections were the best ones for determining rights of entry and abode.

Satvinder Juss approaches some of these issues through a critical appraisal of the United Kingdom's current and historic immigration controls. No book, this one included, will by itself afford a fully satisfying answer, but unless the right questions begin to be asked, and asked through the type of informed critique which this book offers, no progress will be made in an area of law which more than most touches fundamental human rights. When, as has now begun to happen, refugees from tyrannies in the Third World have to flee from racial persecution in the First World country in which they have sought asylum, the immediacy of the issues addressed by Dr Juss and their intimate linkage with one another stand out starkly. If it is through law that state policy on human rights is mediated, lawyers have a particular obligation to understand the issues, to think about them, and to be ready to respond professionally in the interests of the many people to whom other nation-states, or what remains of them, can no longer guarantee security or – sometimes – survival.

STEPHEN SEDLEY

Preface

'Once the people begin to reason, all is lost.' – *Voltaire* (Letter to Damilaville, 1 April 1766)

Oscar Wilde, in the preface to his only novel, *The Picture of Dorian Gray*, urged that 'There is no such thing as a moral or an immoral book. Books are well written, or badly written.' This is bound, however, to be a controversial book. It is about modern British immigration control, and it sets out to give a general account of that control by examining the main aspects of law and policy in this field over this century – a subject-matter that is controversial in itself.

This area is obviously important to particular sections of British society, as well as to advocates of civil rights and to those concerned with maintaining the high standards of law developed so rigorously by British judges in recent constitutional and administrative law. However, the subject has not always received the wide degree of critical interest that it clearly merits. Three times this century British politicians and the media have had the opportunity to debate immigration control – firstly over the wave of Jewish immigration early in the century, secondly over New Commonwealth immigrants, and now over asylum seekers from various strife-torn parts of the world. Yet this debate has always been remarkable in two important respects. On the one hand it has been characterized by what appears to have been an irrational fear of the stranger, coming often from a different culture. On the other hand, and leading on from this, it has been characterized by the way in which immigration was viewed at home as an issue important to electoral politics. It is the nature of this debate, and even lack of it, that ultimately accounts for the manner and style in which the various conflicting interests have been resolved by the major institutions of the state. This work is designed to throw light on this saga.

The method of this book is therefore necessarily not just descriptive but also prescriptive. Much legal writing in the United Kingdom is purely descriptive. This is a useful device where the purpose of the writer is to inform and instruct the reader about the formal law, and it is also an approach that ties in neatly with the traditional view of law-making and adjudication as a discrete activity. Law, however, is not value free. Legal provisions, it is true, are *in vacuo* neither moral nor immoral, but are amoral. However, the effects of any law or enactment are not amoral and that is why we often speak of a law as being a good law or a bad law. The fact is that laws in Western democracies, unlike those in dictatorial regimes, cannot be justified by their functional purpose alone. They must also be compatible with democratic principles. They must be just. That is why in an American immigration case in 1953 Mr Justice Jackson dissented, saying that 'basic fairness in hearing procedures does not vary with the status of the accused', since '[I]f they would be unfair to citizens, we cannot defend the fairness of them when applied to the more helpless and handicapped alien'.

A descriptive account of a bad law would inevitably succeed in reproducing the ideological assumptions of that law. In truth, as every area of public administration comprises a variety of opposing interests concerning the state and the individual, there exists the possibility of wide manoeuvrability for governments and a broad range of choices are open to them. It is the job of governments to respond to pressures, to evaluate their importance, before formulating policy. Laws therefore have to be placed in their appropriate social, political and economic contexts to understand how well governments fulfil their task of governing. Thus viewed, it becomes manifestly plain that both the law and the underlying basis of that law are a matter for legitimate public debate and concern. Indeed, only then can one usefully speak of what is a 'good' and what is a 'bad' practice of the law. Consequently, in an effort to apply the maxim of Mr Justice Brandeis of the American Supreme Court in 1927, that to expose falsehoods one needs 'more speech, not enforced silence', the writer has quoted directly from a wide range of sources – from the opinions of judges, the writings of academics, lawyers, and eminent public figures, to the speeches of politicians and the utterances of remonstrative voluntary organizations – to substantiate his own conclusions about the law in this area, arrived at after some years of researching, lecturing, and finally practising in this particular field of public administration. In so compiling this book the writer has not infrequently felt, like John Keats, that ultimately '[A]ll writing is a form of prayer'.

Chapter 1 of this book deals with the latest clamour for immigration controls, with the asylum issue, and with the need for a coherent and fair immigration policy. Chapter 2 focuses on a brief history of modern British immigration control, from the Aliens legislation of

1905 to the British Nationality (Hong Kong) Act 1990, and emphasizes the link with nationality law. Chapter 3 examines the development of New Commonwealth immigration and the gradual promulgation of controls, but uses the comparative technique in relation to the earlier Jewish influx as a device to identify the main problems of law and administration in this area. Chapter 4 is an analysis of freedom of movement in Europe, which is expounded at length to demonstrate how an open-door policy is still practicable for industrialized countries in specific cases. Chapter 5 is the first of two sections explaining the legal process in this area, and looks at the apparatus of the immigration appeals system, entry clearance Officers, the Home Office, and the work of representative organizations. The second section on the legal process is Chapter 6 which describes and analyses the immigration rules and extra-statutory discretionary immigration control.

The writer wishes to thank Professor Paul O'Higgins for his unceasing guidance and friendship over the years ever since he first supervised him in Cambridge many years ago. He is most grateful to the Honourable Mr Justice Stephen Sedley, a High Court Judge, for the contribution of a Foreword to this work. He wishes also to record his very warm thanks to Dr Robert Blackburn for his earnest enthusiasm for the inclusion of this work in Mansell's Citizenship and the Law series, and for the many helpful remarks that he subsequently made to assist the writer. Thanks are likewise due to Miss Veronica Higgs, Mr Peter Harrison and the publishers for their patience and encouragement. Oxford University Press kindly gave permission to publish material that appears in Chapter 6. The writer must single out for praise the talent and commitment of Miss Kathryn Bates, who cheerfully proceeded to type each chapter in manuscript form almost as fast as the subsequent one was being written up. A great debt is owed by the writer to his family. To his two brothers and sisters-in-law, Tarvinder and Baljeet, and Warinder and Kanwal, he owes an incalculable debt for their constant affection and support over the years and for this work. It is hoped that the end product meets up with their expectation. To his parents, the writer owes his deepest gratitude. They set an example for hard work and industry, even in old age, to which he can only aspire. Last, but by no means least, the writer thanks his wife, Rani. As she does everything better than he, she would no doubt have written this book better than the writer, had she first applied her mind to it.

This book is lovingly dedicated by the writer to his parents.

December 1992   SATVINDER S. JUSS
                                                         4 King's Bench Walk
                                                     Temple, London EC4Y 7DL

Table of Cases

Table of Statutes

Table of Statutory Instruments

1

Contemporary Issues in British
Citizenship Laws*

'Democracy passes into Despotism' – (*Plato*)

INTRODUCTION

In 1783 Boswell found Dr Johnson to be 'a stern true-born English-
man', and one who was 'fully prejudiced against all other nations'.
Boswell did not say whether other nations were any less prejudiced but
went on to comment on that 'cold reserve too common among
Englishmen towards strangers'.[1] Blackstone found the position in law
to be no different. He had earlier observed that whilst the children of
aliens born in England were 'natural-born subjects', Jews did not share
in the same civil privileges as their fellow subjects.[2] Yet Blackstone it
was who also recorded that 'Great tenderness is shown by our laws not
only to foreigners in distress . . . but with regard also to the admission
of strangers who came spontaneously.'[3] Such remarks betray an
obvious ambivalence and paradox in public policies in respect of
people who are seen, and sometimes continued to be seen (as Blackstone himself recognized), as strangers. Dicey, in his pre-eminent
definition of the British Constitution, wrote that 'here every man,
whatever be his rank or condition, is subject to the ordinary law of the
realm and amenable to the jurisdiction of the ordinary tribunals'.[4]
Yet the definition of who 'belongs' to the state is not assisted by the
idea of equality before the law. When recently two distinguished
writers on immigration and nationality law wrote that 'The history of
British nationality law is a story without a central character'[5] it was
this inconsistency and ambivalence in public attitudes that they were
referring to.

Immigration control should be taken seriously because it tells us
not only about a country's attitude to those without, but also to those
within it. It is trite to say that how a country treats its immigrants is a

1

reflection of its commitment to civil liberties. It is less well recognized that through its definitions of belongers and non-belongers, of desirables and undesirables, a community is able to define the sort of internal society it wants. A government may use immigration laws to define its internal political priorities. Perhaps the most striking example is Israel, which under its Law of Return permits all Jews to return. Despite its small size and heavy reliance on outside aid its population has expanded fourfold since its inception. Everyone who returns is assisted on arrival with subsidized housing, intensive instruction in Hebrew and help in finding a job. A more instructive example is Sweden, which, whilst formally recognizing the status of 'guest-workers' for some immigrants, nevertheless aspires to a sense of community with other Nordic countries and maintains a liberal policy on refugees. The effect internally is that not only do over half Sweden's foreign subjects come from these Nordic countries but that education, medical care, rent subsidies and loans for housing to newly-wed couples are available to all just as they are to Swedes. Moreover, there is an ethnic press, subsidized by the government, which serves minority groups.

This is what may be termed a nation's immigrant policy, and it is directly linked to its immigration policy. Immigrant policy refers to all the conditions under which resident immigrants live. It refers to education, medical health, and housing facilities, to social services and social benefits, to cultural amenities (including language instruction), leisure activities and voluntary associations. It refers to working conditions, membership of trade unions and participation in political affairs. If there is a harsh immigration policy in respect of some people it is unrealistic to expect an immigrant policy to succeed in being kind to those very same people. The problem could not have been more admirably expressed than by Lester and Bindman in their seminal work, who explain how the law would therefore have two faces:

> One face confronts the stranger at the gate; the other is
> turned towards the stranger within. They express the
> ambivalence of public policies. The hostile expression of our
> immigration law casts doubt upon the friendly expression of
> our race relations law. However much our legislators might
> wish it otherwise, the hostility is taken more seriously than
> the friendliness – on both sides of the colour line. . . . If our
> immigration laws are racially discriminatory in their aims and
> effect, it becomes difficult to persuade employers, workers,
> property and house-owners to treat people on their merits,
> regardless of race.[6]

Sir Norman Anderson in his Hamlyn Lectures, *Liberty, Law and Justice*, also remarked that:

it is idle to imagine that a law which discriminates against the admission of further coloured immigrants will not blunt the effect of legislation designed to lessen the prejudices which undoubtedly exist against those who are already here.[7]

Clearly, therefore, what is needed here is a uniform and coherent approach by a state to all its laws, including its immigration, nationality and citizenship laws, for as the Reverend Kenneth Leech has recently commented, '[R]acism is indivisible. It cannot be opposed at one point and supported at another'.[8]

Immigration control is a necessary function of the modern nation-state and an inevitable reality of the modern world. Under international law statehood is dependent upon the right of nations to exclusive competence in respect of their internal affairs,[9] so the regulation of a country's population through its municipal law is an essential attribute of its sovereignty. Thus in 1905 the first modern piece of British immigration legislation was passed in the form of the Aliens Act to curb Jewish immigration from the pogroms of tsarist Russia and 'to prevent this country being made a receptacle for destitute, diseased and criminal aliens'.[10] The Commonwealth Immigrants Act 1962 was the second modern piece, passed some fifty years later during a period of increased New Commonwealth immigration from the colonies, to check 'unemployment, overcrowding, and to foster racial harmony'.[11] Yet those surveys that had been undertaken were generally favourable to immigration.[12] Now in the 1990s, world problems in Eastern Europe, the Middle East and Africa have brought about the spectre of a third spate of large-scale immigration – the largest since the Second World War – to the borders of Western Europe and to Britain.

This book sets out to explain how throughout this modern period the underlying issues of immigration control have remained substantially unchanged. Issues of immigration, nationality and freedom of movement have raised the same time-worn questions of basic individual rights and the state interest. Yet, despite a century's experience of modern immigration control and more than thirty years' experience of post-war colonial immigration, each time the government of the day has shown itself to be inept in the handling of these issues. Nothing has been new in this regard save the novelty of the event in a new historical setting. Policymakers, it is submitted, must now learn from their experience and look more widely at the nature and phenomenon of migration if they are to develop a rational immigration policy that meets the demands of the late twentieth century in a world that is increasingly volatile.

THE ISSUES

Throughout its long history, Britain has actually operated an unplanned open-door immigration policy. In the words of Geoffrey Robertson QC, in his *Freedom, the Individual and the Law*:

> Historically, the United Kingdom has a more liberal record than most: the blue-plaques around London bear testimony to the home it was to Marx, Mazzini, Garibaldi, Lenin, Engels, Kropotkin, Kossuth and Sun Yat-San.[13]

Vaughan Bevan, in his excellent *The Development of British Immigration Law*, states that 'the United Kingdom's record in immigration is far from unique', and is actually favourable.[14] This record is no doubt owed to the common law tradition, which was generally regarded as the law of freedom. Basic freedoms did not have to be defined, only the restrictions upon them did, with the result that what was left over was referred to as the subject's residual freedoms. For aliens, the open door ended only after the 1905 Aliens Act. For Commonwealth citizens the ending of the open door was delayed until the Act of 1962 because of the Crown's distaste for placing restrictions on a subject's liberty, a distaste that emanated from the common law traditions of allegiance and protection, the twin pillars that determined the subject's freedom. In these circumstances, when control came eventually, it was *ad hoc* and reactive, and not planned and proactive. Control was not based on any a priori determination of the needs of housing, education, public health and employment, which alone can decide a country's capacity for social absorption. The result was the enactment of an exclusion policy rather than an immigration policy properly so called. To develop a more modern system of immigration control it is necessary to abandon the old shibboleths.

The Immigration Act 1971 provides the legal basis for the modern control of immigration in Britain. Yet in the debates on that Act basic alternative views as to whether immigration constitutes a 'problem' and, if it does, according to what principles a solution should be sought were not developed. Nor was the basis of the policy which the machinery established by the Bill was supposed to implement made clear at any stage in the debates on this critical piece of legislation. There was, and there has since been, little interest in immigration of patrials, EC nationals or foreign nationals, and immigration figures have been rarely placed in the context of net migration, which has resulted in a net loss of population in the post-war period. It is frequently said, however, that the majority of those leaving are white whilst the majority of those entering are black; but there has for many years now been a net outflow of people to the West Indies.

Immigration law in the United Kingdom has not been discussed in terms of its intended policy, nor has it been looked at in the broader context of post-war European immigration. Always it has been discussed in terms of numbers and always with a view to keeping these down. Discussions of numbers alone is meaningless if only because between 1971 and 1983 more than 450,000 more people left the United Kingdom than entered it. Moreover, as Ann Dummett has explained in *A New Immigration Policy*:

> No country has, or can have, a policy on immigration whose sole purpose is with the numbers of people entering that country, year by year. . . . We must ask: what kind of people are encouraged to come and what kind are refused admission? What are the reasons for preferring some kind to others? For what purposes are they admitted? What conditions are attached to their stay?[15]

In fact, according to *Social Trends*, the Government's annual statistical survey, with the ageing of the larger generation born after the Second World War, deaths could exceed births around the year 2030, whereupon the population will begin to decline in Britain unless immigration acts as a balancing factor. The International Labour Organisation (ILO) has also found that although the industrialized economies of the Western world would be reluctant to welcome new migrants, skilled labour is going to be needed in the future if sustained economic growth is to be maintained.

This means that manpower needs and economic effects are essential criteria for consideration alongside the matters of social absorption that we have discussed above. A properly called immigration policy must deal with such cogent and cogitable criteria. Parliament – or the European Community inasmuch as it is at that level that immigration policy will now be fashioned in its major parts – should take it upon itself to discuss the nature of migration, and a variety of differing forms of immigration control before taking away vested immigration rights.

Parliament should ensure, and the British Parliament alone *can* ensure, that any new development in this area does not abridge its historic relationship with the New Commonwealth. At present, citizens of the Commonwealth countries are not aliens because those countries are not foreign countries, the Commonwealth being in law an amalgam of equals. There should be discussion, if at all possible, of the optimum levels of population and discussion of how such optima can be determined. International and humanitarian obligations should not be ignored, including the United Kingdom's obligation to the Hong Kong Chinese; they were, after all, not ignored in respect of the Falkland Islanders. The discussion, moreover, should be placed in the context of Irish immigration and UK membership of the EC, which ensures the free admission to Britain of workers from member countries.

Britain can begin this process by examining the nature of post-war European immigration more closely. The British policy of favouring colonial immigrants, although inevitable in the circumstances, being based on a common bond of citizenship and the continuance of post-independence links overseas, has nevertheless had the effect of delaying for the time, or preventing, the formulation of a well structured, coherent and balanced immigration policy. Britain has not been alone, however, but has, together with such countries as France and The Netherlands, received large-scale post-colonial immigration that has been the direct result of the more benign aspects of an imperial relationship between the mother country and its subject peoples. No country in Western Europe dealt with the large-scale labour migration of the 1960s with a ready-made proactive immigration policy. The attitude of most countries was *laissez-faire*, with immigration being left largely to the decisions of employers and job seekers on the labour market. Only Germany actively recruited foreign labour for temporary work on a guest-worker basis.[16] The exception, however, was Britain, which, unlike such countries as France, The Netherlands and Sweden, was not *laissez-faire*, choosing to engage in the control of New Commonwealth immigration. Unlike many other countries in Western Europe, Britain also saw immigration as an area of political controversy and partisan conflict. Political parties competed for the control of immigration. Zig Layton-Henry explains that:

> it was the electoral victory of Peter Griffiths in the General Election of 1964 that had the most decisive impact on policymaking. After a strong anti-immigrant campaign Griffiths captured the Labour constituency of Smethwick, unseating Patrick Gordon-Walker, the prospective foreign secretary. His achievement was dramatic because he gained a swing to the Conservative Party of 7.5 per cent in an election where the national swing to the Labour Party was 3.2 per cent.[17]

Consequently, Britain instituted controls much sooner than other major European countries such as France and Germany, being much more concerned about the social and political aspects of immigration from the New Commonwealth. To quote Zig Layton-Henry again:

> The growth of the British economy in the 1950s and 1960s was slow and punctuated by crises over the balance of

payments and the role of sterling and by worries about inflation. It was also a period of rapid withdrawal from imperial commitments and a realisation by British leaders and people of their declining world status. In such a situation immigration was seen as an added burden – not as a valuable asset.[18]

Yet the fact is that Britain need not have taken this route in the way that it did. A comparison shows that although other European countries differ in their approach to immigration for a variety of traditional, historical and geographical reasons, they do share a common experience of two world wars, of similar ideologies, and of similar political and economic conditions which suggest that Britain did not have to take such a political stance on immigration nor to institute controls so quickly. Moreover, whilst it is true that the post-war economic boom is now over and that all European countries have seen fit to restrict immigration in the slump that followed the first oil crisis of the early 1970s, The Netherlands has still managed to relax the rules for family reunification to protect human rights, which is a cornerstone of its foreign policy. There was, and is, no reason why family reunification cannot be a matter of the highest priority for Britain in dealing with the cases of New Commonwealth immigrants and other newcomers. Indeed, Sweden has learnt early from its experience with a common Nordic labour market – as Britain should have learnt from its special relationship with the Commonwealth – to balance ideas of free movement with protecting its economic interests. Instead, Britain continues even today to take measures that adversely affect the most vulnerable groups in society. Recent initiatives to impose fines[19] on airlines that bring in immigrants without proper documentation strike at asylum seekers as the largest single group. Yet the statement by Peter Lloyd, the Immigration Minister, that 'nearly all Western countries have similar provisions' is belied by the facts that only five countries in Western Europe impose sanctions and none as harshly as Britain.[20] The irony is that asylum is not just a moral but an international legal commitment; and wrongfully to deny it is, as Sir Louis Blom-Cooper QC says, 'a betrayal of some of the finest and bravest people in the world, as well as of a decent society in Britain'.[21]

The second thing that Britain can do is to play a lead role in Europe because as from 1992 it no longer has absolute control over the development of its immigration policy. Its role in this regard is gradually being whittled away by Community law, which will determine who enters and who settles in a Community country. If Britain does not forge ahead here it will find that other countries with a more sober experience of immigration control will leave Britain with an ever-diminishing role over matters, such as its Commonwealth ties, over which it should rightfully show the most paramount concern. At Maastricht in December 1991 Britain, perhaps short-sightedly, insisted that immigration should be one of the areas of policymaking that should be taken outside the competence of the European Commission. The result is that it is now handled by an *ad hoc* group of interior ministers on immigration under the auspices of the Trevi Ministerial Group on security and counter terrorism. Had the matter been left to be dealt with under the Brussels Convention there would have been open public and parliamentary debate in both the European and national legislatures. Instead, changes to policy can now be made quite surreptitiously by European interior ministers.

This is what happened recently with the draft European frontiers convention regarding unwanted aliens that was agreed in 1991, but which had not been signed because of a dispute between Britain and Spain over the status of Gibraltar. This draft convention contains a common European blacklist of undesirable aliens and is generally regarded as paving the way for a common European visa. Some observers believe that it will eventually impose a restriction on Commonwealth citizens who wish to enter Britain and who have previously not required entry permits. Yet, when these matters were put by a *Guardian* journalist to the British Home Secretary, Kenneth Clarke, he confessed to ignorance of the draft convention because it is kept secret from the public, press and Parliament.[22] When on 1 July 1992 Britain assumed the presidency of the Community, and the Home Secretary the chair of the interior ministerial group for the next six months, it should have taken the lead and insisted on the publication of this draft.

This is wishful thinking, however. Recent calls by Germany for a national quota for placing refugees fleeing from the former Yugoslavia and Soviet Union were rejected by Britain and other European Community countries.[23] At Maastricht it was Germany, not Britain, that tried in vain to argue that once the internal borders of the Community came down in 1992, it will be fairer and easier if there is a common policy by which member states can share out the burden of vetting, housing and eventually integrating refugees and asylum seekers. Yet *The Times* must have spoken for many when it said, '[I]n the greatest human upheaval on the Continent since the Second World War it was important that '[H]aving failed to stop the fighting, the world must not fail the refugees'.[24] After Germany received a record number[25] of refugees (265,000 in 1991) rioting broke out in August 1992 at the eastern German port of Rostock[26] and, unpalatable as it may seem, changes to Germany's Basic Law, which guarantees the automatic right of all refugees to claim asylum, now seem imminent. Yet Bonn's Commissioner for refugees, in her annual report in July 1992, referred to the irrepressible fact that without Germany's six million foreigners, whole sections of the economy would close down or operate only with extreme difficulty. It was time to take emotionalism out of the debate over whether Germany was a country of immigration, she said.[27] On the other hand, an influx of new immigrants was also said to threaten France,[28] Spain[29] and Italy.[30] As *The Times* explained only too well, however:

> the statistics do not support any belief that Western Europe is being 'invaded' by immigrants from east and south. In 1973 immigration to the 12 countries of the European Community was 1.2 million. In 1990, it was down to 800,000. INSEE, the French state institute of statistics that published these figures, has caused uproar in France by saying that on current demographic trends the country will need more, not less, immigrants next decade than the current 125,000 a year to keep the population stable. England's fertility rate is similar to that of France. Across Western Europe, ageing populations are stretching social security budgets. In Italy, there are already more people over 60 than under 20. Unmet demands for skilled labour will increase over the coming decade.[31]

Bernard Levin argued that for centuries Britain had gained from immigrants and should go on welcoming them. To Home Office claims of a thousand new applicants a week, Mr Levin, in his characteristic way, replied: '50,000 a year is a million in 20 years, about one fifty-fifth of our present population – which . . . is steadily falling. Can we really be afraid of a couple of percentage points?'[32]

THE AMBIVALENCE AND PARADOX IN PUBLIC POLICIES

The fundamental problem is that the importance of immigration is not recognized by British policymakers; it is not that the importance of immigration control is not appreciated by others. Not only has the immigration debate gone wrong in this respect, it has gone drastically wrong. Even though it cannot be said of Britain, as Professor Legomsky says of America, that there 'immigration touches everyone' (as the 'vast majority of us are either immigrants ourselves or the recent descendants of immigrants'), so that to that extent 'the effects of United States immigration policy are pervasive',[33] nevertheless, Professor Legomsky recognizes its importance to be no less relevant in Britain:

> The magnitudes of the sometimes competing national and individual interests, the foreign affairs ramifications, the

economic impact of immigrants, the environmental issues, and the social, cultural, racial and philosophical questions raised by immigration control all coalesce to make this area a prime target for heated argument.[34]

A. Dummett and A. Nicol draw attention to the subject's 'enormous contemporary importance' because it raises vital questions 'about law-making in general' and about 'changing ideas concerning the nation and the body politic in British history' and about 'contemporary national and international politics'.[35] J. Hutton rates the study of immigration law highly on at least two fronts: 'First, the questions of immigration and nationality have consistently been one of the most politically controversial areas of post-war legislation', and secondly, the subject 'provides a delicate combination of statutory and non-statutory rules together with a burgeoning volume of judicial precedent' so that mastery of 'a highly complicated legal framework and eventually the ability to operate these rules in courts and in tribunals' is required.[36] Thus the importance of immigration law is recognized as a subject by lawyers, academics and other specialists.

Yet the consensus is that, on the whole, British policymakers have not understood that importance. In the post-war era, according to Zig Layton-Henry, British politicians saw immigration and race relations 'as emotional, irrational and intractable matters, not amenable to the reason, negotiation and compromise which characterized economic and class issues'. Consequently, they wished 'to avoid or suppress'[37] such issues and not confront them. The emphasis therefore fell on immigration control and restriction, which has quite plainly had the effect of throwing out the baby with the bath water. Three areas of potential difficulty which have figured most prominently in the British immigration experience may be examined in support of this thesis. These are (1) employment and economic problems; (2) cultural and social problems; and (3) political and electoral problems.

Employment and Economic Problems

In his comparative study on the French and British attitude to post-war immigration, Gary Freeman explained that on the employment front 'only the French have even the rudiments of such a policy. The manpower aspects of British immigration decisions must be interpreted as wishful thinking at best and a ruse to cover up racial discrimination at worst.' The British, he believed, had failed 'to understand that immigration could contribute to the resolution of their economic woes',[38] and at the time '[T]he Conservative Party behaved as if the economic health of the country were the furthest thing from its mind'.

He concludes by saying that once it was decided to institute controls, 'no proper and rational basis for choosing one system over another was ever uncovered'.[39]

If we examine the first major immigration legislation of the post-war period, we find that the Commonwealth Immigrants Act of 1962 was passed on the grounds of 'unemployment, overcrowding, and to foster racial harmony'. Implicit in the unemployment argument is the theme that the changing requirements of British capitalism in the 1960s necessitated the shift in state policies on New Commonwealth immigrants from settler-citizen to migrant contract-worker. The shift would preserve the stratum of cheap labour for the British economy to carry out essential jobs which the indigenous white workforce was unwilling to perform. The truth, as Freeman's study shows, is otherwise. Ben-Tovim and Gabriel in their analysis demonstrate that there were additional autonomous ideological and political factors at play here which impinged on the economic sphere and thereby prevented the government of the day from fully addressing the unemployment issue in any proper way.[40]

When in 1985 three women from Britain complained before the European Commission of Human Rights that being settled in the UK they were prevented from being joined there by their husbands, the Government replied that allowing them to be so joined would pave the way for 5700 new entrants who would harm the employment situation at home. The women alleged sex discrimination because men could bring in wives but the women could not bring in husbands, and they alleged infringement of family life. The Commission rejected the Government's argument on the grounds that the pro-posed figure (revised from the Government's initial 2500 figure of prospective entrants) constituted only 0.02 per cent of the working population and would therefore make no significant impact on employment in Britain. Besides, such economic arguments could not justify sex discrimination and the detrimental consequences on the family lives of the women concerned. Moreover, the Commission also found unacceptable the argument of 'public tranquillity', as the Government had not shown that the measures in question enhanced good race relations, for although they may respond to the fears of a certain section of the population, they may create resentment in that part of the immigrant population which views the policy as unfair.[41]

A case such as this demonstrates that there are other less logical and rational forces at play here. In 1962 the Conservative Party applied for the first time controls to Commonwealth citizens while still maintaining an almost mystical reverence for the Commonwealth. Equally remarkable was the context of subsequent legislation where the liberal ethic of 'equal rights' in both parties was not considered to be irreconcilable with unequal treatment for New Commonwealth immigrants in those laws.[42] There was no ideological paradox felt by the Labour Party in arguing for universal brotherhood and internationalism while passing the second Commonwealth Immigrants Act in 1968. Neither the Government of the day in arguing its case, nor the Opposition in attacking its proposals, has thus far dealt with the problems of the nature of migration, on what basis it should be controlled, and what kind of control mechanisms it would be proper to adopt. Political considerations and not economic needs have in essence been uppermost in the minds of policymakers.

Cultural and Social Problems

It is said that cultural and social problems are caused by increased immigration. We have seen earlier that for some years now more people from the ethnic minorities have been leaving Britain than entering it, so that this in itself puts paid to any simplistic argument concerning social problems. Culture is more closely associated with national characteristics, and certainly these are worth preserving and protecting. But the concept bears closer scrutiny. Boswell for his part had no doubt that 'there is no permanent national character; it varies according to circumstances.[43] Orwell, passionate patriot that he was, recognized in his essay 'England Your England' that on coming to England from any European country one cannot mistake the fact that '[T]he beer is bitterer, the coins are heavier, the grass is greener, the advertisements are more blatant. The crowds in the big towns, with their mild knobbly faces, their bad teeth, and gentle manners, are different from a European crowd.' But even so, Orwell was the first to recognize that '[N]ational characteristics are not easy to pin down, and when pinned they often turn out to be trivialities or seem to have no connexion with one another'.[44] The fact is, as Dummett and Nicol explain in their recent work:

> we are unlikely to see British culture – for example – defined
> in terms of sport, drink, dodging authority and having a
> good laugh, or of English poetry and drama, or of a mixture
> of common sense, eccentricity and bloody mindedness,
> though any of these could reasonably be called characteristic.
> You can pick what you like to be a culture or even invent
> one if you are in power, and there will be a strong
> temptation to pick one that suggests excluding people you
> want to exclude anyway.[45]

The Universal Declaration of Human Rights refers to each person in Article 22 'as a member of society' having the cultural rights 'indispensable for his dignity and the free development of his personality'. Article 27 states, 'Everyone has the right to freely participate in the cultural life of the community, to enjoy the arts and to share in scientific advancement and its benefits'. In the same way, the UN Covenant on Economic Social and Cultural Rights 1966 defines cultural rights in an expansive and not restrictive form, giving every person the right to an educational and cultural life and to partake in the gains of scientific development. Consequently, to quote Dummett and Nicol again, 'culture is a matter of personal development, to be pursued in association with others as one chooses, within a social framework that has no necessary correlation with the boundaries of a state'.[46]

There is nothing therefore to protect as such; but there is something to promote and enhance, and that is pride in our inheritance and an inculcation of values in ourselves and our citizenry that preserves our culture in literature, the arts, and the sciences. That does not require cultural aggressiveness on our part, and it does not require the prevention of indigenous cultural practices in immigrants. Contrary to popular belief, the immigrants' culture, in the words of Bernard Levin, 'isn't just food; the cultures and religions they brought have given us philosophies, insights and profundities of immense value to us all'.[47] Increased freedom of movement across borders will arguably enhance the cultural rights of all, not diminish them. Yet, when the Immigration Act 1971 was passed, Reginald Maudling, the Home Secretary, spoke of 'the simple fact . . . that some control had become necessary in the interests of society in this country',[48] and the 1962 Commonwealth Immigrants Act was passed, in part, to prevent 'overcrowding and to foster racial harmony'.[49]

There was no evidence or investigation of any rationally assessable harms that it could be said would eventuate in the absence of these and other legislative enactments. To speak of 'racial harmony' presupposes that a racial problem existed in 1962 and that the best way to deal with it was by cutting numbers through a new Immigration Act. Numbers can, of course, be reduced in this way but there is no evidence to suggest that any of the Immigration Acts have helped race relations in Britain. If anything, the contrary seems to have been true.[50] Why these initiatives were taken can, however, be better understood if we turn to our third and most important analysis.

Political and Electoral Problems

It is in the political arena that we see the most vivid manifestation of all the salient features of immigration and its control. In the General Election of 9 April 1992 immigration played a minor role as an issue.

Early in the campaign the Foreign Secretary, Douglas Hurd, described the Government's proposed Asylum Bill as 'an honest attempt to streamline and accelerate the system of identifying refugees'.[51] Little was then heard of this, except when the prospect of a Conservative defeat grew ever more likely in the opinion polls. Three days before the election the immigration issue was then seized upon dramatically by the Home Secretary, Kenneth Baker. Seasoned observers saw in this a last-ditch attempt to prevent Tory support slipping among skilled workers and their families. The Home Secretary dealt with the more important electoral issue of proportional representation in Britain from the Liberal Democrats by coupling it with an inevitably less vigorous control over immigrants and bogus asylum seekers that he said could unleash extremists.

When the leader of the Liberal Democrats, Paddy Ashdown, said '[I]t remains our view that we should honour the rights of passport holders in Hong Kong' and that Britain should absorb a 'significant influx' of the 4.5 million Hong Kong Chinese, Kenneth Baker strongly criticized him even though Paddy Ashdown was of the opinion that not all would want to come.[52] In fact, the use of the 'immigration card' for political gain in a General Election was not actually necessary, for the Conservatives were only too easily returned to power. Indeed by this time the number of applicants had fallen by more than half, possibly because various measures had by then been taken by the Government, such as that since November 1991 asylum seekers had been required to go in person to the Home Office to make their application rather than just apply by post. The figures for the first three months of 1992 showed an average of 1730 applications a month compared with 3730 a month in 1991,[53] a figure that has remained fairly static since then.

Was the rigorous stance on the immigration issue by the Government really necessary, therefore? How do political parties decide to react to this particularly sensitive issue? Do they have any choice? Do party politicians have a choice? In her book, *Immigration and Social Policy in Britain*, Catherine Jones compared the two major influxes of immigration this century and asked how it was that politicians responded so much more quickly to the New Commonwealth immigration of the 1950s than to the 'alien' migration of the 1900s. In her view, this may have been because there exists today 'the enhanced political importance of popular opinion' which is 'inherently of greater import, given a system of government, that was supposed to act not merely on behalf of, but as the spokesman for the mass of the people'.[54]

However, it is by no means clear that vote-seeking politicians always act by responding to a perceived undertow in the minds of the electorate. Professor Michael Dummett and Ann Dummett take the view that 'the activities of the politicians have not merely mirrored, but have been the primary cause of'[55] current attitudes to immigration control. In their recent classic work, *Subjects, Citizens, Aliens and Others*, Dummett and Nicol graphically explain that if politicians did always respond to public feelings and expectations, then:

> there was an alternative popular tradition which British political leaders might have developed after the Second World War . . . the tradition of welcome for refugees; popular solidarity in support of personal freedom and against authoritarianism; the large public for Defoe's satire; the eighteenth-century London 'mob' protecting runaway black slaves; the readiness to inter-marry which shocked the *Morning Post* in the eighteenth century (as it did the city fathers of Liverpool in the early twentieth); demonstrations in support of Dreyfus; the welcome for black GIs during the second World War, and strong hostility to a 'colour bar'. Leadership could have played on British sentiments of openness and fairness . . .[56]

Manifestly, therefore, British politicians had a large field of options open to them in their approach to immigration, and were not compelled just to follow one course of action. In fact, an aspect of British immigration control is the way in which it is, as we have seen, highly politicized. In his comparative study, *European Immigration Policy*, Tomas Hammar has compiled an analysis of six countries: Sweden, The Netherlands, Great Britain, France, Germany and Switzerland. From this, he concludes that '[T]here were no political controversies or partisan divisions over immigration in any of the project countries, with the exception of Britain, where political parties competed in their efforts to restrict colonial and post-colonial immigration'.[57] Professor Michael Dummett, Fellow of New College, Oxford, and Wykeham Professor of Logic at Oxford University, took a similar view when in 1974, in what is a little-known masterpiece in this area, *Immigration: Where the Debate Goes Wrong*, he remonstrated that:

> No one subject . . . not the Common Market, or unemployment, or inflation, or housing, or the Trade Unions, or education . . . has been so persistently, repeatedly and repetitively discussed. For nearly two decades it has been our major preoccupation. It is the one issue of which the whole electorate has heard and on which all have opinions; it is the *only* issue of which the politically illiterate have heard.[58]

15

Other writers have tried to explain this state of affairs further by drawing a distinction, such as that between 'populists' and the 'progressives' in the Conservative Party, who they say 'articulate distinctive views on race'. According to the 'populists', apparently, 'good race relations emanate from the assurance that the indigenous population has had from politicians that strict control of immigration endures'. They have entrenched views 'about society, the state, law and the individual' which are 'unexpressed touchstones in the hearts and minds of many Conservatives'.[59] Their actions cannot therefore always be rationalized as a response to what their electorate expects of them.

However, those who say this should not overlook the unique tradition of political liberalism in Britain. Political liberalism and its offspring, liberal democracy, is the greatest political gift of Britain to the rest of the world. Even the right wing of the Conservative Party ideologically divides into two. There are the 'economic liberals', who are free-market radicals and who may, or may not, be morally conservative; and there are the 'libertarians', who are both economically and morally radical and who see economic freedom as a gateway to a wider general freedom. Political liberalism in the nineteenth century was a very large movement spanning the whole of Western Europe as well as America. Its greatest development, however, took place in England. In Germany this liberal philosophy was mostly academic, and French liberalism remained for the most part the social philosophy of a class. Only in England, which throughout the nineteenth century was the most highly industrialized country in the world, did liberalism with its mixture of Christian charity and humanitarianism achieve the status at once of a national philosophy and a national policy.[60]

British politicians, according to Professor Dummett, should take a moral lead and guide the electorate on the immigration issue, and not succumb to gratifying its prejudices simply because those prejudices exist:

> No-one, whether or not he has a role, is *entitled* to irrational hatred, contempt, fear or prejudice, directed against whole groups of people. No politician has any duty to respect or abet irrational feelings of this kind; for instance, to advocate anti-semitic policies because anti-semitism is prevalent. . . . All that you need, to overcome racial prejudice, is a social climate in which it does not pay and earns public dispproval; it will then rapidly vanish without residue.
>
> For this reason, not only is it false to say that politicians have a duty to pander to popular prejudice, but it is equally untrue to say that such prejudice is a stubborn fact with

which they are forced to come to terms. On the contrary, politicians are freer to say what they believe on this issue than on any other; the general public is more likely to mould its attitudes, in this matter, in conformity with what it believes to be the socially acceptable ones as determined, in large part, by those evinced by public figures, than in any other area.[61]

On this basis, it seems that if the public were assisted by politicians of all parties to understand the historical origin and nature of Britain's immigration commitments, such as to the Hong Kong Chinese or internationally to refugees displaced from other countries, there might be a greater public support for a more liberal immigration policy.[62]

This lead has already been taken by the Home Affairs Select Committee on Race Relations and Immigration. The Committee has been looking at immigration and race relations now for approximately a quarter of a century, during which time it has 'been applauded, as well as reprimanded, for its unanimous reports', in the words of Hamelfarb.[63] This committee has done valuable work, making constructive proposals for the reform of administrative procedures in immigration control in its 1982 Report. But its boldest comments have come from its Tory-dominated committee of 1990 which in its Report began by proclaiming that '[T]he effectiveness and fairness of immigration control affects both the maintenance of good race relations at home and Britain's standing in the world'. On this premise it then described as 'inexcusable' the inefficiency in the handling of citizenship applications by the Home Office and as 'indefensible' the 27-month queue for naturalization. Many people, it declared, were caused 'severe personal hardship' and an 'understandable suspicion' therefore arose that civil servants were using red tape as an unofficial method of immigration control.[64]

However, the Select Committee has never conducted an investigation into immigration policy. Hamelfarb observes how in 1969 'it chose to examine the administrative details of immigration control and deliberately evaded questioning policy in order to avoid internal controversy'[65] and in 1990 the Committee at the outset declared, '[W]e have not conducted a comprehensive analysis of immigration policy . . .'.[66]

In its 1992 Report, *Migration Control at External Borders of the European Community*, the Committee again did not consider policy. Yet as the Refugee Council said in its Memorandum to it, 'it is impossible to separate certain aspects of asylum policy from that of control of the external frontiers of the EC'.[67] Given its considerable experience in this area there is no doubt, that, if it chose to, the

Committee could make the most invaluable contribution to the debate about immigration policy, which is of such fundamental importance in the current state of international affairs.

In the meantime, the following approach outlined by Hannah Rose as to the most effective way of evolving policy in Parliament could with advantage, it is submitted, be applied to any administrative or political process of decision-making in respect of immigration matters. Policy formulation, Rose contends, should involve six stages. These are: (1) the identification of a 'problem'; (2) to think of a situation in which the 'problem' no longer exists; (3) analysis of the existing 'problem'; (4) desired situations to discover how the problem could be removed and a solution achieved; (5) the choice of the best and appropriate policy; and finally, (6) its discussion, refinement, enactment and enforcement. In the end what is sought is the most perfect result that can be achieved along these lines.[68] Subsequent events, however, demonstrate the singular absence of such a considered approach to immigration control and a recourse, yet again, to more irrational methods.

THREE NOTEWORTHY EVENTS

Three events, more than any other, epitomize the contemporary issues in British immigration and citizenship laws. Each event was characterized by governmental inexpertise and uncouthness and each arose to catch the public eye in the most dramatic of circumstances. Each event drew much adverse comment, concern and criticism at the time and each occurred against the backdrop of a climate of increasing hostility to refugees and newcomers, not just in Britain but throughout the whole of Western Europe. These are firstly, the Tamil Refugee Case of 1989; secondly, the Zairean school-teacher's deportation of 1991; and thirdly the Asylum Bill of 1991–93. Each one of these three events deserves first to be factually described and then to be contextually analysed for its true significance.

The Tamil Refugees and the European Court

In 1989 five Tamil refugees were returned to Sri Lanka. Four of the five men subsequently suffered torture and inhuman treatment. One of the five arrived in England in February 1987 with a group of 58 others whose asylum claims were rejected by the then immigration Minister, David (now Lord) Waddington, as 'manifestly bogus'. The group escaped immediate repatriation because on the runway at Heathrow airport they protested by stripping down to their underclothes. The other three arrived in the summer of the same year, only to have their applications likewise rejected. The existing law is that no appeal against refusal may be made until after removal from the United Kingdom, so the claimants questioned the Government's removal order by an application for judicial review challenging the validity of the decisions. This was duly lost in the House of Lords.[69] In February 1988 the five were returned to Sri Lanka, from where they appealed to an Immigration Adjudicator in London. He found that the men were indeed genuine refugees who had been wrongly returned to a situation of risk in Sri Lanka. The adjudicator said, 'It could not be forecast what the day would bring by way of tension, interrogation, detention and even physical harm and destruction of property' for these five men. The Government appealed, still presumably believing that their claim was 'manifestly bogus', but lost. The men were returned to Britain, where they resubmitted their asylum applications. Subsequent events, however, were to be still more bizarre.

The five men had launched separate proceedings before the European Commission of Human Rights. They challenged the absence of a right of appeal in the United Kingdom before removal and they challenged their enforced return to Sri Lanka. The Commission overwhelmingly accepted (by 13 votes to 1) that the British Government had not provided an effective remedy against the mistakes of Government officials, which it was bound to do (breach of Article 13), but by a narrow margin, on the President's casting vote (making it 7 to 7), found the applicants not to have been exposed to torture or inhuman or degrading treatment or punishment (no breach of Article 3), although the minority, moved by the adjudicator's findings, felt that there was a serious risk of ill-treatment. Remarkably, the European Court of Justice then found against the applicants on all counts. The British Government, it held, had not been in breach of Article 13 (by 7 votes to 2) and had not been in breach of Article 3 (by 8 votes to 1).[70]

The Home Secretary and the Zairean Teacher

In the second of the three events, some similar issues were raised once again. This was the deportation of the Zairean teacher in 1991. The teacher, known as M, had also applied for and had been refused political asylum. He was about to be removed to Zaire on the evening of 1 May 1991. Shortly before this, he made an application for leave to move for judicial review of the decision. This was rejected. Immediately afterwards fresh solicitors and counsel acting for him applied again to the High Court. They alleged new grounds and this time the judge, Garland J, wished to have a postponement of the applicant's departure. He required time to consider his application, so he sought from counsel for the Secretary of State an undertaking to this effect. Unwittingly, it seems, the latter conveyed this to the judge. Overnight, however, M was then mysteriously removed. In Paris an hour later, the Immigration Minister, Peter Lloyd, and the Chief Inspector of the Immigration Service considered the possibility of returning M to England, but decided against it.

On the night of 1 May Garland J, having heard of M's removal, then made an *ex parte* order requiring the Home Secretary forthwith to procure M's return to the jurisdiction of the High Court and demanded that his safety be ensured pending such return. The Home Office accordingly arranged for M to be met on arrival at Kinshasa and the first available return flight was booked for him. During the afternoon, however, the Home Secretary was then informed of the new situation. On legal advice he decided that the judge had no jurisdiction to make a mandatory interim injunction order against an officer of the Crown, so that rather than comply with it, he decided he would at the earliest possible opportunity apply for its discharge. He cancelled all arrangements for M's return to the United Kingdom. On 4 May, on the Home Office's application, Garland J's order was then set aside.

Four days later M brought contempt proceedings against the Home Office. In the High Court Mr Justice Simon Brown held that the court had no contempt jurisdiction against the Crown. In the Court of Appeal, however, the majority held that Crown officers are just as amenable to contempt proceedings as any other citizen and that the rule that injunctions do not lie against the Crown was inapplicable here. The court held that if the order by Garland J was improperly made, the proper course of action was to make an application to have it set aside. Until this was done the order could not be treated as void since it was made by a court of unlimited jurisdiction. Accordingly, the Home Secretary had been in contempt of court.[71] A year later this judgment was upheld by the House of Lords on appeal in what is widely regarded as one of the most important constitutional law rulings this century, with Lord Templeman holding that the Government's view would, 'if upheld, establish the proposition that the executive obey the law as a matter of grace and not as a matter of necessity, a proposition which would reverse the result of the Civil War'.[72]

The Government and the Asylum Bill

The third event is the Asylum Bill. Originally this was published on 1 November 1991. It reached the Committee stage of the House of Lords early in 1992. As the Government prepared to go to the polls in the General Election of 9 April, it was then shelved. Returned to power, it declared its intention[73] to reintroduce it in the new session of Parliament. The genesis of the Asylum Bill lay in the fear of ever-increasing asylum applications. In January 1991 the Government's annual statistical survey, *Social Trends*, stated that some 30,000 applications for refugee status were expected by the end of the year, almost double the 1989 figure.[74] In the event, a record 44,743 applications were received, which was ten times the number in 1988 when 5000 applied, rising to 22,000 applications in 1990. Almost 28,000 of these applications came from Africa, 10,400 from Asia and 3800 from Europe and America.[75]

To curb this development the Home Office began to look at a series of options such as tougher visa requirements, more thorough checks on asylum applications, and bigger fines on airlines carrying passengers without a right of entry.[76] In one week alone in February 1991 British Airways paid out £3 million in fines under the existing Immigration (Carriers' Liability) Act 1987, which required an airline or shipper to pay a £1000 fine for every passenger brought without a visa. Subsequently, this was raised to £2000 by Statutory Instrument.[77] The Government's Asylum Bill had as its chief characteristics compulsory fingerprinting of all refugees, new quicker appeal arrangements without an oral hearing, fast-track removal of 'bogus' applicants, and removal of a family right to council housing pending the determination of a refugee's case.

CONTEXTUAL INTERPRETATION OF RECENT EVENTS

Why Contextual?

The late Professor Otto Kahn-Freund believed that lawyers should look at every concrete situation not only 'in a strictly and rigidly dogmatic way' but 'as a social situation requiring the solution of a social problem' if they are to understand 'the realities of the situation and to what for example a court wanted to achieve (probably without saying so) or in fact did achieve with its decision . . .'[78] Two writers in an influential article have more recently also said that lawyers and legal scholars all too often 'see a "decision" at a particular point in the legal process as an isolated matter, as something logically separable from what surrounds it in the processing of cases' and thereby end up doing 'violence to the inherent complexity of decisions which are made in a variety of legal settings'.[79]

A broad-based approach is necessary not only if one is to understand why a legal situation is what it is, but also if one is to enquire into what the function of law is, or ought to be, in society. According to John Rawls, justice is the pre-eminent objective of law, and this value is non-negotiable: 'Justice is the first virtue of social institutions, as truth is of systems of thought', and '[B]eing first virtues of human activities, truth and justice are uncompromising'. The conception is based on each person, as a person, possessing 'an inviolability . . . that even the welfare of society as a whole cannot override', with the inexorable result that 'in a just society the liberties of equal citizenship are taken as settled; the rights secured by justice are not subject to political bargaining or to the calculus of social interests'.[80] Yet it is political bargaining and the calculus of social interests which can alone account for the nature of these three events.

Europe, Maastricht and the European Court

If we reconsider the Tamil refugee case we find, revealingly, that the judgment of the European Court was not actually expected by the British Government. On the contrary, it had anticipated defeat in Strasbourg. In so anticipating, it had decided to include limited rights of appeal in a new Asylum Bill. This Bill was announced in the Queen's Speech only the day after judgment was given.[81] In fact, the European Court's judgment also surprised liberal observers at home, who had for years looked to Europe for guidance in the finer appreciation of their own democratic rights. Europe after all had Bills of Rights and written constitutions which Britain did not.

The judgment, however, could be explained only in the broader context of Europe's developing refugee problem. The European Community had failed to deal with this because it had not found enough common ground to forge a joint Community immigration policy and the 17 Commissioners were sharply split on this issue.[82] Britain opposed any erosion of its sovereignty but Germany, facing a flood of ethnic Germans, Poles and other East Europeans, wanted the Community to share in the burden of accepting new arrivals. At the Maastricht summit, which was to take place only the following month in The Netherlands, the development of a common European immigration policy was the most urgent item on the agenda as 1992 approached with the prospect of the harmonization of frontier controls. The fact was that for most participants at Maastricht economic union was a foregone conclusion. What was not, was the thorny question of a European immigration policy.

It was well known that Britain was the only member of the European Community that opposed any move towards European competence in immigration policy.[83] No doubt Britain felt that it did so for the best of reasons because the Select Committee on Immigration had found in June 1990 that between 1984–85 and 1989–90 the number of arrivals at United Kingdom ports was expected to rise by 39 per cent. It found there to have been an even more marked increase in the number of applications for refugee status and for British citizenship.[84] Demand for entry clearance (which consists of a visa, an entry certificate or a Home Office Letter of Consent) was growing throughout the world, and the Head of the Foreign and Commonwealth Office Migration and Visa Department went on record to say that this was 'a reflection of the vastly greater volume of people wanting to travel today, either wanting to travel or wanting to travel and settle'.[85] It was recognized, moreover, that much of the pressure came from Eastern Europe.

From 8 June 1990 the British Government allowed the former nationals of East Germany to enter Britain without visas and the Select Committee for its part welcomed this, saying, 'we have no doubt that the process of democratisation will be aided by exchanges at all levels between our countries'.[86] Leading European politicians, however, continued to express their concern. Wolfgang Schaube, the West German Interior Minister, said in 1990 that he expected 400,000 refugees from the Eastern bloc and the Third World to seek entry into Western Europe. Moscow, with its empire in its dying throes, warned at the time of a mass exodus of three million Soviet citizens to the EC from 1991.[87] The view of the International Labour Organisation was that the total migrant population would increase substantially throughout the world from its present estimated 100 million by the end of the decade.[88]

This unhappy and troublesome period provided the context for the European Court's judgment in the Tamil refugee case. At Maastricht subsequently, agreement was reached that 'The Council acting by unanimity . . . shall determine the third countries whose nationals must be in possession of a visa when crossing the external borders of the Member States.' The agreement represented a hardening of attitudes in Europe, and the European Court's judgment was only a harbinger of that change in attitude. Maastricht was the beginning of a common immigration policy, when from 1996 there would be a gradual harmonization of asylum policies in Europe. Harmonization meant a tightening up and not a loosening of the rules for entry for economic migrants as well as for family members to join relatives already legally settled in Britain.[89] How this will work out in practice is a different but no less important question. Democratic politicians are bound to seek to control patterns of inward migration through the exercise of veto.[90] In May 1992, Britain, only weeks before taking over the presidency of the European Community, indicated that it intended to continue with passport checks at ports and airports on all travellers to identify non-EC citizens so as to preserve its island status.[91]

Contempt, the Home Secretary, and Political Decision-making

The deportation of the Zairean asylum seeker by the then Home Secretary, Kenneth Baker, in contravention of a High Court judge's ruling, also requires a similar further analysis. The case raised large questions of constitutional practice and the rule of law. One source remarked, 'No minister in British history has ever faced a contempt of court action. Mr Baker has not only had the case against him allowed, but has also been found guilty'.[92] With hindsight the most curious aspect of this case is not the finding of guilt for contempt. It is the court's assertion that Kenneth Baker's culpability was at the lower end of the scale as he had acted only after taking advice from Treasury counsel. Was this really correct, however? A leading constitutional law expert, Mr Geoffrey Marshall of Oxford University, feels that, 'This perhaps is not quite an accurate description of his decision. His decision was a political one made in the light of the legal advice'. He cannot, as the rules on ministerial responsibility make only too plain, shift the consequences of his decision onto the shoulders of his legal advisers. Otherwise for every action that is 'impolitic or immoral' he could disclaim all responsibility. Mr Marshall states, 'A minister who decides to disregard a court order must be aware that he is stirring up trouble, even if his advisers tell him that this action has a legal justification.'[93] In fact, Kenneth Baker made other decisions as Home Secretary which are just as unsatisfactory.

Just four days after this case the High Court ordered Kenneth Baker to reconsider his decision to deport a Sikh independence campaigner to India. Mr Justice Popplewell confessed to having 'enormous anxiety' over the case of Karamjit Singh Chahal and said that Mr Baker had failed to make clear whether he accepted an Amnesty International report that Sikhs had been persecuted in India and failed to make clear whether the findings of the report had any relevance to Mr Chahal's claim for political asylum. Therefore, said Mr Justice Popplewell, '[H]e must reconsider the matter in the light of this judgment'.[94] The High Court also criticized Kenneth Baker for failing to provide reasons for agreeing to surrender a person who had devoted himself to creating a settled family life and a business to the United States in extradition proceedings brought by that country. The United States had 'over many years showed complete indifference to the whereabouts and way of life' of the person in question and extradition proceedings were not instituted for ten years after his conviction and sentence for an offence. Lord Justice Watkins 'failed to see how any Home Secretary acting reasonably could possibly use his discretion other than to refuse the request . . .'.[95] It is a nice question whether these were all 'political' decisions by the Home Secretary. They were certainly not properly reasoned legal decisions. For what it is worth, in the Zairean deportation case Kenneth Baker made a separate statement to the House of Commons some months afterwards to say that asylum applications from Zaire currently stood at 6000 people,[96] and this, perhaps more than anything else, provides a better explanation for the nature and manner of that decision in respect of the deportation of M.

Of Economic Migrants, Bogus Claimants and Staff Shortages

As for the Asylum Bill, when it was first published it was attacked by churchmen. The Right Reverend Peter Selby, Bishop of Kingston upon Thames, said, 'To work on the basis that such claims are likely to be fraudulent unless proved otherwise, is to brand many of the world's most vulnerable with accusation of deceit and to run the risk of sending people to torture and death.'[97] The Archbishops of Canterbury and Westminster declared, 'There is little virtue in proclaiming a willingness to open the door to genuine asylum seekers if the path to it is effectively blocked by provisions which obstruct rather than facilitate access to fair adjudication on appeal.'[98] The Law Society and the Bar Council both attacked the Bill on the grounds of natural justice. The Law Society saw the refusal of automatic appeal rights and access to legal advice as a 'barrier to justice'. Asylum seekers, it said, should be brought into the existing appeals process and a duty scheme for suspects held in police stations.[99] The same severe criticism came from the Council on Tribunals and from Lord Ackner, who in a House of Lords debate inveighed against the removal of a right to an oral hearing. 'It will', said Lord Ackner, 'cost the Government nothing to be generous.'[100] The growing criticism forced the Government to undergo some change of heart so that by 10 February 1992 it had decided to continue the 'green form' legal aid system for asylum seekers.[101]

Statistics, however, can mean different things to different people. If the official figures were high that was because they covered up the Government's own ineptitude. The criticism from the various quarters had been harsh for this very reason. The Home Office gave a low priority to public spending on its immigration division. There was a shortage of staff and other resources for asylum work. When after 1989 the number of applications for entry began to rise, the Home Office did not respond with more resources to deal with these, as the responsibility for social security and housing fell to be borne not by the Home Office, but by individual local authorities in the country. In fact, an increase in the asylum applications since 1989 came primarily not from new arrivals but from people who had already been admitted to the United Kingdom as visitors or students. A letter by the immigration Minister, Peter Lloyd, to *The Times* frankly admitted that 'most applications are made by people already in the UK in order to prolong their stay', and that 'only about a quarter are found to be genuine refugees'.[102]

So severe were the staffing problems induced by cuts in the Immigration and Nationality Department (IND) that the Home Affairs Committee on Race Relations and Immigration said in 1990, 'We would not wish the IND to be the Cinderella of any future internal Home Office review of expenditure priorities'[103] and that '[W]e very much regret the enforced freeze on recruitment since September 1989 and urge the IND to resume recruitment at once . . .'[104] The result was that a 14-month delay at the Home Office for hearing asylum applications encouraged many visitors and students to attempt to try to remain in Britain by lodging asylum applications. They could then be given 'exceptional leave to remain' were the Home Office to take the view that an applicant had, through prolonged delay, now put down roots.

The result was that the asylum backlog grew to unmanageable proportions and then happened what always happens in such situations; that is, an incentive was created for some people to make bogus claims. Indeed, some even made fraudulent multiple applications. As the full truth about the asylum cases began to emerge the Home Office's arguments began to change also. One source states, '[I]nstead of conjuring up a picture of ever-increasing hordes of economic migrants, it began suggesting a large proportion of the applications already on file might be bogus'.[105] The Government, however, could not play the 'numbers game' both ways. If fraudulent multiple applications were being made then the fact was that fewer people were actually seeking asylum in Britain. Already when the Asylum Bill was being considered there had been a steady decline in the number of people seeking asylum when they first arrive at a British port of entry. By September 1991 the January figure of 1680 applications had fallen to just 578 and there were signs of further reductions for the remaining year.[106]

The serious press denounced the Bill as 'the Exclusion Bill' whose main 'purpose is to pander to the supposed political prejudice of the British electorate' and as being 'opportunistic and mean-minded'.[107] It was argued that the evidence showed that '[S]wift, humane procedures are required to handle applications and eliminate fraud. That is what the bill should contain, not the denial of a fair hearing to new arrivals at the ports.'[108] Nevertheless, after the General Election, the Prime Minister, John Major, said that the Bill would be brought forward 'very soon'; but the new Home Secretary, Kenneth Clarke, now told MPs that it would be delayed and that an opportunity would be taken to examine the Bill more closely and to reflect on some of the House of Lords debates.[109] When a new Bill was eventually introduced on 22 October 1992 it was visitors and short-term students who were now to lose their rights of appeal following refusal under the Government's new proposals, and not asylum seekers. Yet the Government's concern had never been with visitors and short-term students in the initial clamour for immigration controls, but with the increasing number of asylum seekers. The new proposals gave asylum seekers a new right of oral appeal. Yet its earlier measures of fingerprinting asylum seekers and removing from local councils their statutory duty to house them were preserved intact.[110] The Asylum and Immigration Appeals Bill finally completed its passage through Parliament with a last debate in the House of Commons on 7 June 1993. It completed its final stages on 1 July and by the following day a new immigration Act had come into force.[111]

These three events provide an object lesson in how not to deal with immigration control. Their shabby story of official inexpertise and blunders may hardly be surprising for, as Dr Claire Palley states in her Hamlyn Lectures, 'Unless public, officials and lawyers are imbued with human rights ideology, lip service to, rather than respect in practice for, human rights will frequently be the outcome'.[112] This is at least one explanation for the historic way in which these issues have been habitually handled, and to which we must now turn.

NOTES AND REFERENCES

This chapter is an extended version of a paper delivered by the author at the 1992 Annual Conference of the Law and Society Association in Philadelphia, Pennyslvania.

1 Boswell, J. (reprinted 1985) *Life of Johnson*, p. 1213. Oxford.

2 Blackstone, W. (3rd edn, 1853) *Commentaries*, 3, p. 252. This was not remedied until 1826, when it finally became possible for Jews to be naturalized as British subjects.

3 Blackstone, W. (1765) *Commentaries*, 1, p. 252.

4 Dicey, A.V. (1961 edn) *The Law of the Constitution*, p. 193.

5 Dummett, A. and Nicol, A. (1990) *Subjects, Citizens, Aliens and Others*, p. 2. London.

6 Lester, A. and Bindman, G. (1972) *Race and Law*, p. 13. London.

7 Anderson, Sir Norman (1978) *Liberty, Law and Justice*, p. 72. London.

8 *The Independent*, 20 May 1992.

9 See *Mous Taquim* judgment, *The Times*, 8 May 1991 and the authorities cited

therein. Also Crawford, J. (1976–77) The Criterion for Statehood in International Law, *British Yearbook of International Law* 8, p.114; Weis, P. (2nd edn 1979) *Nationality and Statelessness in International Law*, p. 67 Leiden; Lauterpacht, H. (1933) *The Function of Law in the International Community*, p. 300, Oxford; Oppenheim, L.V. (1955) *International Law* 1, p. 643; Schwerzenberger, G. (1949) *International Law* 1, p. 162; Hackworth, G.H. (1942) *Digest of International Law* III IX, p. 1.

10 The Home Secretary, Aretas Allers-Douglas, introducing the Bill: see HC Deb., Vol. 145, col. 468 (18 April 1905).

11 The Home Secretary, R.A. Butler, introducing the Bill: HC Deb., Vol. 649, col. 687 (16 November 1961).

12 See Jones, K. and Smith, A. (1970) *The Economic Impact of Commonwealth Immigration*, Chapter 2. Cambridge.

13 Robertson, G. (6th edn 1989) *Freedom, the Individual and the Law*, p. 315. Harmondsworth.

14 Bevan, V. (1987) *The Development of British Immigration Law*, p. viii. London.

15 Dummett, A. and Nicol, A. *op. cit.* pp. 6–7.

16 These matters have been well discussed in a collection of essays in: Hammar, T. (1985) *European Immigration Policy: A Comparative Study*. Cambridge.

17 *Ibid.* See essay by Zig Layton-Henry, p. 125.

18 *Ibid.* p. 98.

19 See *The Independent*, 8 February 1991. In October 1991 a motion to annul the Immigration (Carrier Liability Prescribed Sum) Order 1991 (SI 1991 No. 1497) which increased the penalty from £1000 to £2000 was withdrawn after debate: HC Deb., Vol. 531, col. 1454.

20 See letter to *The Guardian* by Revd David Haslam of the British Council of Churches for Britain and Ireland on 12 November 1991.

21 See letter to *The Times*, 4 October 1991.

22 See *The Guardian*, 2 July 1992.

23 See *The Times*, 30 July 1992 and 15 July 1992.

24 *Ibid.*

25 *The Times*, 5 February 1992 and 3 July 1992.

26 *The Independent*, 25 August 1992.

27 See *The Times*, 15 July 1992.

28 See *The Daily Telegraph*, 23 September 1991.

29 See *The Times*, 14 February 1992.

30 See *The Times*, 23 October 1990.

31 See *The Times*, 4 December 1991.

32 See *The Times*, 4 December 1991.

33 Legomsky, S.H. (1992) *Immigration Law and Policy*, p. xxi. New York.

34 Legomsky, S.H. (1987) *Immigration and the Judiciary*, p.1. Oxford.

35 Dummett, A. and Nicol, A. *op. cit*, p. xv.

36 Hutton, J. (1986) Legal Education and the Law of Immigration and Nationality. In *Towards a Just Immigration Policy* (ed. by Ann Dummett), pp. 211–12. London.

37 Layton-Henry, Z. (1984) *The Politics of Race in Britain*, p. xiv. London.

38 Freeman, G. (1979) *Immigrant Labour and Racial Conflict in Industrial Societies 1945–1975*, p. 309. Princeton, NJ.
39 *Ibid*. p. 315.
40 Ben-Tovim, G. and Gabriel, J. (1978) The Sociology of Race: Time to Change Course. *The Science Teacher*, 8(4) (pp. 143–71), p. 147.
41 See *Abdulaziz, Cabales and Balkandali* v. *UK*, applications No. 9214/80; 9473/81; 9474/81 (1985) 7 EHRR 471. For a commentary on these cases, see Juss, S. (1987) Time for Parliament to Stop Playing the Numbers Game. *The Independent*, 22 May 1987.
42 Ben-Tovim and Gabriel, *op. cit.* p. 147. Also see Rex, J. and Tomlinson, S. (1979) *Colonial Immigrants in a British City, passim*. London.
43 Boswell, *op. cit.* p. 494.
44 Orwell, G. (ed. 1957) England Your England. *Selected Essays* (pp. 63–91), pp. 64–5. London.
45 Dummett, A. and Nicol, A. *op. cit.* p. 276.
46 *Ibid.* p. 277.
47 See *The Times*, 4 December 1991.
48 HC Deb., Vol. 813, col. 42 (8 March 1971).
49 HC Deb., Vol. 649, col. 687 (16 November 1961).
50 See letter by Canon Ivor South-Cameron to *The Guardian*, 28 November 1984, warning about 'a kind of impatience that could boil over' in Britain's immigrant communities.
51 Speech at Stevenage: see *The Times*, 26 March 1992.
52 *The Daily Telegraph*, 7 April 1992.
53 *The Times*, 7 May 1992.
54 Jones, C. (1977) *Immigration and Social Policy in Britain*, p. 136. London.
55 Dummett, M. and Dummett, A. (1982) The Role of Government in Britain's Racial Crisis. In *Race in Britain* (ed. by C. Husband) (pp. 97–127), p. 100. London.
56 Dummett, A. and Nicol, A. *op. cit.* pp. 226–7.
57 Hammar, T. (1987) *European Immigration Policy: A Comparative Study*, p. 293. Cambridge.
58 Dummett, M. (1974) *Immigration: Where the Debate Goes Wrong*, p. 1. London: AGIN, c/o JCWI.
59 Edmonds, J. and Behrens, R. (1981) Kippers, Kittens and Kipper-Boxes: Conservative Populists and Race Relations. *Political Quarterly* 52 (pp. 342–8), pp. 342, 344, 348.
60 See Sabine and Thorson (1973) *A History of Political Theory*, pp. 608–33. Illinois. Also see Guido de Ruggiero (translated by R.G. Collingwood, 1927) *A History of European Liberalism*. Oxford; and Davidson, W. (1916) *Political Thought in England: The Utilitarians from Bentham to J.S. Mill*. New York.
61 Dummett, M. *op. cit.* pp. 5–6.
62 Nowhere has the plight of the Hong Kong Chinese been better championed than in the pages of the *Spectator*, which argued that there is 'no evidence' for the view that British public opinion will not stand for their entry to Britain (*Spectator*, 17 June 1989) and that 'it is unBritish not to welcome people' (*Spectator*, 10 June 1989) in these circumstances. According to some observers, many politicians in

the future may indeed be forced to take a more liberal line on this issue if they want to win the middle-class Asian vote, and in any case, in view of the growing electoral force of ethnic minorities in urban constituencies: see Rex, J. (1984) Race in the Round. *New Society*, 15 November, p. 254; Layton-Henry, Z. (1984) *The Politics of Race in Britain*, p. 143. London; Layton-Henry, Z. (1978) Race, Electoral Strategy, and the Major Parties. *Parliamentary Affairs* 31 (pp. 268–81), p. 280; Anwar, M. (1980) *Votes and Policies: Ethnic Minorities and the General Election of 1979, passim*. London; Jenkins, J. (1984) The Middle-Class Vote. *New Statesman*, 30 November 1984; Scruton, R. in *The Times*, 5 March 1985.

63 Hamelfarb, S. (1980) Consensus in Committee: The Case of the Select Committee on Race Relations and Immigration. *Parliamentary Affairs* 33 (pp. 54–78); Layton-Henry, Z. (1979) The Report in Immigration. *Political Quarterly* 50 (pp. 241–8), *passim*.

64 See *Administrative Delays in the Immigration and Nationality Department* (1989–90) HC 319, p. 1.

65 Hamelfarb, *op cit*. p. 63.

66 See *Administrative Delays in the Immigration and Nationality Department, op. cit*. p. v.

67 See *Migration Control at External Borders of the European Community* (1991–92) HC 215, p. 85.

68 Rose, H. (1972–83) The Immigration Act 1971: A Case Study in Work of Parliament. *Parliamentary Affairs* 26 (pp. 69– 91), 71. Also note the published decision of the German Federal Government in 1984 to the effect that federal legislation should always be examined by government departments to ensure that it was necessary, likely to be effective and would be comprehensible. Ten broad questions should be asked in the drafting of all federal legislation. For a comment on these, see Editorial (1992) *Statute Law Review* 13(2), iii–iv.

69 See *Vilvarajah* v. *Secretary of State for the Home Department* [1988] AC 958.

70 See *Vilvarajah* v. *UK* [1992] 14 EHRR 248.

71 Simon Brown J. relied on the first Factortame case: see *R* v. *Secretary of State for Transport, ex parte Factortame* [1990] 2 AC 85.

72 For the report of the judgments see *M* v. *Home Office and Kenneth Baker* [1992] 2 WLR 73.

73 See the Queen's Speech, reported in *The Times*, 7 May 1992.

74 *Social Trends* (1991 edn) 21. London.

75 See *The Times*, 7 May 1992.

76 *The Times*, 26 January 1991.

77 *The Independent*, 8 February 1991. See further note 19 *supra*.

78 Quoted from Gray, K.J. and Symes, P.D. (1981) *Real Property and Real People*, p. v. London.

79 Baldwin, R. and Hawkins, K. (1984) Discretionary Justice: Davis Reconsidered. *Public Law* (Winter, pp. 570–99), 580.

80 Rawls, J. (1971) *A Theory of Justice*, p. 3. Oxford.

81 It was proposed to have a new fast-track appeal procedure for deciding cases on paper, which, without giving the applicant the right to appear in person for an oral hearing and without legal support, would result in less protection against bureaucratic errors.

82 *The Times*, 10 January 1991.
83 *The Independent*, 5 November 1991 and 25 October 1991.
84 See note 62 *supra*, p. xvii, para. 45.
85 *Ibid*, p. xii, para. 30.
86 *Ibid*, p. xii, para. 31.
87 *The Times*, 3 September 1990.
88 *The Independent*, 8 February 1991.
89 See Chapter 4, *infra*.
90 *The Times* (Editorial), 4 December 1991.
91 *The Times*, 8 May 1992.
92 *The Independent*, 28 November 1991.
93 Marshall, G. (1992) Ministerial Responsibility, the Home Office and Mr Baker. *Public Law* (Spring, pp. 7–12), 12.
94 *The Times*, 3 December 1991.
95 See *R* v. *Secretary of State for the Home Department, ex parte Sinclair, The Times*, 30 January 1992.
96 HC Deb., Vol. 200, col. 37.
97 *The Guardian*, 12 November 1991.
98 *The Guardian*, 20 January 1992.
99 *The Guardian*, 10 February 1992; also see *Financial Times*, 14 November 1991.
100 See *LAG* (Editorial), June 1992. The United Nations also said that the Asylum Bill breaks refugee rules: see *The Independent*, 14 December 1991.
101 *The Guardian*, 10 February 1992 and 11 February 1992.
102 *The Times*, 9 September 1991.
103 See note 62, *supra*, p. xviii.
104 *Ibid*. p. xx.
105 John Carvel in *The Guardian*, 13 May 1992.
106 See the analysis in *The Guardian*, 31 October 1991, which affords the best insight into the asylum situation.
107 *The Independent* (Editorial), 4 November 1991.
108 John Carvel in *The Guardian*, *op. cit.*
109 *The Guardian*, 10 June 1992.
110 *The Times*, 23 October 1992 and 10 November 1992.
111 The new Act was accompanied by new immigration rules (HC 725) introduced with new Asylum Appeals (Procedure) Rules (SI 1661) and new Immigration Appeals (Procedure) (Amendment) Rules (SI 1662) which were published on 5 July, ready to come into force from 26 July 1993.
112 Palley, C. (1991) *The UK and Human Rights*, p. 3. London.

2

The Growth of Immigration Controls in Britain

'Man's capacity for justice makes democracy possible, but man's inclination to injustice makes democracy necessary' – *Reinhold Niebuhr*

ALIEN IMMIGRATION

The Aliens Act 1905

The modern control of immigration into the United Kingdom begins with the Aliens Act of 1905.[1] Prior to this there was no existing statutory regulation of immigration. The Act was passed at a time of mounting concern over the arrival in the early 1890s of Jewish refugees fleeing from the pogroms and economic hardships of Russia and Eastern Europe.[2] This novel piece of legislation was the device adopted to prevent Britain being made a receptacle for 'destitute, diseased and criminal aliens'.[3]

Aliens were allowed to land only at authorized ports under this Act and immigration officers had the power to refuse leave to land to 'undesirable aliens'. An 'undesirable immigrant' was one who could not 'decently' support himself and his dependants (if any), and appeared likely to become a charge on public funds or was otherwise a detriment to the public. He could also be refused entry on grounds of being undesirable if he had been sentenced for an extradition crime in a foreign country with which an extradition treaty was in force, or if he was the subject of an expulsion order made under the Act. Political refugees, people of British birth and descent and aliens in the country who had been unable to migrate elsewhere escaped the full rigours of the law. The Home Secretary could deport an alien if during the first 12 months of his residence in the UK he was found to be in receipt of parochial relief or he was destitute or living in insanitary conditions.

These provisions suggest that the Act was clearly aimed at minimizing the social cost of immigration that fell to be borne by the United

Kingdom.[4] Nevertheless, in the light of subsequent events the most noteworthy feature of the 1905 legislation appears to be the conferment in law of the right to appeal against refusal of entry to an independent tribunal. As the Act was concerned with imposing controls at the port of entry, immigration boards were constituted for each port consisting of three members from a panel of people with magisterial, business or administrative experience who would hear appeals against refusal of leave to land. This specific provision is of interest because in 1919 a battery of discretionary powers were given to the Home Secretary in another Act[5] to deal with the expulsion of enemy aliens who had sought refuge in the United Kingdom after the war. The 1905 Act was repealed in the war-time atmosphere which gripped the nation, and with it the rights of appeal were swept away. This meant that between 1919 and 1969 when the Immigration Appeals Act was passed to counter claims that immigration decisions were 'arbitrary and capricious',[6] 'there was virtually no legal guarantee of due process in the administration of immigration law'.[7]

The Immigration Boards which heard the appeals held hearings at designated ports and their decisions were binding upon the Secretary of State.[8] However, they did not determine important justiciable questions of fact and law. For example, Section 1 of the Act prohibited 'immigrants' from landing from an 'immigrant ship' except at a scheduled port and except by permission of the officer. In this connection, what did 'immigrant' and 'immigrant ship' mean? Moreover, when was an offence extraditable or of a political nature?[9] Between 1906 and 1910 the number of aliens refused entry averaged only 4 per cent of those inspected by immigration officers.[10] No doubt this is one of the reasons why 'the Aliens Act 1905 seems in the light of subsequent developments a very modest measure'.[11] Nevertheless, the Immigration Boards allowed a variable number of appeals against refusal of entry ranging from 55 per cent in 1906 to 18 per cent in 1909. This averaged about 60 per cent of would-be immigrants losing their appeals every year.[12] The reasons for refusal, as far as these figures were concerned, were 'want of means' and 'medical grounds'. According to Landa success in appeals was very difficult because 'the Boards have developed into mere bodies for confirming and registering the decisions of the immigration officers when they are challenged'.[13] Given that such charges comprise the main thrust of the criticism levied at present-day Immigration Appeals Tribunal, there would appear to be substance in the claims of one writer that 'the 1905 Act marked the beginning of demands for increasing restrictive measures'[14] and of another writer that it constitutes 'the foundation stone of immigration restrictions'.[15]

Alien Immigration and the Background to the 1905 Act

The basis of the Aliens Act 1905 lay in the recommendations of the Royal Commission on Alien Immigration in 1903 which was convened to inquire into and report upon the 'character and extent of the evils which are attributed to the unrestricted immigration of aliens' and 'to advise what remedial or precautionary measures it is desirable to adopt . . . having regard to the absence of any statutory power to exclude or expel' any alien. Between 1881 and 1901 the alien population of London alone had risen from 60,000 to more than 135,000, which included 53,000 Russians and Poles, four-fifths of these living in the Borough of Stepney. The other cities – Manchester, Liverpool and Leeds – had a combined alien population of almost 27,000 in 1901. An estimated 286,000 aliens were resident in the United Kingdom at this time constituting 0.75 per cent of the population. This could be compared with 20 years earlier when there were 135,000 aliens, 0.45 per cent of the population.[16] The aliens were mainly, but not all, Jews. There were non-Jewish Russians, Poles and Germans as well, all arriving in fluctuating numbers. Between 1881 and 1883 about 5000–6000 settled each year; between 1884 and 1886 about 2000–3000 settled. The Russian laws of the time increased the influx so that 7000 settled in 1891, 3000 in 1892 and stabilizing at around 2500 for the rest of the decade. A further fillip to the migration of Jews was added after 1899 arising from the afflictions of famine and violence. In 1905 the pogroms in Russia exacerbated the plight of Russian Jews, leading to a further sharp rise in migration.[17]

The 'evils' which the Royal Commission had in mind were: that the newcomers were largely paupers and thus liable to become a charge on public funds; that they constituted a criminal class; that they were a non-assimilating community; that their religious practices led to their becoming a 'distinct colony'; that because they lived in 'limited localities' the 'native dweller' had become dispossessed of his house accommodation; that they worked for lower wages and continued to do so even when they became skilled;[18] and that they practised 'insanitary habits'.[19]

It is worth noting that a Select Committee of the House of Commons had delved into this question earlier in 1888. It had inquired into 'the subject of immigration of destitute aliens, and as to the extent and effect of such immigration into the United Kingdom; and to report whether it [was] desirable to impose any, and if so, what, restrictions on such immigration'. This Committee reported in 1889 but did not advocate control for the present. It found that immigrants arrived in terrible conditions on the ships, and that their physical condition was inferior to that of British workmen, but their health appeared to be good, notwithstanding their neglect of sanitary laws. They had good qualities and were inoffensive as citizens, but generally dirty and uncleanly in their habits.[20]

By the turn of the century, however, the alien immigrants were beginning to feel the brunt of widening anti-alien hostility for a number of reasons. Populist politicians pandering to the anxieties of sections of the populace demanded immediate remedial legislation, arguing that the problems of indigenous poor workers were directly attributable to the immigrants.[21] The Conservative Government of the day found itself to be in some quandary over the issue of introducing controls, not least because of the novelty of such a course of action. The anti-Semitic stance taken by some of those who argued for control also worried the leadership.[22] A good deal of anti-Semitism existed in a latent form and the Government was concerned lest it became a dominating factor in the debate.

The case for alien restriction was compounded also by the fact that immigration control had long been the rallying cry of those who clamoured for tariff protection. Thus Garner has written that 'The origin of the Aliens Act of 1905 lies in the search for politically profitable protectionism and in the modern superstition of race.'[23] Tariff reform was to protect the British worker against foreign goods. Immigration control was to protect the British worker against foreign workers. The two, it was argued, went together hand in hand. *The Spectator* in 1903 stated that calls for restricting alien immigration were 'the demand of certain London workmen for protection against foreign rivals'.[24] To be sure, trade unionists at the turn of the century had expressed their hostility. The alien was regarded as an incurable 'sweater', an unfair competitor and a bad trade unionist. The Trades Union Congress passed resolutions to restrict immigration in 1892, 1894 and 1895. Thereafter, and during the period of maximum immigration in 1902–1905, it was quiescent.[25] Faced with all this the Government responded by setting up a Royal Commission in 1903.

Unlike the Select Committee of 1888, the Royal Commission reported in favour of statutory regulation of immigration.[26] In so far as the specific 'evils' were concerned the Commission found that there was no substance in the claim that aliens were a health hazard or that they carried contagious diseases,[27] despite the deplorable conditions on the ships in which they arrived. It recommended, however, that immigrants with infectious diseases, lunatics and idiots should be excluded as undesirable aliens.[28] The Commission also found that although workers in some trades had undoubtedly suffered from new competition, immigrants were not the cause of unemployment. 'On the whole,' it declared, 'we arrive at the conclusion . . . that it has not been proved that there is any serious displacement of English labour.'[29] Earlier grievances of the Trades Union Congress were also found to be baseless. Lord James of Hereford in the parliamentary debate on the Aliens Bill 1905 said:

> In the course of [the Commission's] investigation we did not find that the trade unionists came and complained of alien competition with unskilled labour. There are no better trade unionists in the world than aliens: they are industrious to a degree; they keep up their wages and they turn against employers as quickly as any class.[30]

The Commission recommended that controls were not needed to protect the labour market. Controls should, however, be imposed on those aliens who arrived in the UK in an impecunious state and had no prospect of gaining employment, as these would become a charge on public funds.

Of more substance in the Commission's view were the allegations that by living in 'limited localities' in certain parts of the city, the immigrant had dispossessed the native dweller of his house accommodation, leading to higher rents, over-crowding and unsanitary conditions in those areas.[31] The Commission took account of the fact that poor housing conditions existed before the arrival of the immigrants, and accepted that much could be done to ameliorate them if the existing public health laws concerning overcrowding and sanitation were properly enforced.

However, it found that some restrictions on alien immigration would be necessary if immigrants were to be prevented from living in what it termed 'prohibited' areas where conditions 'injurious to the interests of the native resident have tended to produce within the affected districts a great amount of irritation and ill-feeling against the alien immigrants who are regarded as "intruders"'.[32] As for whether the newcomers constituted a criminal class, the Commission concluded that aliens were responsible for a disproportionate amount of crime, and that power should be taken to exclude criminals, anarchists, prostitutes, pimps, those who became a charge on public funds, and other persons of 'notoriously bad character'. The necessary powers of exclusion and deportation should, the Commission recommended, be exercised by a court of summary jurisdiction.[33]

Aliens Restriction Act 1914

The Aliens Act was certainly a foundation for the Aliens Restriction Act of 1914, which extended the powers in the 1905 Act in order to deal with enemy aliens at the outbreak of the war. It was passed amid high war-time fervour and xenophobic agitation and was whisked through Parliament in one day.[34] Its provisions were far-reaching in their effect, not least because they introduced an element of unfettered discretionary power exercisable by the executive in a way hitherto not considered necessary.[35] The executive was endowed with virtual *carte blanche* in control over the activities of aliens. As a corollary to the formulation of this power in the Act, there was a corresponding failure to stipulate statutorily the form in which control would take.

Procedural rights for individuals and the principles underlying the refusal of entry or deportation were not to be found enshrined in any statutory document but became a matter of administrative discretion in the hands of the executive. Under the Act Orders in Council could be made to prohibit or restrict the landing or embarkation of aliens, to deport them, to confine them to specified areas, to make them comply with any provisions as to registration, to prohibit or require them to change their abode, or to restrict their travel. The Act was promptly followed by harsh Restriction Orders passed in 1914.[36] Unlike the Aliens Act of 1905 this Act was a temporary piece of legislation. However, when the war ended it was extended by one year during peace-time by the Aliens Restriction (Amendment) Act 1919.

Aliens Restriction (Amendment) Act 1919

The 1919 Act not only extended the ambit of the 1914 legislation by making the powers of exclusion and deportation exercisable 'at any time',[37] it effectively entrenched those powers through the Act's renewal under the annual Expiring Laws Continuance Acts. The 1905 Act was repealed. In accordance with the Act one Aliens Order was passed in 1920 and another in 1953.[38] The Aliens Order of 1953 dealt with the position of aliens right up to its repeal in 1971 when a permanent framework of control was established once again.

The more salient features of the Act were that as it was passed to deal with former enemy aliens it made provision for the Secretary of State to deport any such person unless an advisory committee had previously exempted that person from internment or repatriation, and whose continued residence in the United Kingdom was alleged by a 'credible person' to be undesirable in the public interest.[39] Former enemy aliens were prohibited from entering the country for three years after 1919.[40] There was also a three-year prohibition upon their acquisition of land and involvement in key industries and they were barred from seeking employment on British ships.[41] It was also a criminal offence for an alien to attempt to do any act calculated to cause sedition or disaffection amongst the armed forces or the civilian population, or to promote or attempt to promote industrial unrest in an industry in which the accused had not been a bona fide employee for the previous two years.[42] These and other restrictions[43] indicate that this law was clearly created with the activities of alien spies specifically in mind.

As for the Aliens Orders of 1920 and 1953, these ensured that from now on aliens in general would only be admitted subject to conditions. Aliens who sought entry into the United Kingdom for the purposes of employment would have to be in possession of a work permit issued to an employer by the Minister of Labour.[44] These work permits were available only for certain limited classes of work for which British or resident alien labour was not available. Authority to admit certain categories of workers, for example, doctors, without permits was given by the Home Secretary in his 'General Instructions' in due course.[45] An alien admitted for employment could bring with him his wife and dependent children; so could an alien admitted as a visitor or student, if he was able to maintain them. Once any time limit on his stay was removed, he could also be joined by his parents, if one of them was over 60, or certain other relatives if compassionate grounds justified their admission.

In the context of war-time emergency legislation both the 1914 and the 1919 Acts are, like the Official Secrets Act of the same period, quite comprehensible. The draconian powers conferred upon the executive were strictly for times of 'imminent national danger or great emergency'.[46] The paradox lies, however, in the extension of this legal regime well beyond times of national exigency into peace-time. For once the abnormal conditions of war-time were over there was no attempt to revert to the pre-1914 law, namely the 1905 Aliens Act. The leverage that that Act accorded in terms of the right of appeal for beleaguered individuals was not to be restored until the passing of the Immigration Appeals Act in 1969, and even then the restoration of right of appeal was to be only partial.[47] For over half a century this war-time temporary legislation, enacted in a hurry, stamped its imprimatur on British immigration law and practice. The Aliens Order of 1953 was repealed in 1971 but the 1919 Act is still in force and its effect on British law therefore remains resilient and enduring.

A sharp slump in immigration into the United Kingdom occurred as a result of the combined effect of the aliens legislation and the inter-war economic depression, although refugees continued to be admitted after the Second World War from Europe on humanitarian grounds.[48] In the late 1950s the subject acquired a whole new dimension when immigration from the new Commonwealth began to rise.

COMMONWEALTH IMMIGRATION: BACKGROUND

Immigration from the New Commonwealth in the late 1950s and early 1960s was exceptional on account of the large numbers involved. Its basic characteristics were as follows. There were, firstly, the immigrants from the West Indies. In the years 1939–45 West Indians had come to Britain to take part in the war effort. After the war some stayed; others went back. Thereafter the numbers who emigrated from the West Indies to the United Kingdom were not large until the mid-1950s when there was a sharp increase. This reached its high-water mark between 1960 and 1961, the figures for 1961 being over 66,000 arrivals. The second category of immigrants to the United Kingdom were from the Indian sub-continent. The post-war pattern of immigration here was similar. In the decade after the war the number of entrants from the sub-continent was little more than a trickle, as with immigration from the West Indies at this time. Some 7000 people entered in 1955 but in 1961 nearly 50,000 arrived. It seems likely that this colossal increase was prompted more by the threat of impending legislation to control immigration, which materialized in 1962, than being a wholly natural increase. The figures for 1960, for example, were only 8400 arrivals from the sub-continent.[49]

The Commonwealth Immigrants Act of 1962 affected to check the flow of immigrants into the United Kingdom from the Commonwealth. After the peak of 1960–62 the numbers from both areas of emigration steadily declined. In fact, in the case of the West Indies, within a few years there was an annual outflow of people of West Indian origin from the United Kingdom.[50] Immigration from the Indian sub-continent also declined although this decline was interrupted by an increase in 1967–69 and to a lesser extent in 1974–76. The early immigration comprised mainly unaccompanied men followed in later years by their wives and children together. Fiancés and fiancées have also entered. Many wives and children have yet to join the sponsoring relative in the United Kingdom, though the bulk of these are now largely dependants from Bangladesh. The total number of male fiancés presently entering is small in the context of present-day Commonwealth immigration, as their entry is now rigorously controlled through the immigration rules.

In addition to immigrants from the Indian sub-continent there has also, since 1965, been the issue of Asian refugees from East Africa although this source of entry has now become of declining importance. These East African Asians were predominantly holders of United Kingdom passports[51] with a definite right of entry to the United Kingdom. In 1968 their entry was restricted by the Commonwealth Immigrants Act 1968. However, at the same time an extra-statutory and extra-legal scheme was started known as the Special Voucher Scheme, in recognition of the hardship suffered by heads of household with United Kingdom passports and their dependants who were under pressure to leave their countries of residence in East Africa and had nowhere else to go.[52] The scheme was worked by setting an annual quota of the number of vouchers to be issued to heads of household who could then bring their dependants with them.[53] Its operation was disrupted by the expulsion of Asians from Uganda, when over 28,000 arrived.[54] The present position is that the vast majority of United Kingdom passport holders from East Africa who wanted to settle in the UK have done so, but a sizeable proportion of them were compelled to migrate to India from where they applied for special vouchers. Their claims have yet to be settled and remain outstanding.[55]

This, then, constitutes a brief sketch of immigration from the New Commonwealth in the post-war era. It comprises the basis on which all Commonwealth immigration legislation and all subsequent immigration and nationality legislation was built.

Commonwealth Immigrants Act 1962

The Commonwealth Immigrants Act 1962 abridged 'the basic principles of English law upon freedom of movement of English subjects' by giving vent 'to local pressure of control'.[56] It was introduced by the Conservative Government to tackle problems of 'overcrowding, unemployment and to foster racial harmony'.[57] It was the first attempt both generally and statutorily to restrict Commonwealth immigration. The scheme of the Act was to draw a distinction between citizens of the United Kingdom and colonies and citizens of independent Commonwealth countries, and the right of free-entry would be dependent upon the kind of passport held by the person seeking entry. Under the Act all Commonwealth citizens were subject to immigration control unless they were: (a) persons born in the United Kingdom; or (b) holders of United Kingdom passports issued by the United Kingdom and not issued by the government of a colony. By this was meant that the passport was issued either by the British Government in the United Kingdom or its representative overseas, usually a United Kingdom High Commissioner in an independent Commonwealth country; or (c) persons included in the passport of a person excluded from control in either of the above two categories.

The Act introduced the notion of 'belonging' to the United Kingdom, the basis upon which exemptions from immigration control were made to Commonwealth citizens. Those who 'belonged' were those who had definite tangible ties with the United Kingdom on account of being either born there or, in most cases, in having acquired their passports here. Not surprisingly, such Commonwealth citizens were mostly white.

The 1962 Act did not, however, merge the distinction between aliens and those Commonwealth citizens who became subject to immigration control. The rights of the wives and children of Commonwealth citizens to join them if they were ordinarily resident in the United Kingdom was specifically recognized then, but has since ceased to be a feature of immigration legislation. Although the Act introduced an employment voucher scheme, Commonwealth citizens in receipt of such vouchers had a statutory right to enter and remain unconditionally. Aliens entering under the work permit scheme could not, by contrast, do the same. Significantly, too, Commonwealth citizens could not be deported on the grounds that their deportation was deemed to be conducive to the public good, but aliens could.

Despite this, however, the Act achieved its purpose. As Grant and Martin observe, the concept of citizenship in United Kingdom law no longer necessarily carried with it the right to freedom from immigration control. This 'affected many white people, particularly third generation Canadians, Australians and New Zealanders, [but] it was designed largely to limit black immigration and achieved its object'.[58] The quotas set for the granting of employment vouchers were large in 1962. But in 1964 they were drastically reduced from the initial 51,000 by the incoming Labour Government to 8500 per annum with the condition that such vouchers were to be issued only to those with particular qualifications or with specified jobs.[59] In 1968 the allocation of vouchers became restricted further still, allegedly because a balance had to be struck between individual territories whilst taking into account special cases such as Malta. The effect of all these measures was a drop in those admitted with employment vouchers from 28,500 in 1963 to 4700 in 1967.

Commonwealth Immigrants Act 1968

The Commonwealth Immigrants Act 1968 was passed to impose immigration controls on a group of Commonwealth citizens who had been specifically exempted from control under the 1962 Act, namely the East African Asians. These were people who had acquired their passports through the British High Commission, a category of people that comprised, among others, the majority of settlers in Kenya. Their rights were accorded to them on exactly the same basis as to their European counterparts in these regions. With the policy of Africanization being adopted by many newly independent African countries, the trading activities of Asians were restricted[60] whereupon these people chose to exercise their right of entry to the United Kingdom in large numbers from the mid-1960s onwards.

The second Commonwealth Immigrants Act was aimed at checking this new flow of immigrants. It was transacted rather hurriedly 'in an atmosphere of emergency and with a willingness to surrender liberal and humanitarian decencies generally associated only with the gravest national crisis'.[61] It wafted through Parliament in three days, the House of Lords sitting all night to ensure its speedy passage. Back in Nairobi the British Overseas Airways Corporation, in keen anticipation of the Bill in Parliament, prevented people from boarding flights to London.[62] The frenzy into which the country had been whipped up over immigration and race relations is difficult to countenance,[63] and the parliamentary debates at this time make painful reading.[64] Once again the Government sought to restrict immigration by evoking the notion of 'belonging', albeit this time it was to define it even more narrowly than it did under the 1962 Act.

From now on United Kingdom passport holders were to be divided into two classes; those in one of them would be 'belongers' and have the right of entry, the others would not. Holders of United Kingdom passports whose passports had been issued by the United Kingdom Government were now to become subject to control unless they had an ancestral link with the United Kingdom. This meant that at least one of their parents or grandparents had to be born here. Because of this formulation, white British settlers in Kenya and other African countries had their rights preserved inviolate. The same could not be said of the Asians since hardly any had the requisite ancestral connection. Ancestral link was therefore the crucial mechanism of the Act and it was an ingenious device. As Macdonald vividly explains, 'It is a formula which enables politicians and officials to cross their hearts three times over and proclaim that there is nothing racist about such laws.'[65]

Nevertheless, it is manifest that this Act, like that of 1962, was racially discriminatory in its effect. For although some 83,000 Asians were admitted in this category between 1968 and 1975, in addition to those displaced by President Amin of Uganda in 1972, the United Kingdom Government's pre-eminent design was to deny a group of its citizens the essential rights of citizenship. By refusing them entry it made them 'stateless in substance though not in name'.[66] The position of these citizens was peculiarly unique in that, unlike other colonial citizens elsewhere, they had no other citizenship of, or the right of abode in, any other country. One effect of being in this state of limbo was that when they tried to enter the United Kingdom they found themselves being shuttlecocked around the world or being incarcerated.[67] Those who were allowed to enter did so only if they were in possession of a special voucher under an extra-legal scheme instituted by the Government in an attempt to mollify the full effects of the new law.

The aim of two Commonwealth Acts passed within six years of each other was to strike at non-white primary immigration from the New Commonwealth which was undertaken for the purpose of settlement. The Acts of 1962 and 1968 succeeded in doing this by first defining and then redefining those who 'belonged' to the United Kingdom. After 1968 governmental concern over immigration decidedly shifted from a sole concern over primary immigration to a more wide-ranging concern over secondary immigration. This shift, although by no means absolute, is a crucial development as it is an important indicator of the changing debate about immigration, which is increasingly to do with a reduction of immigrant numbers.[68] This view is borne out if one examines the development of the law generally between 1968 and the present day, where the most significant legislative initiatives seem to have been framed with this objective in mind.

A good example in this respect is the right of a parent to have his children under 16 join him in the United Kingdom, which was abridged by the 1968 Commonwealth Immigrants Act itself. The 1962 Act had preserved this right by stating that 'The power to refuse admission . . . shall not be exercised . . . in the case of any person [who] is the wife of a child under sixteen years of age, of a Commonwealth citizen . . .'.[69] The Act of 1968, however, then retroactively made the right conditional upon both parents being resident in the United Kingdom.[70]

Immigration Appeals Act 1969

In 1969 the Immigration Appeals Act was passed to provide rights of appeal against a refusal of admission or decision to deport by immigration officials. The Act was the Government's answer to widespread criticism that its handling of immigration control was 'arbitrary and capricious'.[71] After making provision for appeals, however, the Act proceeded in Part III of the Act and under the heading, 'Miscellaneous and Supplementary Provisions' to impose a mandatory requirement of entry clearance for dependants who wished to come to the United Kingdom.[72] The granting of entry clearance took the form of a stamp endorsed in the passport of the person seeking entry at British High Commission posts in an overseas country and it constituted proof of relationship. For practical purposes it was to become the highest hurdle in the paths of all prospective dependants as they now had to prove their relationship, often in very difficult circumstances,[73] in their country of origin.

As the National Council for Civil Liberties observed at the time, the rights of appeal enshrined in the 1969 Act was 'a new and positive feature which could minimise the negative effects of control', but the Government had chosen 'to sabotage' the Act 'with the last minute inclusion of yet another control – perhaps the most restrictive of all – the mandatory entry certificate'.[74] After nearly a quarter of a century this view would appear to have been amply borne out. J.M. Evans, adverting to its effects, has remarked that although the new requirement 'excluded many without a genuine claim and has eased the entry of those who had, it has also inflicted serious hardships by delaying, sometimes for years, and in some cases, no doubt, excluding altogether those with legitimate claims'.[75]

The Immigration Act of 1971 dispensed altogether with the right of a wife to join a husband who was a Commonwealth citizen. In all previous legislation this right had been meticulously included. Now it was not. Instead, the Act stated that 'The rules shall be so framed that Commonwealth citizens settled in the United Kingdom *at the coming into force* of this Act and their *wives and children* are not, by virtue of anything in the rules, any less free to come into and go from the United Kingdom than if this Act had not been passed'[76] (emphasis added).

Two consequences flowed from this. Firstly, the rights of family members to join a sponsoring relative in the United Kingdom were no longer statutorily entrenched but were dependent upon the formulation of immigration rules by the Home Office, or by subordinate civil servants within that department.[77] Secondly, such rules did not protect the rights of a Commonwealth citizen who was not settled in the United Kingdom 'at the coming into force of this Act' (that is, 1 January 1973) but who subsequently became so settled. In fact, the immigration rules have not even protected the rights of those who were settled in the United Kingdom before 1973 as they have become progressively more restrictive over the years. This point is of fundamental importance because it shows that they exercised their rights on sufferance of the Home Office.

Two notable examples may suffice by way of illustration. The first is the worsening position of dependent sons and unmarried daughters. The rules prior to the passage of the 1971 Act said that 'it will be proper to admit an unmarried and fully dependent son or unmarried daughter under 21 who formed part of the family unit overseas if the whole family is coming to settle in the United Kingdom . . .'.[78]

The 1980, and now the current, rules say that children over 18 must qualify for settlement in their own right. 'Special consideration may, however, be given to fully dependent and unmarried daughters over 18 and 21 who formed part of the family unit overseas and have no other close relatives in their own country to turn to.' Moreover, the sponsor must also be able and willing to accommodate his dependants without recourse to public funds.[79] Thus the rights of Commonwealth citizens have been abridged in at least three important ways: it is now no longer 'proper to admit an unmarried or dependent son or daughter', although special consideration 'may be given to such cases'; it must be proved that there are no close relatives in the country of origin for the dependent children to turn to; and accommodation must now be provided.

Secondly, the rules regulating the entry of children to join a single parent have also undergone a similar transformation. The 1970 rules held that a child under 16 years of age could join a parent in the UK in certain circumstances, and that 'parent' includes a stepfather or stepmother, an adoptive parent, and the father as well as the mother of an illegitimate child.[80] The 1973 rules modify this by stating that 'parent' includes the stepfather of a child *whose father is dead*; the stepmother of a child *whose mother is dead*; and the father as well as the mother of an illegitimate child (emphasis added). Adoptive parents are included but they must now prove that 'there has been a genuine transfer of parental responsibility on the ground of the original parent's inability to care for the child, and the adoption is not one of convenience arranged to facilitate the child's admission'.[81]

According to the Immigration Appeals Tribunal these rules are not *ultra vires* the 1971 Act, which could mean that further erosion of the rights of resident Commonwealth citizens may continue. The reasoning that the tribunal employs is that although it is true that progressively restrictive rules have been made after the 1971 Act, the fact is that the Home Secretary could have made even more restrictive rules at any time before 1971 because none of these *particular* rights was statutorily reposed in either the 1962 or the 1968 Acts.[82] Accordingly the Home Secretary may do whatever he or she likes with regard to these particular rights of Commonwealth citizens without fear of infringing any statute, including the 1971 Act.

The concern with reducing the numbers of non-white settlers, and through that with secondary immigration, also explains the abandonment of the *jus soli* rule in the British Nationality Act of 1981. Why an Act introduced with the professed aim of rationalizing and updating British nationality law[83] should tamper with a rule of feudal antiquity going back 700 years can only be explained from this standpoint. The *jus soli* rule had meant that a person born within the allegiance, or in the realm, was a British subject or citizen.[84] The British Nationality Act 1981 changed this by providing that from now on rights of citizenship would accrue to a child born after the commencement of the Act only if at least one parent was either a British citizen or settled in the United Kingdom.[85] The immediate affect of this 'single most contentious provision of the 1981 Act'[86] was to exclude automatically from citizenship the children of immigrant parents who were either in the UK illegally or had no leave to remain. Such children were also, together with their parents, eligible for deportation.

Immigration Act 1971

The Immigration Act of 1971 ended the temporary basis of control over the entry and residence of aliens and of Commonwealth citizens and placed it on a permanent footing. It was the first time this had happened since the Aliens Act of 1905. The Act carved out of the motley of Commonwealth citizens a group to be designated 'patrials'.[87] Only patrials had the right of abode in the United Kingdom and were free from any form of immigration control. This group corresponded roughly to those 'belongers' who had already been carefully delineated in the Commonwealth immigrants legislation of the last decade.

The basis of the Act was that it was aimed at reducing the number of people entering the United Kingdom. Yet if this was so, how was the mere interposition of this new notion to help? The answer is that the Act did affect the number of people who were eligible to come but not in the way that the proponents of the legislation had advocated. 'Patriality' was a further accentuation of the formula of 'belonging' already figuring prominently in the previous legislation.[88] It covered people who had either an ancestral connection with the United Kingdom (mainly white), or were citizens of Commonwealth countries with ties with the United Kingdom through birth, descent, settlement or acquisition of citizenship in the United Kingdom (mainly non-white). In his majestic work Fransman writes that '[T]he idea of patriality was that it should serve as a secondary status. Hence, if a given individual was, for example, a CUKC [i.e. citizen of the United Kingdom and colonies], then that person would also have been a patrial or a non-patrial.'[89]

The effect on the numbers did not take the form of a decrease in the overall people who were entitled to come under the new denomination but in a modest increase. This increase was not a matter of concern because it consisted wholly of people in the first category above; that is, those who were of 'European extraction' and had 'special ties of blood and kinship'.[90] Basically, then, the consequences of this Act were twofold and they emanated entirely from the new concept of 'patriality'. Firstly, because non-white Commonwealth immigrants were on the whole 'non-belongers' under this definition, they had no claim of entry, residence and freedom from immigration control. What the Immigration Act of 1971 did, therefore, was to combine for the first time, in one statutory code, the immigration status of British subjects and aliens. It was no longer the type of one's passport but the citizenship one held that determined immigration status.[91] Secondly, those who had 'special ties of blood and kinship' were, in accordance with the more accentuated notion of 'belonging', exempt from immigration control even if they *were* citizens of other independent Commonwealth countries. The one notable exception was citizens of the Republic of Ireland, who were not 'patrial' and did not have the right of abode and yet were free from immigration control.[92]

As with previous immigration legislation the circumstances surrounding the passage of the Act of 1971 are extraordinary. Reginald Maudling, the Home Secretary, introducing the Bill in Parliament, spoke of 'the simple fact . . . that some control had become necessary in the interests of society in this country',[93] and that 'under the Bill the total who come in future will be such as will carry out our undertaking of the election that there will be no further large-scale permanent immigration'.[94] The notion that was abroad in the House was, as Arthur Davidson found, 'that the purpose of the immigration Bill is to cut down immigration', and he could see 'no Government statement to suggest other than that the purpose of the Bill is to have a substantial effect on the number of immigrants entering the country . . .'.[95] But as members soon found out, this was not so. David Steel, for example, let this be known by saying: 'The saddest conclusion I have reached at the end of our discussions is that, regrettably, this was a thoroughly unnecessary measure. . . . This Bill does nothing about numbers. . . .'[96] It is difficult not to avoid reaching the conclusion that the only real reason for the Bill was, as Mr Maudling readily acknowledged, the fulfilment of an election pledge given by the Conservatives in 1970 that more could be and would be done on immigration. It was a story not without previous parallels, which is what gave the Act 'in the longer perspective . . . the inevitability of true Greek tragedy . . .'.[97]

This view is reinforced by the fact that the Government did not have a perception of either the 'problem' or the 'solution' on which it was seeking to legislate. It did not have a clear-cut immigration policy which it sought to place on the Statute Book, and when taken to task by Opposition members it found itself to be in the most difficult position.[98] Indeed, the Bill does not seem to have been prepared by the Home Secretary but by civil servants not necessarily acting on his instructions. It is unlikely that the drafters of the Bill knew what the Minister wanted, nor, having produced it, that the Minister knew what the drafters had produced for him.[99] In fact, the press seems to have been better informed about the minutiae of the Bill than the Government.[100] The concept of 'patriality' was not, apparently, devised by the Home Secretary but – it was being said almost in jest – by the Lord Chancellor, Lord Hailsham, the 'Government's leading classical scholar', who had 'plucked the word . . . from obscurity'.[101]

The joining together in the Bill of non-patrial Commonwealth citizens with aliens into one category had two effects. Firstly, the assertion by the Minister of State at the Home Office that 'the whole complex of law (regarding the immigration status of aliens and non-patrial Commonwealth citizens) should be brought into harmony in a single piece of comprehensive and permanent legislation'[102] was seminal, as it was to pave the way for the British Nationality Act ten years later which, by dispensing with the idea of Commonwealth citizenship, aligned freedom from immigration control with citizenship. Whether or not such a stance seemed ignominious to the government of the time, it clearly made more sense to muster support for the Bill on this ground than to argue that it was aimed at a reduction of immigration numbers. Secondly, such a joining together set the mould for how coloured immigration and immigrants were henceforth to be viewed in British society: that is, if possible, as 'non-belongers'. The most striking evidence of this in the 1971 Act itself is the provision for voluntary repatriation.[103]

AN OUTLINE OF BRITISH NATIONALITY LAW

An incursion into British nationality law is necessary at this stage, for a prominent feature of the post-1950s immigration law is the recourse to nationality law concepts which have been modified in order to meet the ends of immigration control. This is an oddity in British law since in most countries nationality law determines the rights and disabilities of individuals. As nationality is a concept of international law[104] those individuals who are nationals of a state are deemed, within the domestic legal order, to be its citizens. They have the right to enter and remain without let or hindrance and the state uses its immigration laws to prescribe the entry and residence of non-nationals. In the United Kingdom, however, the opposite has been the case. During the past thirty years it is immigration status, defined by immigration law, which has determined the rights and disabilities of nationals. Nationality law has been distorted to achieve the policy objectives of immigration control. This curious state of affairs is best explained by a brief historical analysis.

Historically, there had never been a general right of entry and settlement for people into the United Kingdom. Aliens who settled were subject to severe disabilities.[105] They could not inherit real property[106] and whatever rights they had flowed from the exercise of the royal prerogative. The law on the subject was not as clear-cut and simple as it has often been taken to be,[107] but broadly speaking there were two categories. Those who were born within the allegiance were known as subjects;[108] those born without were aliens.[109] The basis of the concept of a British subject at common law was the correlation of allegiance and protection. In return for his allegiance to his lord, and later to his king, the subject was given protection. This rule is of 'such basic and compelling character' at common law that it is 'irrefutable as a major principle of law'.[110] As correlative legal duties it is necessary, however, to define what we mean by allegiance and protection.

Fundamentally, allegiance signifies the fidelity of the subject and means that he will not commit treason. Protection means the protection of the Crown against the activities of others, but also respect for the subject by the Sovereign in the course of his own activities. The latter is a negative protection but it is necessary if protection is to mean anything as there is not much value in protecting a subject against third parties only to reserve him for spoliation of his lord.[111] Such indeed is the intrinsic durability of these principles that the House of Lords has held that the issue of a passport in modern times imposes upon the Crown the burden of protection and on the holder the duty of fidelity, so that as long as the passport is held the holder may be liable for treason, even though he is an alien and the acts in question are committed outside the realm.[112] Given this settled principle regarding the correlation of allegiance and protection, the alien's position in this respect is no different from that of a British subject.[113]

These principles formed the bedrock of the rule that those born in the British Colonies owed allegiance to the Crown and were thus subjects within the protection of the Crown. Fransman puts it well when he states in this respect that '[A]llegiance was the forerunner of modern nationality'.[114] By the seventeenth century the expansion of colonial rule led logically to the corresponding liberalization of the law so that naturalization was made easier for aliens living in the colonies who, although not born there, owed their allegiance to the Crown. A series of statutes were passed to this end and a doctrine of imperial naturalization grew up.[115] Regular naturalization under statute was introduced by the Imperial Act of 1844. However, in 1847 An Act for the Naturalisation of Aliens laid down that the Act of 1844 did not apply to the colonies, which were endowed with their own legislatures to undertake naturalization of their own volition 'within the respective limits of such colonies or possessions'.[116]

The late Professor Clive Parry writes that the effect of the statute of 1847 was 'both to confirm and to encourage local naturalization', and that a new principle of imperial administration had now come into play 'of territorial division of legislative competence'.[117] By this, power was devolved by the United Kingdom Parliament on executive and legislative assemblies of colonial governments to enable them to deal with a number of local affairs that were deemed to be within their competence. The Act of 1847 laid down that local naturalization by individual colonies, particularly the white Dominion Territories, could be undertaken. As a result these territories embarked upon a course of pursuing racially discriminatory policies directed at people of Asian origin who attempted to emigrate to them after the middle of the nineteenth century.[118]

Chinese emigration to Australia, for example, met with Victoria Act 39 of 1855, which was directed at 'any male adult native of China or of an island in the Chinese seas or any person born of Chinese parents', and restricted the entry of Chinese migrants into Victoria by sea.[119] In New South Wales, after numerous Chinese passengers were refused permission to land illegally, Act 4 of 1888 was passed. Article 2 of this Act conferred retrospective validity upon the acts of any official 'who may have committed any act in preventing the landing of Chinese, or otherwise in relation to Chinese immigrants, or to vessels carrying such immigrants', and no action could then be brought against that official in any court of law.[120]

The importance of such restrictive immigration policies lay not only in enabling the Dominion Territories to determine the racial composition of their population but also to base their nationality laws in large part on the restrictive immigration policies pursued. In Australia, the 'All-White Australian' policy could be made effective only by a linkage of nationality laws with immigration laws.[121] Thus Professor Parry has written that:

> No account of the nationality law of Australia would be complete without a reference to the policy of exclusion of African, Asiatic and Pacific Island aboriginals. This policy in fact proceeded federation and colonial legislation restrictive of Chinese immigration dates back at least to 1861.[122]

In the other Dominion Territories the development of local nationality laws followed the same course.[123]

The tendency of certain colonies to exclude British subjects from their territories was a thorny subject for the British Government in view of its other colonial possessions.[124] The Colonial Conference of

1902 and the Imperial Conference of 1907 were convened to look into the question of naturalization, followed by another Imperial Conference of 1911 when agreement was reached on this matter. The upshot of the 1911 Conference was the British Nationality and Status of Aliens Act 1914, which postulated the concept of the 'common code'.

The Act was essentially an attempt to underwrite links with a fragmenting empire. It was based upon the ancient idea of allegiance and contained no rules at all on how changes in territorial sovereignty would affect nationality. The 'common code' meant that there was an equality of citizenship throughout the empire. The 'common code', however, was only a half-truth for it did not explain that in practice the self-governing dominions were at liberty to discriminate against subjects of the same Crown, and were, in fact, encouraged in this by the home Government. The result was that the much vaunted 'common status' of British subjects did not connote any substantial equality in relation to, in particular, the right to enter or settle in any particular part of British Territory.

A British subject of whatsoever race or condition might indeed enter the United Kingdom freely. But production of evidence of that status had itself no influence on an immigration officer in Canada, Australia, New Zealand or South Africa.[125] The desire on the part of newly independent nations to formulate their own nationality laws was the main reason for reform in 1948. Curiously, however, the policy of the 1914 Act, aiming 'generally to discourage purely local naturalization',[126] was, despite its unpopularity with the governments of the Dominion Territories, re-enacted rather awkwardly in the British Nationality Act of 1948. The hope of the home Government was that the notion of the Commonwealth would, in time, solidify so that citizens of the Commonwealth would have equal rights and privileges by virtue of their shared common association with the mother country.[127]

This was the basis of the two awkward phrases used in the Act of 1948: 'Commonwealth Citizenship' and 'Citizenship of the United Kingdom and Colonies'. Commonwealth citizenship was synonymous with the status of a British subject, the old status at common law.[128] As far as the United Kingdom was concerned, citizens of independent Commonwealth countries fell under this status and were free from its immigration controls as under the common law. 'Citizens of the United Kingdom and Colonies' in reality denoted not only people who had genuine links with the United Kingdom, but also people whose only links were with a United Kingdom dependency; for example, Hong Kong.

It was clear, then, that the United Kingdom did not have an

individual citizenship of its own, any more than Hong Kong or Tanganyika at this time had a citizenship of its own. But why combine the two groups into one? The Lord Chancellor, introducing the Bill in the House of Lords, explained that such a citizenship was designed to help all those who did not have the advantage of belonging to an independent Commonwealth country. It provided the gateway to the 'umbrella' status of British subject and the Government had decided to bestow this citizenship in one single category simply because it was not right 'that we should differentiate between our own people and the people for whom we are trustees'.[129]

This did not obscure the fact that the proposed juxtaposition of citizenship law was artificial. To be sure, this was the nub of the Opposition's attack on the Bill. Why was it necessary to legally define citizenship in this way when the concept of allegiance and British subject had sufficed in the past? If the rights and privileges attached to the status of British subject then, in the words of Lord Altrincham, '[W]hy try to link together in an artificial connection of this kind an immense variety of people who range in their standard of civilisation from the head hunters of Borneo to noble Lords opposite?'[130] In his view citizenship should have a real meaning and should not be used loosely.[131]

In spite of this, the Bill became law. Its more notable features were that it recognized the common law principle that birth within the territories of the Crown conferred citizenship of the United Kingdom and colonies (the *jus soli* rule).[132] Those born outside United Kingdom territories, but of a father who was such a citizen, also acquired citizenship through descent (the *jus sanguinis* rule).[133] A new method of acquisition of citizenship was introduced by registration either in the United Kingdom or elsewhere to (a) citizens of independent Commonwealth countries and Ireland; (b) children; (c) women married to United Kingdom citizens; and (d) certain stateless persons.[134] Aliens could acquire the same status by naturalization.[135]

An interesting aspect of the Act was the creation of what Macdonald refers to as 'a number of residual categories of British subjects'[136] who were neither citizens of independent Commonwealth countries nor citizens of United Kingdom and colonies. Some of these were Irish, and some were foreign women married to British subjects. But the biggest category was those termed 'British subjects without citizenship'.[137] These were British subjects born before 1949, most of whom were inhabitants of Indian princely states, whilst others, although of Indian descent, lived in other Commonwealth countries. The Act also referred to 'British Protected Persons', who were people who lived in any protectorate, protected state, mandated territory or trust territory and who were British subjects 'by virtue of their connection with the protected state or territory'.[138] Most of these territories were former German colonies given to the United Kingdom to administer after the First World War, or territories in the Arabian Gulf.

BRITISH NATIONALITY ACT 1981

The British Nationality Act 1981 bears the full imprint of nationality legislation. The then Home Secretary, William Whitelaw, prefaced its introduction in Parliament with the observation that 'Citizenship and right of abode, which ought to be related, have over the years parted company with each other'.[139] In a sense the law has now come full circle. While the empire lasted Parliament was determined not to follow the road of its white dominions and let immigration law determine the nationality rights of individuals. But in the 1960s such a course of action could no longer be resisted. A Parliamentary Committee affirmed in 1977 that 'the extent to which immigration law . . . interacts with the law on nationality . . . is itself a reminder of our imperial past . . .'. However, this is not strictly true, for although there is interaction between immigration law and nationality law this did not occur during 'our imperial past' but only when the bulk of the empire had broken away. Only the fact of New Commonwealth immigration, it is submitted, is attributable to the imperial past.[140] The Act replaced the scheme established by the British Nationality Act 1948, the principal nationality legislation until 1981. It had long been felt that the framework created by the British Nationality Act 1948 was outdated and in urgent need of reform. That Act created a composite citizenship of the United Kingdom and colonies.

With the advent of post-war independence for the colonies and their formation into separate nation-states, often under a republican form of government, the fundamental inadequacy of a composite citizenship to refer to citizens of other independent Commonwealth countries was becoming increasingly evident, especially when allegiance of such citizens no longer lay with the mother country. At another level, the existence of the composite citizenship meant that the United Kingdom's position with regard to its own nationals was becoming difficult to work out in international law. This was aptly demonstrated when the UK joined the European Economic Community in 1972. Under the Treaty of Rome provision was made for the right to freedom of movement for nationals of member states.[141] The Government had the difficult task of defining its nationals for Community purposes, particularly in the view of the fact that its immigration laws did not discriminate between nationals and non-nationals of the United Kingdom.[142]

In the words of Vaughan Bevan: '[T]he British Nationality Act 1981 is the ultimate recognition of the immigration reality for which junior members of the Commonwealth had catered, however distastefully, for many years and with which the United Kingdom had ingloriously contended since 1962'. He continues, 'Until 1981 the basic concepts of citizenship remained unchanged.'[143] The Act of 1981 replaced the existing scheme by dividing citizenship into three groups. The most valuable of these is British citizenship, corresponding to the 'patrial' status under the 1971 Act and denoting a genuine link with the United Kingdom.[144]

Second in line is citizenship of the British Dependent Territories, conferred upon those citizens of the United Kingdom and colonies who had a connection with a colony by virtue of being born there.[145] Unlike the first category, this one carries no right of entry to the United Kingdom. The term, however, is a misnomer as there is no common travel area matching what appears to be a common citizenship.[146] A person in this category does not have an enforceable right of travel between one British Dependent Territory and another, any such right being dependent upon the local immigration laws of individual colonies. Thus 'to call the three million British Dependent Territories Citizens a "group" begs a question'.[147]

The third category is British Overseas Citizenship. 'If British Dependent Territories Citizens do not *per se* enjoy any enforceable rights, *a fortiori* this is true of British Overseas Citizens.[148] This category is designed for those who do not fall into either of the first two and is a transitional citizenship generally catching those United Kingdom and colonies citizens who were born in former colonies which have subsequently become independent. It confers no right to enter any British territory and is therefore even more of a misnomer than the second category described above.[149] The largest number of British Overseas Citizens are in Malaysia. About 90 per cent of these are Malaysian nationals but will lose this nationality if they attempt to enter the United Kingdom on the basis of their nationality.

Another group are the East African Asians, divided between the East African countries and India. Although they do not have a right of entry, the Government's extra statutory voucher scheme initiated with the aim of facilitating the entry of the 'United Kingdom Passport Holders' has meant that under 10,000 – and not, as the Home Office suggested 39,000 – are likely to come from India, where they have been waiting in long queues for several years.[150] There are also those who acquired United Kingdom and Colonies citizenship by descent and consular registration.[151]

All in all, some 1.5 million British Overseas Citizens were created by the 1981 Act. It may be noted that neither the status 'Commonwealth Citizen' nor that of 'British subject' is wholly transplanted by these new categories. Civic rights still attach to the status of a Commonwealth citizen rather than that of a British citizen, and the class of persons called British subjects without citizenship is preserved under the 1981 Act.[152]

Although the 1981 Act thoroughly overhauls British nationality law there is little doubt that the overriding considerations in its enactment were to do with immigration control. It is as much an immigration Act as a nationality one. Thus in their article on the new law White and Hampson have no doubt that 'the principal motive' for changing nationality law is concern with immigration.[153] Macdonald began the first edition of his book, *Immigration Law and Practice*, with the caustic assertion that:

> the much publicised aims of the 1981 Act in equating
> citizenship with the right of abode is only achieved by casting
> one lot of citizens of the United Kingdom and Colonies into
> the new limbo of British Overseas Citizenship and another lot
> into a polyglot British Dependent Territories Citizenship, in
> which Hong Kong and the Falkland Islands share a common
> citizenship but their inhabitants cannot travel freely to each
> other's territory.[154]

FUTURE TRENDS

Immigration and nationality law concepts continue to interact awkwardly with each other in the future control of immigration. There is little attempt to tidy up the law of nationality. Instead new legislation is geared to stringently controlling both immigrants without and immigrants within the United Kingdom. Ever since the publication of the *First Report from the Select Committee on Race Relations and Immigration* in 1978[155] the thrust of immigration controls has been increasingly directed at immigrants after entry, and not just before. This Select Committee Report made a number of detailed suggestions.[156] In particular, it called for (a) more resources to be allocated for curbing illegal immigration;[157] (b) strict controls on unauthorized employment propped up by sanctions introduced as 'a matter of urgency';[158] (c) procedures to be introduced by the Department of Health and Social Security to institute effective identity checks and improve the issuing of national insurance numbers to new applicants;[159] (d) an independent inquiry to be set up by the Government to look into the system of internal control of immigration.[160]

This partial policy shift is based on a number of assumptions such as that immigration is directly and intrinsically related to the creation of socio-economic problems and the solution is to be found in the reduction of numbers of persons entering the United Kingdom.[161] The Select Committee has never sought to question the basis of its assumptions. It has not examined the relative effects of the periodical rise or decline in non-white Commonwealth immigration on such issues as racial tension, unemployment and social deprivation. Consequently, no rational or coherent policy on immigration has ever been evolved. Nevertheless, the assumptions persist.[162]

Writing about the effects of recent legislation such as the Immigration Act 1988, Dr Claire Palley concludes that:

> a combination of the legislation on immigration and on nationality does cause hardship. The 1988 Immigration Act provides that families of long-settled British and Commonwealth male citizens can join them only if such family will be maintained without recourse to public funds. This strikes at family life. There are also effects on human dignity: social security benefits depend on immigrant status and social security officers, who are not always sympathetic, check passports and ask detailed questions, giving black people the idea that they are agents of immigration control.[163]

The most important changes introduced by the Immigration Act 1988 are the removal of automatic rights of entry for the wives and children of Commonwealth citizens settled here before 1973;[164] a restriction on exercise of right of abode for wives in cases of polygamy;[165] a restriction on the right of appeal against deportation;[166] the creation of a continuous offence of overstaying,[167] facilitating entry of persons exercising Community rights;[168] and making some changes to the law on illegible stamps.[169] However, it is generally agreed that the most striking effect of this legislation is the removal of

> the only statutory right to family unity in British law. It is now the case, as a result of that Act, that *no* British citizen has a right to be joined in the United Kingdom by a spouse of either sex.[170]

The second major piece of legislation has been made in relation to Hong Kong. By virtue of the Joint Declaration of 1984 between Britain and China, reached in anticipation of the expiry of Britain's lease of Hong Kong in 1997, Britain agreed to give up all claims to sovereignty in that year in return for China's promise to retain capitalism there for at least 50 years. There was, however, no agreement on nationality, only an Exchange of Memoranda. Under this Britain declared that all British Dependent Territories Citizens (BDTCS) in Hong Kong would lose their status in 1999, but a new 'appropriate status' would be created permitting requests for consular protection in the form of a British National (Overseas) status which the BDTCs could apply for. These changes were incorporated into the Hong Kong (British Nationality) Order 1986, which was passed by Britain under the Hong Kong Act 1985.[171] The brutal suppression of a pro-democracy student demonstration on 4 June 1989 in Tiananmen Square in Beijing, however, aroused fears and doubts in the people of Hong Kong about the Chinese guarantees in the settlement of 1984. Large numbers of people left the colony to obtain nationality elsewhere, the rate of leaving being 55,000 per annum.

The passing of the British Nationality (Hong Kong) Act 1990 was an ironic move by the British Government to induce a highly selective and highly qualified minority of people, who were essential to the continued prosperity of Hong Kong, to remain there by bestowing upon them an automatic right of abode in the UK.[172] It was felt that, safe in the security of this right, they would not emigrate, even to the United Kingdom. By contrast, when a somewhat similar fear affected the people of the Falkland Islands in 1982, the Government responded by conferring British citizenship, retrospectively to the commencement of the 1981 Act, on all its native inhabitants in the British Nationality (Falkland Islands) Act 1983.

The fear of further entry of new immigrants has also led to the imposition of criminal penalties on carriers. The Immigration (Carriers' Liability) Act 1987 began by imposing a £1000 fine on carriers that brought into the United Kingdom a passenger without a valid passport or identity document or a proper visa or entry clearance from the port of departure.[173] This fine has now been doubled to £2000 by statutory instrument.[174] Carriers have a defence if they can show that the falsity of any passport or visa produced to them by a passenger was not 'reasonably apparent'.[175] But the Act is objectionable and carriers strongly object to it as '[T]here is no way in which [they] . . . can sort out the passengers who qualify for entry and those who do not, unless they take on the role of immigration officer'.[176]

The doubling of the fines on carriers in 1991 was itself directly aimed at checking the arrival of asylum seekers, a measure that was to become the precursor of the Asylum Bill in Parliament. In 1985 the Government had already broken with convention to impose visa requirements on Sri Lanka, a Commonwealth country, in an attempt to prevent Tamil refugees arriving here. This was followed up with visa requirements being imposed on India, Ghana, Nigeria, Turkey (with its Kurdish refugees) and Haiti – all countries with internal strife and fleeing populations.

The Asylum Bill itself, which has comprised the subject-matter of our discussion in Chapter 1, was the flag-ship of the Government's legislative programme in its 1991–92 session. As with many ill-considered initiatives – such as the Government's much vaunted removal of the right to silence for police detainees in 1989 – it had to be shelved for the time being, so damning was the criticism of it from all sections. This raises the question whether it was really all that necessary.

Perhaps governments need to pin-point their case with more exactitude then they have hitherto done. The Foreign Secretary's arguments in Brussels in May 1992 for the retention of frontier passport controls (despite the implementation of the single European market) to combat terrorism and drug trafficking were found by many people to be baseless.[177] *The Times* put it well in its leader when it said:

> Retaining intra-EC passport control will not halt the IRA. If
> it did, the British government would surely have introduced
> it by now between Britain and Ireland. Nor will it stop drug
> trafficking, the iron law of which is that if more restriction
> means more scarcity, that in turn means higher prices on
> the streets and bigger profits to the suppliers. Nor will it
> make a difference to the main flow of non-EC immigrants
> to Britain who enter legally, though it may affect the
> marginal flow of illegal immigration. That is where its real
> significance lies.[178]

In an increasingly uncertain world what is needed, as Sir Norman Anderson once said in his Hamlyn Lectures, is not an 'emphasis on race or colour as the decisive criterion which is both offensive and harmful' in immigration control, but 'a policy of both justice and compassion'. Addressing himself to issues in 1978 that are as relevant today given the plight of British citizens in Hong Kong, and the hardships suffered by Commonwealth citizens and their descendants in being reunited with their families, Sir Norman expounded on his precepts of justice and compassion as follows:

> justice in considering every applicant strictly on his merits
> and giving full recognition to the claims of those who have
> opted for United Kingdom Citizenship to the exclusion of
> any other; and compassion in opening the door freely to
> the *bona fide* marriage partners and dependents of those who
> are already here and to other cases of exceptional hardship.[179]

Those precepts have yet to be applied.

NOTES AND REFERENCES

1 A detailed analysis of the Act appears in Henriques, H.S.Q. (1906) *The Law of Aliens and Naturalisation*, Chap. VI. London. Also see Sibley, N.W. and Elias, A. (1906) *The Aliens Act and the Right of Asylum, passim*. London.

2 See Gainer, B. (1972) *The Alien Invasion*. London; Garrard, J.A. (1971) *The English and Immigration 1880–1910*. Oxford; Gartner, L.P. (1971) *The Jewish Immigrant in England 1908–1914*. London; Landa, M.J. (1911) *The Alien Problem and Its Remedy*. London. For more general studies see Cunningham, W. (2nd edn 1969) *Alien Immigrants to England*. London; Holmes, C. (1978) *Immigrants and Minorities in British Society*. London; Foot, P. (1965) *Immigration and Race in British Politics*. London; Walvin, J. (1984) *Passage to Britain*. London; Dummet, A. and Nicol, A. (1990) *Subjects, Citizens, Aliens and Others*. London.

3 The Home Secretary, Aretas Allers-Douglas, introducing the Bill: HC Deb. Vol. 145, col. 468 (18 April 1905).

4 See Macdonald, I. (1st edn 1983) *Immigration Law and Practice in the UK*, p. 19. London. Macdonald sees the genesis of this approach in the poor laws and vagrancy laws of the eighteenth century, when, during the Industrial Revolution, there was a great movement of people from the country to the towns. These laws allowed for indigent migrant workers to be sent back to the countryside by the signing of a removal order by the justices, thereby effecting deportation (see George, M.D. (1965) *London Life in the Eighteenth Century*, p. 116, London). The earliest alien laws followed this policy of keeping down the social costs to a minimum. See also Landa, *op. cit.* p. 185.

5 Aliens Restriction (Amendment) Act 1919, which replaced the Aliens Act 1914.

6 *Report of the Committee on Immigration Appeals* (August 1967) Cmnd 3381 at p. 27.

7 See Evans, J.M. (2nd edn 1983) *Immigration Law*, p. 9. London. In practice, the full severity of the law was tempered by a number of administrative concessions, as for example an advisory committee set up in 1919 which recommended to the Home Secretary that an enemy alien should not be deported. This system ended in 1939. From 1956 aliens were allowed to put their case before the Chief Magistrate against deportation if they had been resident in the United Kingdom two years prior to receiving notification of deportation. However, the recommendations were not binding on the Home Secretary. Clearly, then, whatever system of administrative concessions was applied it fell far short of a legal right of appeal.

8 It seems that such a decision as that of the Home Secretary in the case of Rodney Perera (*The Times*, 23 May 1984), where the Home Secretary reversed the decision of the Immigration Appeals Tribunal authorizing the appellant's deportation, would not occur under the Aliens Act. This would be so notwithstanding the fact that the Home Secretary made all the rules necessary for the working of the boards under the Act of 1905.

9 The working of the Immigration Boards makes interesting reading. See Landa, *op. cit.* pp. 199–212, 248–58; Gainer, *op. cit.* pp. 199–203; Garrard, *op. cit.* pp. 104–5, 113, 125–217.

10 The vast majority of immigrants entered the United Kingdom unmolested, despite the Act. In 1906, 38,527 entered and only 931 were rejected at first instance. In 1910, 19,143 entered and only 1006 were rejected at first instance (see Garrard, *op. cit.* p. 107). This was in accordance with the remark of the Prime Minister (Balfour) in the House on 10 July 1905 that 'the great mass of alien immigrants was not touched at all. Those who were kept out were but a small number, and they were kept out solely because they were likely to become a burden upon the country if they were allowed in': HC Deb., Vol. 14, col. 157 (10 July 1905). Indeed, the Home Secretary admitted that a criminal who could pay a higher fare for his sea passage from the Continent would be unimpeded in entering the country. See HC Deb. Vol. 159, col. 1257 (19 July 1905).

11 J.M. Evans, *op. cit.* p. 6.

12 *Ibid.* p. 9. These figures are based upon Tables appearing in Garrard, *op. cit.* p. 107 and Landa, *op. cit.* p. 228.

13 Landa, *op. cit.* p. 228. At p. 230 he declared that 'The odds are decidedly against the immigrant who is once refused permission to land.'

14 J.M. Evans, *op. cit.* p. 9. Evans is referring to Gainer, *op. cit.* pp. 202–7.

15 James Walvin, *op. cit.* p. 117.

16 For example, only while the empire lasted was it meaningful to speak in terms of the obligations of the 'mother country' to the colonies. Thus in 1958 Arthur Bottomley MP said, 'We are the most industrialized country in the world and we have a direct responsibility for our colonial subjects when they are poor, badly housed or unemployed.' He went on to say that 'The central principle on which our status in the Commonwealth is largely dependent is the "open door" to all Commonwealth citizens. If we believe in the importance of our great Commonwealth we should do nothing in the slightest degree to undermine that principle': HC Deb., Vol. 596, col. 1576 (5 December 1958). Also see Walvin, *op. cit.* Chapter 9.

17 M.J. Landa, *op. cit.* pp. 58–61.

18 James Walvin, *op. cit.* p. 62.

19 The disposition of immigrants towards working for lower wages and in worse conditions seems to be a matter of antediluvian resentment almost everywhere. For example, the records of the Privy Council during the reign of James I abound with complaints against aliens. The weavers of London are on record as having complained to the Privy Council 'that Aliens injure trade – employ men younger than allowed by Statute – live more cheaply – and therefore sell more cheaply and engross the trade of foreigners' (see *Royal Commission on Alien Immigration 1903* (Cmnd 1742), at p. 2). Present-day New Commonwealth immigrants have emulated their forebears. About 400 small back-street rag trade firms, mostly Asian-owned, are known to be operating in Birmingham, Sandwell, Wolverhampton and Coventry. These employ about 20,000 workers, nine-tenths of them women whose pay packets can be as low as £24.40 for a 40-hour week. The Low Pay Unit in the West Midlands, investigating those firms, states: 'It is hard to believe that some of the premises are factories. Often, there is only one entrance and windows are covered by shutters or corrugated iron. Children under school age play in some shops and babies are sometimes present. After school and during holidays 12 to 16 year old children are employed to do packaging,

thread clipping and pressing with steam irons that are extremely hot. First aid units are rare.' See 'Slave Labour in the Rag Trade', *The Observer*, 5 May 1984.

20 *Royal Commission on Alien Immigration, op. cit.* at pp. 5–6.

21 See *Royal Commission on Alien Immigration, op. cit.* at p. 506.

22 For example, Sir William Evans Gordon (MP for Stepney), who gave evidence before the Royal Commission in 1903: see pp. 406–51. Also see Arnold White at pp. 15–28, 47–55.

23 The General Repealing Act of 1863 had swept off the statute book most laws relating to aliens.

24 For example, Arnold White, *op. cit.* See B. Gainer, *op. cit.* pp. 123–8; J.A. Garrard, *op. cit.* p. 18.

25 L.P. Gartner, *op. cit.* p. 278.

26 *The Spectator*, 12 December 1903. Also see Landa, *op. cit.* p. 184; Gainer, *ibid.* pp. 138–45, 150–1; and Garrard, *ibid.* pp. 37, 56, 90 and 142.

27 J.A. Garrard, *op. cit.* p. 71.

28 *Ibid.* para. 41.

29 *Ibid.* para. 131. On the economic effects of alien immigration, see paras 126–36.

30 Lord James of Hereford, HC Deb. Vol. 150, col. 770 (20 July 1905). It may be noted that Asquith always maintained that labour would not benefit by restriction. As early as 1 December 1898 he had expressed this view at Lowestoft, when Home Secretary, adding that 'from county to county some of the most valuable and vitally fertilizing ingredients in our social structure had come to us by refugees from abroad'. Landa, *op. cit.* p. 183. Also Paul Foot has written that New Commonwealth workers 'joined the union immediately eagerly supporting all moves for higher wages', *op. cit.* p. 127.

31 Royal Commission on Alien Immigration, *op. cit.* at paras 142–71.

32 For criticisms of the 'prohibited areas proposal', see the powerful dissenting memo of Sir K. Digby, Permanent Under-Secretary at the Home Office: *Royal Commission on Alien Immigration, op. cit.* at pp. 48–61. The 1905 Act did not incorporate this proposal, no doubt because of the practical difficulties involved in putting it into effect.

33 *Royal Commission on Alien Immigration, op. cit.* at paras 112–25.

34 Cf. Gainer, *op. cit.* pp. 207–8.

35 The Act entailed the reimposition of a rigid control of aliens such as had not been known in the United Kingdom since the French Revolutionary and Napoleonic Wars: see Parry, C. (1957) *Nationality and Citizenship Laws of the Commonwealth and Ireland*, p. 87, London.

36 Aliens Restriction (Consolidation) Order 1914 SI 1914/1874 and Aliens Restriction (Belgian Refugees) Order 1914 SI 1914/1478.

37 Aliens Restriction (Amendment) Act 1919, s. 1(i).

38 Aliens Order 1920 SI 1920/448 and Aliens Order 1953, SI 1953/1671.

39 Section 9 of 1919 Act.

40 *Ibid.* s. 10. Note, however, that the Home Secretary could make exceptions to this and in doing so was required to publish a list of those to whom he had granted permission to enter.

41 *Ibid.* s. 11, s. 12.

42 *Ibid.* s. 3.

43 *Ibid.* sections 4–8.

44 Aliens Order 1920 SI 1920/448, art. 13(b); Aliens Order 1953 SI 1953/1671, art. 4(1) (b).

45 These 'General Instructions' issued by the Home Secretary are the precursor of present-day immigration rules.

46 Aliens Restriction (Amendment) Act 1919, s. 1(i). In the first two years of the war the Government deported some 21,000 of the 75,000 persons of German or Austrian birth resident in the United Kingdom. A great number, including naturalized British citizens of German origin, were interned under the Defence of the Realm (Consolidation) Regulations 1914, reg. 14B, which the House of Lords in *R* v. *Halliday ex P. Zadiq* (1917) AC 260 held to be *intra vires* of the virtually unlimited powers conferred by the Defence of the Realm Consolidation Act 1914, s. 1(i). (See Evans, *op. cit.* p. 45, note 46.)

47 For example, the Home Secretary's exercise of power of deportation on 'undesirable' grounds was much more limited under the 1905 Act. Leaving aside his powers under the prerogative, under his statutory powers he could only deport an alien roughly for 'want of means' and 'medical grounds' because this was what undesirability meant under the Act. But the important thing was that whatever the grounds of the deportation, he could, in most cases, only exercise his power either on the recommendation of a court which had convicted the alien, or on the basis of a certificate issued by a court of summary jurisdiction establishing that the statutory grounds for deportation existed. (See s. 3 of the 1905 Act.) Basically, the idea of his acting on his own initiative to refuse entry to or deport individuals, which has today gained currency, was not latent in the Act of 1905.

48 Between 1930 and 1945 over 50,000 refugees were admitted from Germany. See Evans, *op. cit.* p. 12.

49 J.M. Evans, *op. cit.* Immigration Statistics, Pre-1962 Act , p. 14.

50 In 1974 there was a net loss of 1500 people to the West Indies and apparently a net loss of 300 per quarter in 1976 and 1977. The United Kingdom was no longer gaining people from the West Indies after 1969. See *First Report of the Select Committee on Race Relations and Immigration* (Session 1977–78) HC 303–I, p. ix, footnote.

51 Citizenship had been acquired by the Asians by birth, naturalization or registration in a former dependency, or by descent from or marriage to such people.

52 From the outset, however, the scheme was applied also to British protected persons and British subjects without citizenship who had East African connections because these categories of United Kingdom passport holders were not differentiated by the East African Governments and were also ander pressure to leave.

53 It may be noted that because the scheme is extra-statutory it is difficult to know what the rights of United Kingdom passport holders are in domestic law. The criterion for eligibility for a special voucher is not laid out in the immigration rules. As a result, there is no right of appeal if an applicant is said not to be eligible, although this may involve disputed questions of fact: *R* v. *Entry Clearance Officer, Bombay, ex p. Amin* (1980) 1 WLR 1530. See also Memoranda submitted by JCWI to First Report from the Home Affairs Committee (Session 1981–82), Immigration from the Indian Sub-Continent (26 July 1982) HC

90–II, pp. 49–54. This does not appear to be the position in international law, for the European Commission of Human Rights has admitted a petition by some United Kingdom passport holders following the 1968 Act holding that their claims were sustainable as the Act 'had racial motives and that it covered a racial group'. Also, the applicants had been subjected to 'degrading treatment' as far as Article 3 of the European Convention was concerned. Quoted in the *First Report from the House of Commons Home Affairs Committee* (Session 1979–80) Proposed *New Immigration Rules and the European Convention on Human Rights* (Session 1979–80). Proposed *New Immigration Rules and the European Convention on Human Rights* (11 February 1980) HC 434, pp. 52–5.

54 See the article in *The Guardian*, 9 September 1992.

55 For the practical difficulties in this area, see Macdonald, I. and Blake, N. (3rd edn 1991) *Immigration Law and Practice*, pp. 84–5. London.

56 K.W. Patchett, English Law in the West Indies (1968) *Int. Comp. and Law Rev.* 12 (pp. 922–66) p. 954.

57 HC Deb., Vol. 649, col. 687 (16 November 1961). The Labour Party strongly rejected these arguments (*ibid.* Mr Gordon Walker, cols 709–10), with some justification it seems: see Jones, K. and Smith, A. (1970) *The Economic Impact of Commonwealth Immigration*, Chap. 2. London. As with the Liberal Party in 1905, however, once in power the Labour Party forgot its principled opposition to the kind of controls that were being inaugurated and hastened to enforce them no less rigidly.

58 Grant, L. and Martin, I. (1982) *Immigration Law and Practice*, p. 3. London.

59 *Immigration from the Commonwealth 1965*, Cmnd 2739.

60 Immigration and trade licensing regulations affected Asians in particular in Kenya, Uganda and Zambia.

61 J.M. Evans, *op. cit.* p. 18. See also David Steel (1969) *No Entry, passim*. London.

62 J.M. Evans, *op. cit.* p. 47, note 74.

63 David Steel, *op. cit.*; Plender, R. (1972) *International Migration Law*. Leiden; Goodwin-Gill, G.S. (1978) *International Law and the Movement of Persons between States*. Oxford; J.M. Evans, *op. cit.* pp. 65–68.

64 HC Deb., Vol. 759, cols 1479–81 (28 February 1968) see Mr Lynn, cols 1479–81; Jo Grimond, col. 1450; Jeremy Thorpe, cols 1433–4; N. Fisher, col. 1464; Norman St John Stevas, cols 1530, 1532; Michael Foot, col. 1701.

65 Ian Macdonald, *op. cit.* p. 11.

66 James Walvin, *op. cit.* p. 123.

67 See *East African Asians* v. *United Kingdom* (1981) 3 EHRR 76; Also see *First Report from the Home Affairs Committee* (1979–80), *Proposed New Immigration Rules and the Europe Conv*; HC 394 Appendix 2.

68 This is recognized by Macdonald when he says, 'one of the difficulties of describing the operation of UK immigration laws is that everyone in the field knows that the main purpose of the law is to stop and if possible reverse coloured immigration to the UK'. Macdonald, *op. cit.* p. 12.

69 Commonwealth Immigrants Act 1962, s. 2 (2) (b).

70 Commonwealth Immigrants Act 1968, s. 2 (2A) (C). This says that a child under 16 of a Commonwealth citizen will be allowed entry if 'both' his parents are resident in the UK, or if both of them are entering or seeking to enter the UK with

him or if one of his parents is resident in the UK and the other is entering or seeking to enter the UK with him.

71 *Report of the Committee on Immigration Appeals* (August 1967). Cmnd 3387, at p. 27.

72 Immigration Appeals Act 1969 s. 20. The interesting thing to note is that the Committee on Immigration Appeals (the Wilson Committee) was itself not in favour of making entry clearance certificates compulsory for Commonwealth citizens. Although its use ought to have been encouraged, in its view, 'as the great majority of aliens who come to the United Kingdom are free from the visa requirements, we consider that it would be out of the question to impose on Commonwealth citizens the same requirement under another name'. Committee on Immigration Appeals, *op. cit.* at para. 70.

73 See below, Chapter 5, generally.

74 *Select Committee on Race Relations and Immigration* (1968–70) (Control of Commonwealth Immigration), *Appendices and Minutes of Evidence* (27 May 1970), 17 xxviii at p. 839.

75 Evans, *op. cit.* p. 19.

76 Immigration Act 1971 s. 1(5).

77 Thus Sarah Leigh has written that the rules are not the result of careful consultation or sociological studies. 'The rules are produced by a system of vetos; the civil service seems to invent the details of them normally without any consultation and produces a White Paper. Representations made by pressure groups are normally ignored . . .'. See unpublished paper presented by Sarah Leigh at AGIN Conference on the Reform of British Immigration Law and Its Administration, July 1983.

78 Commonwealth Immigrants Acts 1962 and 1968, Instructions to Immigration Officers (February 1970), Cmnd 4298, para. 40.

79 *Statement of Changes in Immigration Rules* (20 February 1980) HC 394, para. 45. Also the current rules, *Statement of Changes in Immigration Rules* (23 March 1990) HC 251, para. 55. The requirement that there should not be any recourse to public funds is now a position of widespread and general applicability touching equally upon the rights of wives to join settled husbands here. In both the above rules it appears under the sub-heading general provisions'. See para. 42 and 52 respectively of the above rules.

80 Commonwealth Immigrants Acts 1962 and 1968, Instructions to Immigration Officers (February 1970), Cmnd 4298, para. 38.

81 *Immigration Rules for Control on Entry*, Commonwealth citizens (25 January 1973) HC 79, para. 43. Also see current rules *Statement of Changes in Immigration Rules* (9 February 1983) HC 169, para. 50.

82 *Visa Officer, Islamabad* v. *Saeedan* [1988] Imm AR, 131. See also Juss, S. (1988) Family Life, the Courts and Section 1(5) of the Immigration Act 1971. *Family Law* (April edn) p. 145. This reasoning appears to be suspect and Khurshid Drabu, Tribunal Counsellor at UKIAS at the time, argued that 'assuming though not admitting that the Secretary of State could have made such restrictive rules before 1.7.73, the fact that he did not do so, gives Section 1(5) the proper and logical meaning, i.e. that the Secretary of State shall not do so under the 1971 Act'; See *UKIAS*, circular No. 19/83/KD; 7 November 1983

83 *HC Official Report* (5th Series) Vol. 997 (28 January 1981) at col. 935.

84 The two had always been synonymous in British law.

85 British Nationality Act 1981 s. 1(1).

86 Evans, *op. cit.* p. 77.

87 'Patriality' can only be understood by reference to British nationality law, as discussed on p. 48.

88 The view has been expressed that this entailed the simultaneous introduction of the status of 'contract labour' which 'reflected the diminishing needs of the labour market in the United Kingdom by the late 1960s. The status more closely resembles the "guestworker" status for migrant labourers in West Germany and other Western European States. The status of migrant labourer also underlines the increased reluctance of the United Kingdom to bear the social cost of providing housing, education, health and social services for the worker's dependants, while benefiting from the profits of his or her labour'. See Gordon, P. (1981) Passport Raids and Checks, *Britain's Internal Immigration Controls*, p. 6. London. It has further been argued that 'Under a system of contract migrant labour, migrants do not settle and their families remain at home to be rejoined by the wage earner when his contract expires or he becomes unemployed. This system, common in the developed countries of Europe, is beneficial to the receiving country, since it does not need to provide a social infrastructure for workers' families'. The Immigration Act of 1971 was introduced so that Britain could enjoy the benefits of this system. It destroyed finally the 'anomaly' that Commonwealth citizens were able to settle in the UK whereas aliens could only come as temporary workers. See Freeman, M.D.A. and Spencer, S. (1979) Immigration Control, Black Workers and the Economy. *British Journal of Law and Society* 6 (pp. 53–81), p. 69. Also Rose, H. (1973) The Politics of Immigration after the 1971 Act. *POL Quarterly* 44 (pp. 183–96), p. 188. In Parliament, reference was made by members to an 'indentured labour system' and 'a pool of itinerant cheap labour'. See HC Deb., Standing Committee B, cols 402, 410–11 (27 April 1971).

89 Fransman, L. (1989) *British Nationality Law*, p. 115. London.

90 Reginald Maudling, Home Secretary, HC Deb., Standing Committee B, at col. 243 (1 April 1971).

91 The civic and political rights exercised by Commonwealth citizens remain unaffected however.

92 In fact, they now enjoy more freedom to enter the United Kingdom than that accorded to them as EC nationals under Community law.

93 HC Deb., *Official Report*, Vol. 1.813, col. 42 (8 March 1971).

94 *Ibid.* col. 56.

95 HC Deb., Standing Committee B, cols 209–10, 213 (2 April 1971).

96 HC Deb., Vol. 819, col. 757. Also James Callaghan at col. 763 (17 June 1971).

97 Hannah Rose, *op. cit.* p. 184.

98 See *Sunday Times*, The Unnecessary Bill, 28 February 1971 (editorial). On the Government's confusion, compare the statements by Mr R. Sharples, Minister of State at the Home Office on 1 April 1971 (HC Deb., Standing Committee B col. 210) with his statement on 23 March 1971 (*ibid.* col. 78). The relationship between the Government's proposed policy and the EC's free movement of

labour policy was never adequately explored. For the unfamiliarity of Mr Maud-ling with sections of the Act, see his speech on 11 May 1971, Vol. 817, cols. 1505-6 (20 May 1971).

99 HC Deb., Vol. 813 at col. 461 (8 March 1971).

100 See Rose, H. (1972-73) The Immigration Act 1971: A Case Study in the Work of Parliament. *Parliamentary Affairs* 26 (pp. 69-91), p. 73.

101 *Sunday Times*, 24 January 1971. Also see the *Sunday Times* of 10, 14 and 31 January 1971.

102 Richard Sharples, HC Deb., Vol. 813, col. 155 (8 March 1971).

103 Immigration Act 1971, s. 29. See also debates in Parliament: *ibid.* at cols 53-4 and (HC Deb., Standing Committee B), cols 1311, 1321, 1407, 1410 (25 May 1971).

104 Statehood is dependent upon the right of nations to exclusive competence in respect of their internal affairs. The determination of nationality is one matter falling within the exclusive domestic jurisdiction of states because the grant of nationality is a matter which only states by their municipal law (or by way of treaty) can perform. The exercise of this right goes to the very concept of state-hood because it involves the definition and circumscription of the state's popula-tion. International law, being law which is concerned with the relation between states, confers upon sovereign states the right to decide their own nationality: see note 9 to Chapter 1.

105 For example, Parry has written: 'In the general works on legal history the retro-spective quest for a coherent law of nationality has customarily been halted at the loss of Normandy under John.' (See Parry, *op. cit.* p. 28.) In actual fact, the differentiation between subjects and aliens had been systematically applied for a long period even before then. He explains that 'the consolidation of the customs in 1303 and 1305 marks the end rather than the beginning of *a long regulatory process* the basis of which was the differentiation between alien mer-chants from the point of view of customs rates'. (*Ibid.* p. 30.)

106 See Coke, Sir Edward, *The First Part of the Institutes of the Laws of England* (ed. F. Hargrave and C. Butler, 1788). London.

107 For example, the existence of denizens, apart from the categories of aliens and subject, 'has been largely overlooked hitherto'. (See Parry, *op. cit.* p. 36.) Denizens were aliens who were accorded the same rights as subjects by grants of letters of endenization which had the effect of 'equalizing' the status of particular aliens with that of the subject. (*Loc. cit.*).

108 Thus the historic case of *Calvin* in 1608, grounded in medieval law, established that the relation of king and subject was rooted in allegiance. See *Calvin's Case* (1608) 2 St Tr 559. It also laid down that allegiance acquired at birth was indelible.

109 The Aliens Act 1905 and the Aliens Restriction Acts 1914 and 1919 did not define aliens. For a definition of disabilities affecting aliens, see H.S.Q. Henri-ques, *op. cit.*, and for the law of British nationality prior to the British National-ity Act 1948, see Parry, *op. cit.* Chaps 1 and 2, and Jones, M. (rev. edn 1956) *British Nationality Law*, pp. 51-86. London.

110 H. Lauterpacht, Allegiance, Diplomatic Protection and Criminal Jurisdiction over Aliens. *Camb. LJ* (1941-45, Vol. 9, pp. 330-46), p. 336.

111 Williams, G. (1948–50) The Correlation of Allegiance and Protection. *Camb. LJ*10 (pp. 54–68) at pp. 58, 63. Authority for this appears in *Johnstone* v. *Pedlar* (1921) 2 AC 262.

112 *Ibid.* at pp. 189–90. H. Lauterpacht, at any rate, applauded this approach, stating that 'so far as English law is concerned, there is no innovation implied in the assimilation, for the purpose of allegiance of an alien enjoying the protection of the state for a national' (*op. cit.* at p. 346). In view of the existence and legal position of denizens in the past, this view would appear to be plausible.

113 For Coke, conquest worked a species of 'denization' whether or not the conqueror or conquered willed it. See Parry, *op. cit.* p. 72.

114 See Fransman, *op. cit.* p. 24.

115 See Parry, *op. cit.* pp. 60–76.

116 Section I of the Act.

117 Parry, *op. cit.* p. 65.

118 Indentured and contract labour constituted most of the coloured immigrants into Australia before the discovery of gold. After the discovery of gold there comparatively large numbers of coloured immigrants entered, ushering in a series of problems which the other white dominions were also to face. There was much anxiety over this in New South Wales. The debates during the passage of the Act of 1881, for example, saw tempers in the New South Wales Parliament running high at the supposed attitude of Her Majesty's Government. Huttenback writes, 'John McElhone of the Upper House spoke with rising passion: "I say we should insist upon our right, and we should again and again, press legislation, and tell the home Government in plain terms that unless they will legislate for the protection of our social interests in this matter, and to prevent the Chinese from coming to us, we should sever our connection with England and act independently." ' See Huttenback, R.A. (1916) *Racism and Empire: White Settlers and Coloured Immigrants in the British Self-Governing Colonies 1830–1910*, p. 112. Ithaca, NY. Also Chapters 1 and 2 for the problems faced by other dominions.

119 Huttenback, *ibid.* p. 62.

120 Huttenback, *ibid.* pp. 112–15. Article 15, according to Huttenback, 'provided the usual meaningless sop for the Colonial Office. Chinese who were British by birth and could so prove by means of a certificate signed by the government of a British Colony were exempt from the workings of the Act' (p. 114).

121 For example, Article 3 of the Act of 1888 stipulated that any Chinese person not already naturalized who left the colony was subject to all the restrictions of the Act upon his return.

122 Parry, *op. cit.* p. 530 (note 15). Also see pp. 525, 529. See the 1st edition of Macdonald for a brief discussion of how the immigration laws were to be applied, *op. cit.* pp. 13–15.

123 Parry, *op. cit.* Chapters 9, 11, 12 and 13.

124 Thus Macdonald writes: 'To the Colonial Office the solution was to find "a form which was not open to objections that it persecuted people of a particular race" or as the Secretary of State for the Colonies phrased it in 1897 "to arrange a form of words which will avoid hurting the feelings of Her Majesty's subjects while at the same time it would amply protect the colonies against the invasion of a class to which they would justly object" '. Macdonald, *op. cit.* p. 13.

125 Parry, *op. cit.* p. 25.

126 Parry, *op. cit.* p. 220.

127 Indeed, alone among the countries involved the United Kingdom did not discriminate. Lord Simon in the debates during the passage of the British Nationality Act 1946 said, for example: 'It is a fine thing; it is one of the finest things in the whole of our British Commonwealth that anyone who is a British citizen knows that, without challenge or question, he will be admitted here.' HC Deb., Vol. 155, col. 1013 (11 May 1948).

128 British Nationality Act 1948, s. 1(1).

129 HC Deb., Vol. 55, col. 754 (11 May 1948).

130 *Ibid.* at cols 595, 596.

131 *Ibid.* at col. 957.

132 British Nationality Act 1948, s. 4.

133 *Ibid.* s. 5

134 *Ibid.* ss. 6–9.

135 *Ibid.* s. 10.

136 Macdonald (1st edn), *op. cit.* p. 51.

137 British Nationality Act 1948, s. 13.

138 *Ibid.* s. 32(i).

139 HC Deb., Vol. 997, col. 935 (28 January 1981).

140 See (1977) *A Register of Dependants: Report of the Parliamentary Committee on the feasibility and usefulness of a Register of Dependants*, Cmnd 6698, p. 5.

141 The Treaty refers to the free movement of the 'workers of the member states . . . within the Community' in Article 48. It refers to the 'nationals of a member state' in Articles 52 and 59, however. All the secondary legislation in the form of regulations and directives use the criterion of nationality to confer rights upon workers. A worker must thus have the necessary connection with a member state. See Hartley, T.C. (1978) *EEC Immigration Law*, Chapter 2. London; Evans, A.C. (1982) European Citizenship. *Modern Law Review* 45 (pp. 497–515), p. 497. See further Chapter 4 *infra*.

142 The Government resolved this difficulty by making a unilateral declaration which was appended to the Treaty of Accession and which defined its nationals. This definition was in line with the definition of 'patrials' in the Immigration Act 1971. W.R. Bohning has argued that the declaration is of no legal effect because the Treaty confers the right upon all nationals of member states which, in the case of the United Kingdom, included all the citizens of the United Kingdom and colonies and not just the narrow group of 'patrials'. See W.R. Bohning (1973) *CML Review* 10, pp. 83–4. A contrary view is given by T.C. Hartley, *op. cit.* pp. 73–5.

143 Bevan V. (1987) *The Development of British Immigration Law*, p. 113. London.

144 For an early criticism of this, see *A Report by Justice, British Nationality* (1980).

145 British Nationality Act 1981, s. 11(1).

146 *Ibid.* s. 23.

147 See Macdonald (1st edn) *Immigration Law and Practice, op. cit.* p. 57.

148 See White, R. and Hampson, F.J. (1981) The British Nationality Act 1981.

Public Law (pp. 6–20) p. 10. Also see Blake, C. (1982) Citizenship, Law, and the State. *Modern Law Review* 45 (pp. 179–97), pp. 191–2.

149 *Ibid.* p. 11. Thus the 'Justice' comments on the Labour Party's Green Paper stated: 'British Overseas Citizenship (BOC) is a misleading term in that it expresses no territorial link and so gives no indication of the country to which such citizens while abroad might return.' *A Report by Justice, op. cit.* p. 13.

150 See *House of Commons Fifth Report from the Home Affairs Committee* (1981–82). Immigration from the Indian Sub-Continent, Vol. 2, HC 90 at pp. xxx.

151 British Nationality Act 1948, s. 5(1) (b).

152 British Nationality Act 1981, Pt IV and s. 51(2). These amount to about 50,000 in number.

153 White and Hampson, *op. cit.* p. 7. Also Evans, *op. cit.* p. 85.

154 See Macdonald (1st edn 1983) *op. cit.* pp. 1–2.

155 *First Report from the Select Committee on Race Relations and Immigration* (1977–78) 1, HC 303.

156 For a detailed discussion of these, see Freeman and Spencer *op. cit.*

157 At para. 86.

158 At para. 88.

159 At para. 87.

160 The Committee referred to the practice in 'Continental countries' and to the lack of comprehensive administrative data on immigration. It has been argued that it is likely that 'what the Committee had in mind was a system of identity cards or passes such as those issued in France, West Germany and other states and which were used in conjunction with the National Register in the United Kingdom between 1939 and 1952'. See Gordon, *op. cit.* p. ii. The response of the Labour Party, unlike that of the Conservatives, was hostile to a system of internal controls. Merlyn Rees, the Home Secretary, in view of falling primary immigration said that 'no useful purpose would be served' by this as it would lead to an introduction of identity cards: 'Such a major change in practice and power reaching far beyond immigration control would be objectionable in principle' (see HC Deb., Vol. 947, cols. 647–8 (6 April 1978)). In July 1978 the Government published a Command Paper in response: see Cmnd 7287. William Whitelaw for the Conservatives, at a meeting of the Central Council of the Conservative Party in April 1977, shortly after the publication of the Select Committee's Report, said that the Conservatives would establish a system of internal controls, as well as greater restrictions on stay and a nationality law (see Gordon, *op. cit.* p. iv.)

161 Traditionally, it is the number of immigrants entering which has been seen as being the main problem. The Select Committee (1977–78) was itself preceded by the publication in May 1976 of the Hawley Report by Enoch Powell which referred to the uncertainty of numbers causing widespread concern. In July 1976 Mr Whitelaw said that immigration control procedures can only 'allay many unjustified fears if they introduce some certainty into a situation which alas, today is shrouded in far too much mystery'. HC Deb., Vol. 914, col. 965 (5 July 1976). Of late, many have regarded this argument as unconvincing. For example, Freeman and Spencer state that: 'The numbers game can only lead to an

increase in tension and not the opposite, because any number is too many for those who believe numbers are the problem. The [Select Committee] report implies some optimal figure which can only be less than the current figure, for otherwise there would be no problem'. (See Freeman and   Spencer, *op. cit.*, p. 75).The point has also been made that 'Once the debate is about numbers there are no issues of principle to be discussed, only how many?' (1979) *Current Legal Problems* 32 (pp. 117–42), p. 117.

162 Storey, H. (1984) United Kingdom Immigration Control and the Welfare State. *Journal of Social Welfare Law*, January (pp. 14–28), p. 14. Also see Storey, H. (1983), *Immigrants and the Welfare State*. London. Also more recently, *The Guardian*, 9 September 1992.

163 Palley, C. *The UK and Human Rights*, p. 3. London.

164 Section 1.

165 Section 2.

166 Section 5. On recent developments on the law of deportation, see Juss, S. (1993) Administrative Convenience and the Carltona Principle. *Oxford Journal of Legal Studies* 13(1), pp. 142–5.

167 Section 6.

168 Section 7.

169 Section 8.

170 Dummett and Nicol, *op. cit.* pp. 253–4.

171 See White, R. (1987) Hong Kong, Nationality, and the Agreement with China. *International and Comparative Law Quarterly* 36, p. 483.

172 See HC Deb., Vol. 170, col. 1566–75.

173 Section 1(1).

174 See note 17, Chap. 1.

175 Section 1(2) and (4).

176 See Macdonald and Blake, *op. cit.* p. 24.

177 See letters to *The Times*, 15 May 1992.

178 *The Times*, 12 May 1992.

179 Anderson, Sir Norman (1978) *Liberty, Law and Justice*, p. 72. London.

3

Britain and the Commonwealth

*'I never read books of travels, at least not farther than Paris or Rome.
I can just endure Moors, because of their connection as foes with
Christians; but Abyssinians, Ethiops, Esquimaux, dervishes, and all
that tribe, I hate.' – Charles Lamb.*

INTRODUCTION

In this chapter we consider New Commonwealth immigration. To
understand the development of modern immigration control as it is
today New Commonwealth immigration must not be divorced from
its precursor, the alien immigration of the 1900s. In turn both the
alien and New Commonwealth immigrations are a progeny of an illus-
trious tradition of immigration going back many centuries. This was
recognized by the Royal Commission on Alien Immigration in 1903
when it declared that the 'Alien Immigrant is no newcomer to this
country'. It observed how successive generations of immigrants had
come to Britain since the Norman Conquest; some in order to escape
political or religious persecution, others for 'gain and benefit', and
others still because of their 'desire to live in a land of good government'.[1] The effect of this tradition, as one writer has more recently
found, was to make 'the British . . . clearly the most ethnically composite of the Europeans'.[2] The response of the host country to the
newcomers, as the Commission noted, was invariably hostile, with
statutes regulating their movement being passed almost every year
from the reign of Richard II. But the immigrants brought with them
many benefits and the Commission was quick to acknowledge the fact
'that the immigrants in past times made us their debtors cannot be
controverted'.[3]

Accordingly, there is an undoubted interrelationship at various
levels in the immigration experiences of the host community during
this period. It has been said that generally 'every mass immigrant
group was liable to be pronounced unconventional, unclean, unprin-
cipled, and generally unwelcome'.[4] This interrelationship, in the

71

words of another writer, is 'conspicuously similar' in the case of the alien and New Commonwealth immigrants, the similarities being 'so close as to point tentatively to a number of rather surprising generalizations about the English reaction towards immigration'.[5] Even though these two migrations are separated by a time span of fifty years, they are in this century the only sustained mass of migration to the United Kingdom to date. They therefore provide an insight into how future problems in immigration are apt to be dealt with. In appropriate cases, accordingly, the detailed discussion of New Commonwealth immigration in this chapter will be related to the experience of alien immigration to allow for proper inferences and comparisons to be drawn.

The Background to New Commonwealth Immigration

In 1965 Richard Crossman referred to immigration as 'the hottest potato in politics' and expressed the fear that 'immigration can be the greatest potential vote-loser for the Labour Party if we are seen to be permitting a flood of immigrants to come in . . .'.[6] In 1967 the Labour Government made what Crossman subsequently described as 'plans for legislation which we realized would have been declared unconstitutional in any country with a written constitution and a Supreme Court'.[7]

Yet in sharp contrast to the alien immigration of the earlier part of this century, New Commonwealth immigration arose as a direct result of active encouragement on the part of British industries and the British Government, and Commonwealth immigrants came, not looking for asylum, but for jobs in certain key industries which required filling up for want of desperate shortage of indigenous labour. Britain's economic base after the war 'was in parlous state', being 'run down, antiquated, ill-prepared for economic change', and with 'little or no money for vital redevelopment'.[8] But the immediate post-war years were also a time of full employment and economic growth which together with the reconstruction programme avidly sucked up the returning soldiers. Shortage of labour soon followed. The King's Speech in the first Conservative administration after the war highlighted the problem: 'My Government views with concern the serious shortage of labour, particularly of skilled labour which has handicapped production in a number of industries.'[9] For more than a decade after 1945 the United Kingdom was in need of urgently required labour in such industries as transport, catering, textiles, heavy metal and the National Health Service. New Commonwealth immigrant workers seemed to be the best group to attract into this void. Paul Foot believes that if Britain had had to seek European labour after 1951 then 'she would have had to drop the Aliens Acts, and to allow much freer right of entry, and offer adequate inducements to attract aliens away from the high wages of expanding Germany, France, Switzerland and Belgium'.[10]

But, in fact, European labour was wooed. Irish immigrant labour, as in the past, proved to be invaluable at this time with 100,000 net Irish arrivals between 1946 and 1957. By 1959 the figure was an estimated 352,600. London Transport recruiting teams first went out to Ireland and only after 1956 to Barbados.[11] Workers from other parts of Europe were similarly encouraged. Between 1945 and late 1957 more than 350,000 Europeans emigrated to Britain.[12] Thus immigration into the United Kingdom in the post-war period did not wholly consist of New Commonwealth immigrants.

In this respect Britain was not untypical of other major European countries, many of which also needed foreign labour urgently. Germany set up recruitment offices in Spain, Greece, Turkey, Italy and Yugoslavia. Switzerland depended on spontaneous immigration from countries nearby. France actively engaged in state-directed recruitment although employers themselves also recruited in other countries to the extent that by the end of the 1960s about 80 per cent of all immigrants (coming from Portugal and Africa) were entering the country illegally. Sweden recruited both publicly and privately from such countries as Yugoslavia and Greece.[13]

The needs of British industry could not, however, be fully met by Irish and European workers. A more active recruitment campaign was thus taken up in the New Commonwealth countries. The British Hotels and Restaurants Association, the Regional Hospital Boards and individual representatives from the textile industry all appointed agents or launched campaigns to recruit labour in these countries. All these bodies made direct arrangements with the Barbados Government to recruit skilled labour and the Barbadian authorities (still under British colonial rule) provided loans and assistance for migrants.[14] There was even competition between various shipping lines with some lines offering the inducement of a representative waiting for immigrants at Waterloo to meet them and make the necessary arrangements if immigrants booked the passage with them.[15]

The effects of the campaign were startling. It has been estimated that 85 per cent of the people leaving Jamaica between 1953 and 1964 were heading for Britain.[16] The entry of New Commonwealth immigrants rose from 21,000 in 1953 to 58,300 in 1960. In 1961 there were 125,400,[17] but this figure is more the result of the threat of impending immigration legislation than a natural increase. Contrary to popular belief, of those who came during this period only 13 per cent of the men and 5 per cent of the women had no skills whatsoever.[18]

Research on Jamaican immigration indicates that the only catalyst in the migratory process at such a time was the labour demands of the United Kingdom. As T.E. Smith explains, 'Emigration cannot take place unless there are countries willing to accept immigrants',[19] and for the United Kingdom only immigrants could make the existing labour situation soluble.[20] The much quoted study by Cori Peach in 1968 shows that although the existence of unemployment and population pressure in the West Indies were relevant factors it was the British demand for foreign labour that provided the direct stimulus to emigration.[21]

In fact, emigration in the 1950s occurred against a background of economic improvement. Unemployment was not the determinant factor because in the 1930s unemployment was at its worst, yet there was then no net emigration even to the United States, whose door was still open. Between 1953 and 1962 Jamaica had one of the world's highest rates of economic growth and it was at this time that Jamaican emigration reached its apogee.[22] The determining factor in emigration was an external one and this was the fluctuating labour demand in the United Kingdom. Only in 1961 did the correlation between labour demand and New Commonwealth immigration break down with news of imminent immigration control being instituted.[23]

Contrary to popular belief, the developments at home during this time confirm this situation. The *Smethwick Labour Exchange Report* in 1955 candidly stated:

> Shortage of labour is the concern of almost every employer in the town. A policy of importation is now being pursued . . . Coloured labour from the Commonwealth is greatly easing the labour shortage. The labour turnover among these immigrant workers is lower than the average . . . The employers would be very worried if coloured labour were withdrawn. All employers readily pay tribute to the valuable contribution this type of labour is making towards industrial output.[24]

In his pioneering work on race relations E.J.B. Rose asked, 'In what types of jobs and in what industries did the coloured immigrant initially find work?', and answered:

> Usually it was in an industry that was losing ground as far as pay and status were concerned (for example, public transport), or in those jobs that were considered unpleasant by the host community (for example, in foundries), or that entailed long and awkward hours. In general, the employment most easily available for the newly-arrived

coloured immigrant was the sort of employment that the English worker did not want. In times of full employment with the demand for more and more skilled and/or highly-paid labour the local labour force became more upwardly mobile. This movement upwards left a vacuum into which replacement labour had to be attracted.[25]

Even at the time, it was openly admitted that immigrants were being attracted into especially harsh and inhuman work. In Parliament one member described how Jamaicans arriving at the ports of London were told to go straight on to Sheffield for work: 'They went there and found that the work available for them was labouring work in the steel works in very hot conditions, alternating with taking barrow-loads of material out into very cold conditions, and they could not stand it.'[26]

It is relevant at this stage to point out that work was not the only inducement held out to potential immigrants in the New Commonwealth. All such immigrants were British subjects, and although this fact may have been 'an accident stemming from the "benevolence" of British imperialism', it was considered to be a matter of much pride that all the Crown's subjects could come to the 'mother country'.[27] The immigrants came on this understanding. Thus, Chris Mullard explains that:

The London Transport Executive medical officer and interviewer who went to Barbados in 1956 pointed out to potential applicants that besides a job they could expect no racial discrimination, full citizenship rights, and a 'sunny future' in the mother country. Those invited to the Midlands to begin and stay 'at the lower end of the occupational ladder' received similar pledges either directly through employers or indirectly through the projected image, fostered and maintained in the West Indies by the Colonisers, of the mother country's benevolence and recognition of rights to all those who wished to migrate.[28]

When the first batch of 492 Jamaican immigrants landed on 22 June 1948 on the ship *Empire Windrush*, the *London Evening Standard* greeted them with the headlines: 'Welcome Home'. One writer comments, 'Officialdom, at both government and local levels, moved swiftly to make the Jamaicans feel welcome and find them accommodation and work.'[29]

The same formula was adopted for applicants from the Indian sub-continent:

The need, on the employers' part, to purchase cheap labour for an outmoded, under-capitalised, and almost bankrupt textile industry centred in West Yorkshire and South-East Lancashire, led personnel officers often with colonial and wartime experience, to Pakistan; the belief of Pakistanis, on the other hand, that they would be accorded full rights as citizens, and that hostel or lodging-house accommodation in cities such as Bradford was plentiful, helped to complete the exchange – citizenship for labour, jobs for rights.[30]

Other writers have also hinted at this phenomenon. Peter Fryer has referred to the esteem in which British institutions and British values were held by the peoples of the Commonwealth: 'Their ideas about Britain were largely derived from a Colonial education system in which Britain was revered as the "mother country".' Quoting from another writer, Nicholas Deakin, he says that 'They "took their British Citizenship seriously, and many regarded themselves not as strangers but as kinds of Englishmen. Everything taught in schools . . . encouraged this belief." What they found here dismayed and shocked them.'[31]

An interesting question is raised here. If this last point is correct, why did New Commonwealth immigration continue to persist? More to the point, why did it continue to do so in the light of increasingly restrictionist legislation designed to discourage and terminate this flow? The entire thesis of one book is that New Commonwealth immigration has been historically determined. The fact of twentieth-century immigration is attributable to the nature of the essentially imperial relationship between the 'mother country' and the colonized peoples: 'In common with other imperial powers, the British relationship with their colonies had been fundamentally exploitative, however benign or beneficial some of the attitudes and consequences might have been.' This led to the subjection of millions of people to direct or indirect control.

> When that control began to disintegrate, as it did so rapidly in the British case after 1945, many of the subject peoples justifiably looked to Britain for more than the former control and guidance. The British had, especially in wartime, introduced their imperial subjects to the material virtues of the mother country, just as they had exposed or nudged them towards the virtues of the English language, culture, education and political system. When, in the post-war years, the bonds of empire were rapidly loosened, the material attractions of Britain proved irresistibly enticing to growing numbers of people around the world who had already experienced them, or even merely heard of them.[32]

Whether or not this was due to exploitation, there is little doubt that such a situation had arisen (and still persists) in many colonized and formerly colonized countries. Fryer explains how the Caribbean people were only too glad to emigrate because of 'the miserable poverty that was their countries' chief legacy from imperial rule'.[33] In the first parliamentary debate on immigration in this country over Commonwealth immigration the Member importuning for a public inquiry on immigration was quick to admit that:

> it is worth noting that the conditions in Jamaica and elsewhere have been allowed to develop under our rule and control. It is, therefore, not enough merely to say that they must put up with the conditions in their own territory and that they cannot come and benefit by our social security.[34]

When this fact was linked with the ideas with which colonized peoples were inculcated, immigration had a self-generating quality. Once the tradition of migration was established then, as Aurora suggests, it acted as a 'social force' with many people being sucked into it who did not have an economic reason to migrate.[35] More recent research by Anwar on the migration of Pakistanis to the United Kingdom also suggests that the economic 'push' and 'pull' has 'slowly developed into a "chain migration"'.[36]

THE CONTROL OF NEW COMMONWEALTH IMMIGRATION

Socio-economic Problems: Unemployment, Vagrancy, Crime, Disease

In 1962, as we saw in Chapter 2, the first Commonwealth Immigrants Act was passed. Under this Act provision was made for the Department of Employment to issue employment vouchers to regulate the entry of workers. In 1969 the Select Committee recounted how in evidence to it, the Department of Employment saw this as a means of limiting numbers and not as 'a manpower supply scheme specifically tailored to the needs of British industry'.[37] As Vaughan Bevan observes, '[T]his staggeringly short-sighted admission illustrates perfectly the lack of planning in British immigration policy. The opportunity to shape that policy in a practical, relevant and useful fashion was ignored in preference to a reflexive and expedient response.'[38]

It was certainly nothing more than a reflexive and expedient response that could account for the way in which Commonwealth immigration was controlled and managed during this entire period. In the first debate ever held on Commonwealth immigration, in 1954, almost exactly the same issues were raised as before the Royal Commission on Alien Immigration in 1903. The motion for debate was moved by John Hynd. He spoke of Jamaicans leaving their country because of over-population and unemployment, but that 'here we have full employment!'.[39] Nothing, however, could be further from the truth, and the Minister of State for Colonial Affairs told him that under the present circumstances, any talk of a 'high level of employment' was 'purely academic'.[40] Hynd then referred to the 'problems' of housing, vagrancy, racial conflict, and to 'social questions'. Social questions, he explained, had

> nothing to do with colour, but are questions associated with any large settlement of virile young men removed from all social restraints, family, religious, and others, in a foreign country, where they require relaxation, association with their own and the opposite sex and where, having lost all their restraints and restrictions which apply to them in their own family and religious circles, they are inclined to get into trouble.[41]

On vagrancy, he was concerned that:

> In the London County Council there are no less than 300 coloured children, many of them illegitimate. It is impossible to get anyone to adopt them. Again, it is not because people do not like the colour of their skin; in fact, many people think they are the most charming children of all. But when people consider the problem that arises when they have grown up sons and daughters, and all the difficulties associated with the adoption of such children, they naturally hesitate.[42]

In Sheffield there had also been cases of scuffles breaking out at some dance halls. John Hynd explained here that:

> The fact is that these local dance halls have been set up for the purpose of allowing the local boys and girls to get together and enjoy themselves and if there is a sudden influx of outsiders, whether they are Jamaicans, Poles, Welshmen, or Irishmen, it upsets the balance and a great deal of adjustment has to be made.[43]

And housing was a problem, in Mr Hynd's view, because immigrants were living in 'condemned houses'.[44] The impact of new immigrants upon localities was a favourite theme during both the alien and the Commonwealth immigrations. Sir William Evans Gordon argued in 1902 that whole communities were destroyed in the following way: 'Ten grains of arsenic in a thousand loaves would be unnoticeable and perfectly harmless, but the same amount put into one loaf would kill the whole family that partook of it.'[45] Enoch Powell said in May

1981, 'What has happened is that for the native people . . . of Birmingham and Wolverhampton their own town has become a strange place, a place of fear and confusion.'[46]

Feelings that Commonwealth immigrants spread infectious diseases were as widespread as they had been during the aliens legislation of the 1900s. In December 1980, the House of Commons Home Affairs Committee was asked by the Government in its Race Relations and Immigration Sub-Committee 'to carry out a review of the objects and nature of all medical examinations in the immigration control context'.[47] The report produced by Sir Henry Yellowlees and his colleagues was later considered by the Committee. The basis of the report and of the ensuing discussion by the Committee was that immigrants have, or are assumed to have, more communicable diseases.

Tuberculosis, for example, was the subject of particular discussion by the Committee. Two members of the Committee, John Hunt and Alex Lyon, expressed especial concern at the findings of the Yellowlees Report because the report had been 'seized on by the anti-immigrant organizations in this country who have spread scare stories on the basis of it'.[48] Both members, therefore, questioned the Committee further as to its conclusions. It emerged from the questioning of Dr Evans, Deputy Chief Medical Officer at the Department of Health and Social Security, that incidents of tuberculosis within the indigenous community were not necessarily attributable to infection passed on by immigrants as a distinction had to be made between patent infection and pre-existing latent infection which has surfaced in later years. Dr Evans, one of the authors of the report, accepted that:

we are many of us exposed in early life to tuberculosis and can have this latent form of tuberculosis which does not normally break down and give active disease but which under certain circumstances of stress and so on, may do so.[49]

The Yellowlees Report, on the other hand, had not drawn this distinction.

This information when taken in conjunction with some other data wrenched from Dr Evans by Alex Lyon painted a very different picture. Dr Evans went on to concede that out of over 6000 reported cases of respiratory tuberculosis in 1979, 'rather more than 4000' [i.e. over two-thirds] were among the indigenous population; compared to twenty or thirty years earlier the figures now 'are enormously better'; and that the indigenous figure had not shown any sign of increase since the beginning of immigration from the New Commonwealth in the late 1950s.[50] As for Dr Evans's earlier statement that in 1979 there were 824 deaths, John Hunt placed it on record, with Dr Evans's concurrence, that a number of these deaths were due to old age and therefore not necessarily attributable to tuberculosis.[51] This was not the only time that the issue had been raised.

In 1965, for example, Lord Elton rose in the House of Lords to say that 'in respect of leprosy the new regulations as to immigrants are inadequate, and that unless the flow of immigrants suffering from this disease is checked, in ten or twenty years time one may find leprosy endemic in Britain'.[52] Lord Sorenson replied by referring Lord Elton to the findings of Dr Cochrane in his report that 'the possibility of its [i.e. leprosy's] transmission under normal social conditions in this country is virtually negligible'.[53] It was concerns such as these that eventually provided the foundation for the Commonwealth Immigrants Act of 1962 with its targeting of over-crowding, unemployment and race relations.

Yet this development of the 1950s and 1960s was not without its precedents. During the passage of the Aliens Act of 1905, Balfour, the then Prime Minister, and Akers-Douglas, the Home Secretary, were the only two people to speak in support of the Bill and did so, in the words of Mr Balfour, on grounds that 'What actually happens is that these foreign immigrants go into a small area of the East End of London, and they produce the evil of overcrowding . . .'.[54] Yet on 10 July, he admitted that:

the great mass of alien immigrants are not touched at all.
Those who were kept out were but a small number, and they
were kept out solely because they were likely to become a
burden upon the country if they were allowed in.[55]

Mr Akers-Douglas told the House on 19 July that it was 'perfectly true' that a criminal who could pay a higher fare for his short sea passage from the Continent could enter the country.[56] It was also accepted that the protection of the labour market at home was not important since in reality there was no desire to keep out an alien 'able to maintain himself and live up to the public health requirements, simply because he might compete with the labourers of this country'.[57]

As Will Crooks explained, the real grievances were those of 'sweating' and the 'amelioration of the lot of the people and to waste time on a measure like this was positively abominable'.[58] Winston Churchill wanted to know why 'a criminal, a lunatic, an idiot, a prostitute, or a diseased person [could] come into this country immune from the provisions of the Bill simply because he or she could afford to take a cabin ticket' but the poor could not.[59] Indeed, as a class the Americans, who provided the largest group of criminals and vagrants, had only ten of their number excluded in the four years from 1906 to

1909 inclusive. By contrast, 1022 Russians were excluded in the same period.[60]

Adjudication through Tribunals

The Immigration Appeals Act 1969 set up an Immigration Appeals Tribunal consisting of three persons where various appeals against decisions of the Home Secretary and other immigration officials could be heard. This was not without precedent, however, for the Aliens Act 1905 also set up Immigration Boards comprising a panel of three people with magisterial, business or administrative experience to hear appeals. Both forms of tribunal have been criticized in their time. M.J. Landa, a Jewish journalist employed by the *Jewish Chronicle* to inquire into the working of the Aliens Act, wrote of the Immigration Boards that they remain 'the most remarkable of English Tribunals', being 'non-judicial, non-legal, non-professional' and 'the most autocratic body in our whole organization of government'.[61] B. Gainer referred to its 'allegedly unjust and autocratic Star Chamber proceedings'.[62] The Immigration Appeals Tribunal was also referred to as a 'Star Chamber in the Strand' holding its 'unilateral sessions' following the famous *Dutschke Case*,[63] which jostled liberal democratic opinion in the UK.[64] Bob Hepple (now Professor) also drew attention to the fact that:

> One cannot fail to be struck by the paradox of a 'Star Chamber in the Strand' . . . in the same historical period in which the Royal Courts of Justice, on the other side of the Strand, are developing their expansive notions of openness, fairness and impartiality.[65]

In 1905 much concern was expressed over the setting up, without any previous precedent, of an extra-judicial body in the name of the Immigration Boards. What powers would the Immigration Boards have when hearing appeals?[66] What was the extent of its competence in dealing with such pivotal and tortuous questions as lunacy, disease, extradition and crimes of a political nature? Why were these matters not entrusted to the hands of the ordinary courts of the land?[67]

Administrative law, however, has come a very long way since the 1900s and especially in the past 25 years. In fact, in a wide range of specialized areas administrative tribunals are seen as the best way to offer quick and cheap remedies without excessive legalism, whilst at the same time doing so with a degree of specialized knowledge. If criticism still attaches it does so not because tribunals are not open, fair and impartial but because of their inherent difficulties as they take on more and more work. In the industrial tribunal, the Alison Halford sex discrimination case against the Chief Constable of Merseyside, the Home Secretary, Northamptonshire Police Authority and the Inspector of Constabulary highlighted some of the difficulties facing tribunals generally. In an article 'Tribunals Don't Work' David Pannick drew attention to such matters as the absence of legal aid, the increasing load and complexity of cases, how the tribunal cannot award interest, how it has no power to require the employer to promote a woman who proves her case, and how it was inappropriate for the tribunal here to be asked to consider 'the implications of "liquidacious" dinners at which an assistant chief constable may have eaten his potatoes with his fingers . . .'.[68] Rarely is the focus nowadays on openness, fairness and impartiality.

Yet these concerns are of sufficient importance to be raised in immigration adjudications where a tribunal may be asked to find whether it thinks that a man and woman will lie together as husband and wife;[69] whether a student stands a chance of succeeding in his studies;[70] whether a business will succeed;[71] or whether adequate accommodation will be available.[72] Changes in an applicant's circumstances since the decision appealed against are not normally admissible and yet they may be crucial to the determination of all these matters.[73] There are, moreover, no powers of discovery in the tribunal.[74] Two aspects particularly affect the fairness of immigration appeals.

Firstly, in most cases where a person is denied entry he cannot, unlike the Home Office, appeal from within the United Kingdom but has to go back to the country of departure before doing so. As appeals turn on the credibility of witnesses, this has serious implications.[75] Where witnesses are able to be present, adjudicators often permit all manner of questioning on them to destroy their credibility, a practice that the judge in *ex parte Patel*[76] found to be of limited benefit to anyone if the witness did not speak English.

Secondly, it is still the case that throughout the appeals process individual appellants are subject to strict time-limits whereas the Immigration and Nationality Department (IND) is subject to none in the preparation of Explanatory Statements. The Select Committee in 1990 recommended that to reduce delays the IND be subjected to a 15-week time limit on the preparation of explanatory statements.[77] When produced, however, such a document is often the only evidence by the Home Office against the appellant and often includes hearsay and opinion. The existence of an appeals machinery does not therefore by itself guarantee quality in decision making.

In some cases, however, there is not even this right of appeal, and this is by no means because they are unimportant. Thus there is no right of appeal against certain claims to a right of abode;[78] against a

personal decision of the Home Secretary making someone a prohibited immigrant;[79] against decisions on grounds of national security;[80] against refusal of special vouchers to British Overseas Citizens
or delay in doing so;[81] against refusal of a work permit;[82] against
variation in leave after expiry of existing limited leave;[83] against
refusal to extend time during which a person has to leave;[84] and
against variations of conditions for leave made by statutory instrument.[85] In some cases there is no appeal on the merits but only on
the legality of the decision.[86] Additionally there are delays in getting
appeals heard. The Select Committee in 1990 found this 'quite
unacceptable'[87] and urged that the 'backlog of appeals should not be
used as an excuse for reducing rights of appeal'[88] – advice that was
obviously lost on the proponents of the Asylum and Immigration
Appeals Act 1993.

When the case is eventually heard there may be additional problems. Unlike such tribunals as the Employment Appeal Tribunal and
the Supplementary Benefits Appeals Tribunal, the Immigration
Appeals Tribunal may be presided over by lay members even though
it is pre-eminently concerned with resolving legal questions. Similarly, adjudicators alone, who may or may not have legal qualifications, are burdened with deciding disputed questions of fact, law and
discretion. This is worrying given that, as Mr Langdon, the head of the
IND, declared before the Select Committee in 1990, the appeals
system 'is probably of a more legalistic nature now than was originally
anticipated . . .'.[89] Part of the problem also is that the Wilson Committee, which preceded the 1969 Act, considered informality and
flexibility to be important attributes. The way hearings are conducted,
therefore, under the Immigration Appeals (Procedure) Rules 'can differ widely from adjudicator to adjudicator, allowing some adjudicators to work in a way which is mainly adversarial and others to lean
towards the vastly different inquisitorial approach'.[90] It is unlikely
that in the present climate the system will be reformed. Delay,
expense and impracticability are the most frequently cited objections
to improvements, and the financial difficulties of the Home Office are
more likely to make themselves felt in the IND, whose work is given
a low priority, than anywhere else.

The Working of the System

This leads us naturally onto a discussion of how the system is worked
in practice. The institutional and structural imbalance is reflected and
replicated, not surprisingly, in its administrative workings. Under the
Aliens Act, there was strong criticism that many refusals were made
because the testimonies of witnesses were 'deemed discrepant',[91]

many immigration officers cross-examined Jewish immigrants before the Boards when they clearly had no power to do so (this function being reserved for the individual Boards themselves),[92] and that many Jewish immigrants had their testimony deliberately misinterpreted to achieve a refusal.[93] Exactly the same criticism is made in the context of current immigration.[94] Although unfamiliarity with the cultures and social mores of migrant communities can undoubtedly help explain some misunderstandings,[95] as we shall see they do not explain most such decisions.

The circumstances surrounding the detention and deportation of Adol Owen-Williams, who arrived at Gatwick Airport in April 1992, is one such example. Mr Owen-Williams was a black American who arrived in Britain with £2850 for a five-month tour of Europe. His visit here on 30 April coincided with the outbreak of rioting in Los Angeles. According to him, immigration officials accused him of 'probably' fleeing to the United Kingdom to avoid criminal prosecution in the United States. He was, he said, interrogated for several hours, detained for about two days in a urine-smelling cell, given little to eat, then deported 'due only to the fact that I was a black male in my late twenties in the wrong place at the wrong time'.[96]

The incident provoked widespread criticism in the press. Mrs Shirley Williams, a former Home Office Minister, wrote from Harvard University to draw attention to 'the courtesy shown by US immigration officers to visitors to the United States' and to express her 'shame and disgust' on this occasion; whilst Professor Michael Dummett felt it 'intolerable that such outrages should be committed in the name of Britain'.[97] The Home Office took the highly unusual step of commenting on one of its cases by denying allegations of racism in its ranks and defended its officers.[98]

At the same time, David Burgess of Winstanley-Burgess, a foremost firm of solicitors specializing in immigration work, wrote to explain that such cases were not unusual. In 1991 the Home Office paid out substantial compensation in settlement of proceedings brought by 23 asylum seekers when they alleged fraud, assault, false imprisonment and unlawful removal from the United Kingdom by immigration officers. All the men were brought back, but not until at least one had been tortured after being thus returned.[99] According to another commentator, what was needed was a 'Citizen's Charter' to be applied 'to the Immigration Service in order that the culture of the service becomes one of viewing visitors as customers, not insurgents'.[100]

The change of culture and attitude is certainly what is needed most in immigration cases. For example, the Immigration Appeals (Procedure) Rules 1984 plainly mandate immigration officers to 'prepare a written statement of facts relating to the decision in question and the reason therefore . . .'[101] and to provide the appellant with this statement. This is known as the 'Explanatory Statement'. As Grant and Martin state, however, the authorities 'frequently do not supply full information in the explanatory statement or at the hearing',[102] a criticism which, as we have seen earlier in this chapter, is still prevalent today. Cases involving New Commonwealth immigrants are the most telling even when they go to appeal.

In *Fultera Begum* an immigration adjudicator refused categorically to accept evidence of a marriage certificate as constituting valid documentary proof of the appellant's marriage because of the 'facility with which [marriage certificates] could be obtained' on the Indian sub-continent 'with the relevant details inserted, to suit any occasion'.[103] In *Zarina Jan* an adjudicator refused to believe a witness of the sponsor who testified to knowing the sponsor's wife and children simply because he appeared as a witness for the sponsor![104] On the other hand, Dr (now Professor) Pearl, when sitting as an adjudicator in one case, held: '[A]s the sponsor is a British subject, I simply make a finding that I am satisfied on a balance of probabilities that the relationship is as claimed . . .'.[105] This demonstrates what can be done if there is a will to do so.

One of the more notable examples of departmental pressure making itself felt on the immigration appeals process is the tribunal decision in the case of *Vinod Bhatia*.[106] The case involved an interpretation of the concept of 'primary purpose of . . . marriage' in the new immigration rules brought into effect in February 1983. The Home Office view of these rules was that a man who seeks to settle in the United Kingdom on the basis of his marriage to a female British citizen must prove that the 'primary purpose' of his marriage is not settlement. Applications at posts overseas were decided on this basis so that it very soon became the main basis for the refusal of foreign husbands and fiancés. In 1982, 19 per cent of refusals took place on this ground. In 1983 the proportion leapt to 85 per cent. In the first half of 1984, just before the tribunal decision in *Vinod Bhatia*, 74 per cent of all husbands and fiancés applying from New Delhi were refused – 93 per cent on the 'primary purpose' ground.[107]

In a series of cases in 1984 the tribunal tried to reverse this trend. It held that where it was found that the couple genuinely intend to live together, the husband should normally be admitted. In its view, it was for the Secretary of State in such circumstances to adduce evidence to rebut the presumption that the permanent association of the parties was the *primary* purpose of the marriage.[108] Following these decisions, the Joint Council for the Welfare of Immigrants (JCWI), a voluntary organization, wrote to the Home Office requesting that it change its practice on the interpretation of the 'primary purpose' rule. The Home Office wrote back saying, 'We are not satisfied that the Tribunal's approach was right',[109] and declined to do so. It asked the tribunal to reconsider its decisions.

In September 1984, a specially constituted tribunal, consisting of three chairmen, sat to look at the 'primary purpose' rule again in *Vinod Bhatia*. Unusually for the tribunal, it gave a split decision. Two members endorsed the Home Office view and held that the tribunal had previously been wrong to decide the issue as it did. The third member, Professor Jackson, gave a thundering dissent. 'It is not', he declared, 'for the Tribunal to act as surrogate for the Secretary of State.' This was an area where the 'individual rights of British citizens are at stake'. The law, in his judgment, 'must be construed bearing in mind the balance to be struck between the powers of the Secretary of State and the responsibility to British citizens and to *potential immigrants*' (emphasis added). Echoing Lord Atkin's celebrated dissent in *Liversidge* v. *Anderson* he used the very words there used to express his disapproval of the tribunal changing its mind in this way:

> 'When *I* use a word', Humpty Dumpty said in a rather scornful tone, 'it means just what I choose it to mean – neither more nor less.' 'The question is', said Alice, 'whether you *can* make words mean so many different things.' 'The question is, said Humpty Dumpty, 'which is to be master – that's all.'[110]

Unlike *Liversidge* v. *Anderson*, however, the determination of a specially constituted tribunal, on a matter of great particular and general interest, in the case of *Vinod Bhatia* has never been reported. The case speaks volumes, not on the clarification of an important rule of law, but on the uses and abuses of administrative discretion. To this aspect we must now turn.

Officials and the Abuse of Administrative Discretion

Immigration officials not infrequently misuse their powers. This is not surprising given that, as Mr Geoffrey Robertson QC, says,

> The twin features of modern immigration control are administrative discretion and administrative secrecy: the broadest of legal powers are bestowed upon officials, who exercise them according to secret guidelines approving procedures (such as the X-raying of children and 'virginity tests') which cannot be justified once they see the light of day.[111]

The odd thing is, however, that immigration officials do not just misuse their powers, when they do, because they are complying with secret instructions. In fact, the evidence suggests that they may comply with such instructions only when they actually approve of them, choosing otherwise to act as they will. This is a method of decision-making that can only be described as an area of administrative lawlessness since it detracts so massively from decision-making under a system of law. In the words of Geoffrey Robertson QC, it is 'the price we pay for our commitment to executive discretion which permeates immigration law more deeply than any other field of civil liberties, preventing the courts from getting to grips with the merits of decision-making'.[112] The examples are numerous, but it is nevertheless worth pondering why this should be so.

Under the 1905 Aliens Act the onus of proof for refugees claiming political asylum was placed on a person claiming the status of a refugee. Following the Russian pogroms in 1905, Herbert Gladstone, the Home Secretary, gave instructions in March 1906 to members of the Immigration Boards that 'the benefit of the doubt where any doubt exists' in such matters 'may be given in favour of immigrants who allege that they are flying from religious or political persecution'. His circular explained why this was necessary:

> The [1905] Act was passed for the purpose of checking the immigration of undesirable aliens. Parliament, in the judgement of the Secretary of State, never intended that . . . [the rules] should be applied with a rigidity which excludes considerations as to whether refusal of leave to land would involve great personal hardship or suffering in the case of women and children. So, too, a man who is free from any infections or objectionable disease may be in a critical state of health, and to refuse him leave to land might expose him to cruel hardship. Again the statements of a man claiming to be a political or religious refugee may be insufficient or inaccurate, yet he may be exposed to serious risk from political causes if he is forced to return.[113]

This guidance was clearly intended to abate the harsh effects of the law by enabling officials to allow not only cases that were clearly proven, but also cases where there was some doubt. It was, however, ignored by officials, who did not regard themselves to be bound by it. In fact the officials formulated, and put to immigrants, questions which totally negated the instructions in the circular. Landa, who sat in on hearings of the London Immigration Board for over three years, reveals that:

greater and more lamentable ignorance of conditions in
Russia was displayed by the question, 'Did you belong to any
revolutionary organisation?' I have seen the look of alarm on
the face of more than one immigrant when that query has
been put. The answer has generally been, 'I! Heaven forbid!'
and . . . the Immigration Board have triumphantly
exclaimed,' 'Well, if you were not a member of any such
body, we don't see what you had to fear'. Admission of
membership would be regarded as tantamount to a
declaration that the alien was a terrorist and consequently the
worst form of undesirable immigrant.[114]

The effect of adopting such a procedure was that the 'benefit of doubt'
was rarely given, with the instructions being completely overlooked.
The figures for those refugees admitted under the 'benefit of the
doubt' order were 505 in 1906, 43 in 1907, 20 in 1908, 30 in 1909,
and 5 in 1910.[115] Many genuine refugees fleeing from the massacres
of the Russian Revolution were turned away and complaints to the
Home Secretary proved to be singularly ineffective. Small wonder,
then, that it was remarked at the time that 'the odds are decidedly
against the immigrant who is once refused permission to land'.[116]

There is a parallel here with the immigration practices of today.
The outstanding immigration commitment for many years has been
that of dependants seeking to join members of their families settled
here. Entry for dependants is conditional upon satisfying an immigration official that they are related to their sponsoring relative in
the United Kingdom and their acquiring an entry clearance certificate. In 1972 the Divisional Court of the Queen's Bench held
that the standard of proof contemplated by the immigration rules
was the civil standard, on balance of probabilities, and not proof
beyond reasonable doubt.[117] Although restrictive interpretations
of the rules are promptly applied through the immigration system,
the court's ruling did not filter through in any subsequent instructions to immigration officers overseas. Unaware of this ruling, two
years later when Alex Lyon became Minister of State for Immigration in February 1974, he gave instructions while in the Indian sub-
continent to immigration officers that the proper test which all dependants should satisfy was proof on balance of probabilities. As he
explained later:

The fact is that I told every Entry Clearance Officer in the
sub-continent that he ought to apply that standard . . . and I
did so because I thought it was right to do so. I thought that
was the right interpretation of the law. What I did not know
when I went out there was that the Divisional Court, sitting

under the Lord Chief Justice, had decided that in 1972, in a case which ought to have been reported to me and ought to have been reported to every Entry Clearance officer.[118]

Mr Lyon's new instructions shook the system by the roots. In 1975 and the first half of 1976 the ratio of applications refused to applicants granted fell at Dacca, Bangladesh, from 1:16 to 1:6, and at Islamabad, Pakistan, from 1:23 to 1:5.[119] Soon after, however, Lyon was sacked from office. He was sacked, as he explains below, because civil servants refused to abide by his instructions and that made his position untenable. After his dismissal in June 1976 there was a dramatic upsurge in the ratio of applications refused to applications granted. In fact, the refusal rate became even higher than it was in 1974, before Lyon arrived at the Home Office – in the second half of 1976 this was nearly 1:1 in Dacca and 1:2 in Islamabad.[120] The oddest thing about this is that the increase resulted without any fresh instructions being issued by Mr Lyon's successor. In his evidence to the Select Committee on Race Relations and Immigration Lyon relates these events as follows:

> I really got the sack because I believed, simplistically perhaps, that a Minister ought to rule in his Department, and if he makes the decisions the officials must carry them out. I think you can see, if from nowhere else from the graph that comes out of my figures from the processing of figures in the applications, that the officials have taken it in their heads to do exactly as they want in the sub-continent. The graph that was shown in *The Times* . . . shows perfectly clearly that although no new instructions have been given to the Entry Clearance Officers since I left, the rate of refusal has gone up dramatically in Dacca and Islamabad and in Delhi. It has gone up just because the officials have taken it into their own heads to do it, not because any Minister has said so. Whether I am right or wrong, my view is that I was the Minister and what I said had to go. That, I am afraid, caused a certain amount of tension.[121]

According to Alex Lyon, as far as the figures are concerned, 'the increased rigidity which is reflected . . . in the number of refusals has been decided by civil servants'. It is, in fact, quite implausible to assert that the sharp fluctuations within such a short time-span reflect changing proportions of genuine and bogus applications. Mr Lyon adverted to this, arguing that it was 'absurd that in Dacca in the last quarter of 1976 only 481 applications were granted out of 2168 processed', as it was impossible to maintain that 75 per cent of the cases were bogus. His hard words, 'The idea that the officials are *merely* responsive to ministerial direction is nonsense',[122] are an inescapable conclusion, therefore. At this stage the parallel emerges with the practices of the immigration officials under the 1905 legislation. In both cases the door was slammed on people who were entitled under the law to enter and in both cases this was done by officials acting at their own behest.

In the administration of immigration control officials do wield enormous power – more so at times than even the appellate authorities and the courts. Thus in its 1987 Annual Report, the United Kingdom Immigrants Advisory Service (UKIAS) drew attention to 'new trends' which 'undermine the effectiveness and indeed the very existence of the appellate system' in that officials continued to refuse to issue entry clearance certificates to persons whose appeals had been successful. In its view 'little or no regard is paid to findings made by adjudicators and tribunals' in such cases.[123]

Such a development should not, however, have been surprising. The exercise of deviational discretion contrary to mandatory rules of legal competence had by the 1980s become so well established that it stretched in some cases from the lower echelons of the immigration service to the highest levels. A prime example is the admission of foreign spouses, which has constituted one of the most severely restricted categories of New Commonwealth immigrants in the past two decades. The provenance of this restriction lies in the rule that curtailed the entry of foreign husbands. Men were seen as heads of household and to give them the green light was to pave the way for further primary immigration. By 1980 husbands could enter to join wives in Britain only if they could show that their 'primary purpose' in marrying them was not to seek settlement in Britain.[124]

New imigration rules published in February 1983 maintained the application of the 'primary purpose' rule but now also required a woman to be settled in Britain. When in 1985 three women challenged this situation before the European Court of European Rights on the grounds *inter alia* of sex discrimination, the European Court, as we saw in Chapter 1, found in their favour.[125] The Government, however, faced with defeat, rather than up-grading the rights in the immigration rules which the court had found so wanting, sought to comply with its ruling by down-grading all rights. The present position is that the rules draw no distinction between husbands and wives but refer merely to the admission 'as the spouse of a person who is present and settled in the United Kingdom', whilst still making such a spouse subject to the primary purpose rule.[126]

The question which had not been definitively answered was what was to be meant by the 'primary purpose' of a marriage. As we saw, the tribunal in *Vinod Bhatia*, despite being specially constituted for this task, left the matter in an unsatisfactory state. Immigration officials had, however, formulated their own tests which they felt helped them in the determination of the parties' true intentions when they married. At the time that the Government first changed the immigration rules in February 1983, the Home Office issued secret instructions to Entry Clearance Officers. Copies of these instructions were acquired by *The Guardian* as well as the Joint Council for the Welfare of Immigrants (JCWI). Although the rules have now been changed to apply to spouses of both sexes, there is no reason to believe that their import does not continue to be applied. Of the eligibility of a husband to enter, the instructions said, 'if there is no clear evidence either way . . . or if the question of whether he has met the criteria seems evenly balanced he should no longer be given the benefit of the doubt'.[127]

The fact was that under this provision an increasing number of men were refused even when their marriage was known to the Home Office to be genuine. This was never intended by Parliament or even necessarily by the Home Secretary. Someone somewhere had, however, decided to give this instruction to officials. *The Guardian* moreover explained that its copy of the instructions enjoined Entry Clearance Officers to ask three questions which, as the recent case of *Mohammed Safter*[128] vividly demonstrates, still form the basis of questioning today: 'If your fiancée did not live in the United Kingdom would you still marry her?' Alex Lyon, the former Labour immigration Minister, in January 1984 told a meeting of about 80 politicians, lawyers and immigrant welfare workers at the House of Commons that in asking such questions, immigration officers were making an impossible psychological judgment about a couple's motives for marrying, since

> it is a central feature of the arranged marriage system that the families consider the economic prospects of each partner. It is therefore inevitable that one factor in a marriage to a British girl would be the desire for the man to come to Britain.[129]

In the words of Lord Scarman, these instructions were 'an attack on the social habits and customs of a people, who have come to this country and who are living according to the customs in which they were brought up', not adding in any way to the control of immigration.[130] The third question which the guidance stipulates is, 'If your family had asked you to marry a local girl would you have done so?'[131] Muslim men applying to join their fiancées in the United Kingdom have, as a result, been taken through their family tree by an immigration officer and asked why they are not marrying eligible local cousins rather than a girl in Britain. In interviews fiancées have been asked:

'Do you want to go to the United Kingdom?' Because they are applying to do so they normally consider it wise to say yes. This, however, is taken as an admission that the marriage is primarily for the purpose of settlement. This practice continues even today as such recent well-known cases as *Mohammed Safter* and *Sumeina Masood* make only too clear.[132]

Entry Clearance Officers working in British missions[133] abroad are, it seems, under some pressure by their superiors to put leading questions and to get people to admit that their main reason for marrying is to enter Britain.[134] The result is that the most intrusive techniques have been used. According to Whitehall sources, husbands are asked whether their marriage has been consummated and what their living and sleeping arrangements will be in the UK. Letters between couples have also been opened and there is at least one case where it was said that the letters were not affectionate enough for a proposed marriage to be genuine.

Even if a person escapes all these pitfalls his or her application may still fail. This is because the secret instructions prescribe that even if the replies suggest that the marriage is not primarily for the purpose of settlement 'an officer will still need to assess the applicant's credibility and integrity'. This means that if there was a record of a previous application for settlement this could cast doubt on the credibility of the applicant. The instructions also warn that a subsequent appeal to an adjudicator or the IAT might overturn a refusal made solely on the grounds that a man was going to work in his fiancée's business. But if he had secured a job elsewhere in the United Kingdom before applying for entry as a fiancé, a case for refusal would exist.

It is generally accepted in Whitehall that the existence of these practices means that immigration officials have greater powers to intrude into people's lives than almost any group of civil servants.[135]

This almost unbridled exercise of arbitrary discretionary power by officials does not stop here. The corollary of unlawful instructions given with the intention of frustrating the legitimate rights of immigrants is the deliberate failure by the Home Office to send instructions where these would assist the application of immigrants. Thus we have seen how the Home Office failed, following a High Court decision in 1972 on the burden of proof, to inform entry clearance posts overseas of the true tests that immigrants had to satisfy. In February 1984 the Minister in charge of immigration, Mr David Waddington (as he then was), admitted in a letter to John Hunt MP that the liberalizing effects of another High Court decision occurring as long ago as January 1983 had also not been communicated to posts overseas until well over a year later.[136] But when giving evidence on 6 February to the Select Committee, the Minister stated that instructions *had been* issued after the decision when plainly they had not been.[137] The decision was important in establishing that elderly parents whose children could support them in the UK could not be turned away if other relatives overseas could not actually support them. Hitherto, this had been unclear because the immigration rules referred only to entry being refused for parents and grandparents if they had 'other close relatives in their own countries to turn to',[138] without specifying if this included financial support. In his letter to John Hunt, the Minister admitted later that instructions had not been sent at the time he gave his evidence on 6 February. They were sent only on 15 February – nine days after his reply to the Committee.[139]

Conclusions

The combined experiences of the alien and New Commonwealth immigration to the United Kingdom points to some significant similarities in the responses of the host country at its various critical points – the agitation for restrictionist legislation, the political responses that shaped policy, the attempts to impose some vestige of administrative legality and adjudicative fairness through a system of tribunal hearings, and the dubious actions of officials outside this system. It is fair to conclude that such improvements as have been made have met with limited success because the phenomenon of immigration has throughout been analysed in terms of emotionalism and not rationalism or empiricism. It is this which also accounts for the choice of 'government by executive discretion'[140] with its inevitable abuse of power in many cases. The interesting question is, however, why there should be abuse when there are strict rules directed at structuring the exercise of a discretion in the sort of situations that we have seen in this chapter. It is as difficult to answer this question definitively as it is to bring oneself to accept that there is official abuse of power. The problem has been considered to be of sufficient importance and intractability for A. Dummett and A. Nicol to lament that,

> A few years ago, it was possible to consider how legislation and its administration should be reformed, in the context of an expectation that the law would be observed by the authorities . . . But there are now some 'mistakes', particularly concerning refugees, which brazenly disregard not just the spirit of the law, but conformity to hitherto unquestionable standards of basic decency.[141]

It is submitted, however, that the answer arguably lies precisely here, in the promulgation of new reforming legislation that can compel a change in the practices of administration that have through long years become entrenched. There are two reasons why there may be the official abuse of power. Firstly, and most obviously, no one section in society can be said to have a monopoly of vice. If politicians can be said to be open to partisan or prejudicial sentiment, so can officials at posts overseas issuing entry clearance certificates. But secondly, and much more importantly, it must be the case that so long as the fundamental law of a particular regulatory structure is flawed on the basis of being racially discriminatory, officials are bound to proceed on the assumption that they are doing their job best when they apply a discriminatory law in a discriminatory fashion. In this general milieu individual guidances in particular cases instructing officials to give the benefit of the doubt are likely to be seen as aberrations and ignored, in the face of the basic law which detracts so much from the rule of law and from the basic standards of fairness that we all expect from officialdom and have become so accustomed to in our lives. For this reason, it is submitted, it is imperative that the critical initiative first comes from Parliament in its reforming legislation, putting the law on a sound and rational basis. At present immigration control is formally arbitrary, and so long as it is arbitrary it cannot be fair and just.

These arguments apply with equal force to the appeals system. Take, for example, the controversial 'primary purpose' rule which we have already much discussed. There was a time recently when the courts began to expose it for the nonsense it was. In *Kumar* Lord Donaldson MR said:

> If . . . the wife is already settled here, is a British citizen and wishes to continue to live here, it is idle for her to marry a man who does not wish to obtain admission to the United Kingdom. Yet it is fatally easy to treat his admission that he does indeed wish to obtain admission as evidence that this is the primary purpose of the marriage.[142]

In *Matwinder Singh* Mr Justice Simon Brown referred to the 'enormity' and 'improbability' of people marrying for life just to obtain admission into this country.[143] In *Kandiya* Simon Brown J again laid down a guideline that was on appeal endorsed by the Court of Appeal, that each case should be looked at 'sensibly' and 'realistically' and adjudicators in their decision should not follow 'slavishly some preordained route, let alone . . . recite routinely as an incantation certain assumptions or conclusions . . .'.[144] In the leading case of *Mohammed Safter* Lord Prosser in the Scottish Court of Sessions even accepted that although the parties' marriage was, consistent with both partners' wishes, dependent on the husband being able to come to Britain, there was 'no basis in it for doubting . . . that the parties' prime concern was anything other than marriage'.[145] In an excellent article,

'Primary Purpose: The End of Judicial Sympathy', Rick Scannell argues, however, that the continuing tendency to take on judicial review 'primary purpose' cases has now resulted in a shift of sympathy by the judiciary.[146] In *Sumeina Masood* accordingly, the Court of Appeal has now reversed the entire jurisprudence above by holding that unless a spouse is content *not* to live in the United Kingdom following his marriage, he may or may not join his British citizen partner in the United Kingdom.[147] Such reversals of judicial policy are being made possible because of a flawed and arbitrary law. Try as they might, the courts are bound in particular cases to give vent to its underlying purpose, which is to exclude people whose marriages may well be genuine.

The European Court of Human Rights in July 1992 held the 'primary purpose' rule, a key principle of British immigration law, to be incompatible with Community law.[148] In the case of a woman who left Britain to work in Germany between 1983 and 1985, and then upon her return was refused entry to her husband, the court held that immigration officers could not ask them what the primary purpose of the marriage was. The judgment, compelling as it is, does not apply to the admission of spouses from non-Community countries. But the message for the British government is clear. It should abolish the 'primary purpose' rule forthwith.

NOTES AND REFERENCES

1 *Royal Commission on Alien Immigration 1903* (Cmnd 1742), p. 2. Also Foot, P. (1965) *Immigration and Race in British Politics*, esp. Chaps 5, 6, 7, 9. London; and Jones, C. (1977) *Immigration and Social Policy in Britain*, pp. 133–54. London.

2 Geipel, J. (1969) *The Europeans: An Ethnological Survey*, pp. 163–4. London.

3 See *Royal Commission on Alien Immigration*, *loc. cit.* This view was echoed in 1960, at the height of post-war New Commonwealth immigration, by J.A.G. Griffith, lecturer at the London School of Economics: 'There have always been clear advantages in the reception of foreigners. For centuries, the immigrant into the United Kingdom has come for one of two principal reasons. For the very great majority, the reason has been personal economic betterment; for the important minority, it has been the seeking of a sanctuary'; see Griffith, J.A.G. (1960) *Coloured Immigrants in Britain*, p. 157. Oxford.

4 Jones, C. *op. cit.* p. 133.

5 Garrard, J.A. (1967–68) Parallels of Protest: English Reactions to Jewish and Commonwealth Immigration. *Race* 9 (pp. 47–67), p. 47.

6 Crossman, R. (1964–65) *Diaries of a Cabinet Minister* (1975 edn) Vol. 1, pp. 149, 150.

7 *The Times*, 6 October 1972 (quoted in Bevan, V. (1987) *The Development of British Immigration Law*, p. 81. London).

8 Walvin, J. (1984) *Passage to Britain*, p. 136. London.

9 Paul Foot, *op. cit.* p. 124.

10 *Ibid.* p. 123.

11 Walvin, *op. cit.* pp. 106, 108.

12 Rose, E.J.B. (1969) *Colour and Citizenship: A Report on British Race Relations*, p. 178. Oxford. Also see Walvin, *op. cit.* p. 112.

13 Hammar, T. (1987) *European Immigration Policy: A Comparative Study*, p. 245. Cambridge.

14 Rose, *ibid.* p. 78. Also Walvin, *ibid.* p. 108.

15 See speech by Lieutenant-Colonel Marcus Lipton MP (Brixton) HC Deb, Vol. 532, col. 832 (5 November 1954).

16 See Jefferson, O. (1972). *The Post-War Economic Development of Jamaica.* Kingston.

17 Paul Foot, *op. cit.* p. 106.

18 Fryer, P. (1984) *Staying Power: The History of Black People in Britain*, p. 374. London.

19 Smith, T.E. (1981) *Commonwealth Migration*, p. 7. London.

20 Thus Castles and Kosack have written that 'Every period of economic expansion since the war has led to labour shortages, which have been alleviated through the recruitment of immigrant workers'. See Castles, S. and Kosack, G. (1973) *Immigrant Workers and Class Structures in Western Europe*, p. 27. Oxford. For the options available to British industry, see Rose, *op. cit.* p. 80.

21 Peach, C. (1968) *West Indian Migration to Britain*, p. 3. Oxford. Note that the first systematic study of Jamaican emigration was by Roberts and Mills, who regarded rather unemployment as having provided the 'push' inducing emigration to the United Kingdom. See Roberts, G. and Mills, D. (1958) *Study of External Migration Affecting Jamaica, 1953–55*, p. 2. Institute for Social and Economic Research, UCWI.

22 Peach, *ibid.* pp. 24–7.

23 Figures for the years up to 1961 are: 1959: 16,000; 1960: 50,000; 1961: 66,000. See Foot, *op. cit.* p. 126; and Walvin, *op. cit.* p. 111.

24 Paul Foot, *op. cit.* pp. 11–12.

25 Rose, *op. cit.* p. 74. Also see Chapter 30 for economic costs and benefits of immigration.

26 John Hynd (Sheffield Attercliffe) HC Deb., Vol. 532, col. 823 (5 November 1984).

27 See speech by Mr Henry Hopkinson (Minister of State for Colonial Affairs), *ibid.* col. 827. Also see Paul Foot, *op. cit.* pp. 124–5.

28 Mullard, C. (1976) Racism in Britain: Management of Concepts 1948–1975. *Case Studies in Human Rights and Fundamental Freedoms* 5 (pp. 199–225), p. 205. The Hague.

29 Fryer, *op. cit.* p. 372.

30 Mullard, C. *op. cit.* p. 204. Mullard refers to the formula as 'the double attractive

migration principle: the purchase of needed labour with the currency of citizenship', basing this on a study by Clarence Senior on Race Relations and Labour Supply in Great Britain. See Mullard, *op. cit.* p. 203.

31 Fryer, *supra*, p. 374. Also Deakin, N. (1970) *Colour, Citizenship and British Society*, p. 283. London. Also see Paul Foot, *op. cit.* p. 125.
32 Walvin, *op. cit.* p. 114.
33 Fryer, *op. cit.* p. 373.
34 John Hynd (Sheffield Attercliffe) HC Deb., Vol. 532, col. 822 (5 November 1954).
35 Aurora, G.S. (1967) *The New Frontiersmen: A Sociological Study of Indian Immigrants in the United Kingdom*, p. 27. Bombay.
36 Anwar, M. (1979) *The Myth of Return: Pakistanis in Britain*, p. 21. London.
37 (1969) Select Committee Report, Q.2101, 2146. Also see summary of evidence at para. 34.
38 Bevan, *op. cit.* p. 78.
39 HC Deb., Vol. 532, col. 822 (5 November 1954).
40 Henry Hopkinson, *ibid.* col. 830.
41 *Ibid.* col. 824.
42 *Ibid.* col. 825.
43 *Ibid.* col. 823.
44 *Ibid.* cols 824-5.
45 Sir William Evans Gordon.
46 HC Deb., Standing Committee F, col. 2088 (14 May 1981).
47 House of Commons Home Affairs Committee, Race Relations and Immigration sub-committee, *Immigration Topics* (December 1980); HC 89, p. 6.
48 *Ibid.* p. 30; Q.153.
49 *Ibid.* p. 25; Q.107.
50 *Ibid.* p. 27; Q.120, Q.121, Q.122. After this, Mr Lyon said to Dr Evans: 'You have deliberately gone out of your way to make this a national issue in a very sensitive area and unless you did so on the strength of clear scientific evidence it was an irresponsible thing to do' (p. 27, Q.125).
51 *Ibid.* p. 30; Q.154. Mr Hunt ended by asking of Dr Evans: 'Do you not . . . want to register concern that your report has been treated in this wholly slanted and unreasonable way?' *Loc. cit.*
52 HL Deb., Vol. 270, col. 439 (16 November 1965).
53 *Ibid.* col. 43.
54 HC Deb., Vol. 145, col. 803 (2 May 1905).
55 HC Deb., Vol. 148, col. 157 (10 July 1905).
56 HC Deb., Vol. 149, col. 1259 (19 July 1905). His only defence was that the expulsion provisions in the Act could be used against undesirables.
57 *Op. cit.* Vol. 148, col. 853 (3 July 1905). This was in line with the findings of the Select Committee that alien workers did not compete in the labour market at home.
58 *Op. cit.* Vol. 148, at cols 865-6 (3 July 1905). The same view was expressed by Sir Charles Dilke, who explained: 'There was in 1903, the last year for which they had the Board of Trade Return, no increase of alien population in this country and the alien population was trifling as compared with the alien population of

every other country in the world. At this moment France had just extended to the Italian workmen, who were more numerous by far in France than all the workmen of all foreign countries were in England, the whole of the old-age pensions provisions, the whole of the insurance provisions of their law, and this by treaty. It would be a retrograde step unworthy of this country to adopt these means of restrictions and exclusion in face of an evil, which, except in a district here and there, was trifling.' He suggested that 'the evils complained of should be dealt with by anti-sweating legislation'. *Op. cit.* Vol. 145, col. 472 (18 April 1905).

59 *Ibid.*, col. 295.

60 Landa, M.J. (1911) *The Alien Problem and Its Remedy*, pp. 230–51. London.

61 Landa, *op. cit.* p. 214. Also see Gainer, B. (1972) *The Alien Invasion*, p. 284. London; and Garrard, *op. cit.* p. 125.

62 Gainer, *op. cit.* p. 200. Also see Landa, *op. cit.* p. 199.

63 Immigration Appeal Tribunal, Appeal No. TH/381/70, December 1970.

64 (1971) A Strange Death for Liberal England. *The Spectator*, p. 59, 15 January.

65 Hepple, B.A. (1971) Aliens and Administrative Justice: The Dutschke Case. *Modern Law Review* 34 (pp. 501–19), pp. 501–2.

66 See Mr Atherley-Jones, HC Deb., Vol. 145, col. 459 (12 May 1905).

67 *Ibid.*, cols 460–1. For the debate on Tribunals see cols 459–65.

68 *The Times*, 22 July 1992.

69 *Patel* [1986] Imm AR 440.

70 *Rajendran* [1989] Imm AR 512.

71 [1976] Imm AR 114.

72 *Azad* (unreported) (5993).

73 *Visa Officer, Karachi* v. *Hassan Mohd.* [1978] Imm AR 168; *R* v. *IAT ex parte Weersuriya* [1983] 1 All ER 195; *R* v. *IAT ex parte Kotecha* [1988] 2 All ER 289.

74 *R* v. *Carl (Adjudicator) ex parte Secretary of State* [1989] Imm AR 432.

75 *Ex parte Aurangzeb Khan* [1989] Imm AR 524; *Ex parte Halima Begum* [1989] Imm AR 547.

76 [1986] Imm AR 208.

77 (1989–90) Report, *op. cit.* p. xvi.

78 Section 13(3) of 1971 Act as amended by BNA 1981, 39(5), and Immigration Act 1988, s. 3.

79 Section 15(4) of 1971 Act.

80 *Ibid.* s. 14(3) and s. 15(3).

81 *R* v. *ECO, Bombay, ex parte Amin* [1980] 2 All ER 837.

82 *Pearson* v. *IAT* [1978] Imm AR 212, CA.

83 *Suthendran* v. *IAT* [1977] AC 359.

84 *R* v. *IAT ex parte Ahluwalia* [1979–80] Imm AR 1.

85 Section 14(4) of 1971 Act.

86 Section 16(1) of 1971 Act; Section 5 of 1988 Act modifying Section 15 of 1971 Act.

87 (1989–90) Report, *op. cit.* p. xv.

88 *Ibid.* p. iv.

89 *Loc. cit.*

90 (1981) *The Pivot of the System: A Briefing Paper on Immigration Appeals*, p. 22. London.
91 Landa, *op. cit.* p. 207.
92 *Loc. cit.*
93 *Ibid.* pp. 209–11.
94 (1981–82) House of Commons Fifth Report from the Home Affairs Committee, Immigration from the Indian sub-continent. 1, HC 90. p. xviii, para. 43.
95 One member of the Board, it appears, castigated as 'nonsense' the reply by a Jewish witness, who kept a provision shop, that he did not sell bacon, unacquainted with the general knowledge that bacon was the forbidden flesh for Jews: see Landa, *op. cit.* p. 213.
96 See letter of Mr Adol Owen-Williams to *The Independent*, 12 May 1992.
97 Letter to *The Independent*, 14 May 1992.
98 Letter to *The Independent*, 20 May 1992.
99 Letter to *The Independent*, 15 May 1992.
100 Letter by Mr R. Woodgate, *loc. cit.*
101 Immigration Appeals (Procedure) Rules 1984, SI No. 2041.
102 Grant, L. and Martin, I. (1982) *Immigration Law and Practice*, p. 312. London.
103 *ECO, Dacca* v. *Fultera Begum* TH/64779/80 (2221) d. 4.12.81 (unreported).
104 *Visa Officer, Islamabad* v. *Zarina Jan* TH/53001/79, (2300) d. 2.2.82 (unreported).
105 *Sofia Begum* v. *ECO, Dacca* TH/113201/85 d. 6.3.85 (unreported).
106 *Vinod Bhatia* v. *ECO, New Delhi* TH/11935/83 (3456) d. 31.8.84 (unreported).
107 (1983/84) *JCWI Annual Report*, p. 3. Also see (1985) *Immigration Control Procedures: Report of a Formal Investigation*, p. 65. London.
108 See the decisions in *Naresh Kumar* (3278), *Ravinder Singh* (3352) and *Lahmber Singh* (3353).
109 (1983/84) *JCWI Annual Report*, p. 5.
110 [1941] 3 All ER 338, p. 361.
111 Robertson, G. (1989) *Freedom, the Individual and the Law*, p. 315. Harmondsworth.
112 *Ibid.*, p. 330.
113 Landa, *op. cit.* pp. 315–17.
114 Landa, *op. cit.* p. 225.
115 Landa, *op. cit.* p. 225; Gainer, *op. cit.* p. 203.
116 Landa, *op. cit.* pp. 226, 230.
117 *R* v. *Sec. of State for the Home Dept, ex parte Hussein* (1972) (unreported).
118 An outstanding example of this is how the decisions in *Subramaniam* (1976) Imm AR 155, and *Suthendran* (1977) Imm AR 44 were applied through the system. Even some cases which had already been heard (or were being heard) were adversely affected; e.g. see the decision in *Wee Yee Mak* (TH/915/76, (1243), d. 25.5.76 (unreported), at p. 6).
119 (1977–78) *First Report from the Select Committee on Race Relations and Immigration* Annexes and Minutes of Proceedings; HC 303-I, pp. 107–10.
120 *Ibid.*, p. 192.
121 *Ibid.*, p. 193.
122 *Ibid.*, pp. 114–15. The figures are given in Appendix 1. There has been some

confirmation of this. *The Guardian* reports: 'It has been known for senior Home Office officials to remark openly to colleagues that it was a good thing that the Conservatives, with their tougher line on immigration, were now in power and that Mr Alex Lyon – a liberal Labour Minister once in charge of immigration – was sacked.' (See *The Guardian*, 2 April 1984.)

123 (1987–88) *UKIAS Annual Report*, pp. 31–2, quoted in Dummett and Nicol, *op. cit.* p. 256.

124 (1980) *Statement of Changes in Immigration Rules* (20 February) HC 394, paras 50 and 52.

125 See Chapter 1, note 41.

126 (1990) *Statement of Changes in Immigration Rules* (23 March) HC 251, para. 50.

127 (1984) *JCWI Bulletin*, May, 1(9), p. 1.

128 *Mohammed Saftar* v. *Secretary of State for the Home Department* [1992] Imm AR 1.

129 *The Guardian*, 27 January 1984, where Clare Short MP also pointed out that 'In an arranged marriage system a man's willingness to live in the United Kingdom is assumed.' Indeed, this view was accepted by the IAT even earlier under Professor Jackson in *Rokeya Begum* v. *ECO, Dacca* TH/99709/82 (2936) d. 7.10.83 (unreported) where it was accepted that marriage 'logically indicates that they would both live in England'.

130 (1979-80) *First Report from the Home Affairs Committee, Proposed New Immigration Rules and the European Convention on Human Rights*, HC 434, p. 31.

131 *The Guardian*, 21 March 1984 and 2 April 1984. Also *JCWI Bulletin, op. cit.*

132 *Mohammed Saftar, op. cit.* and *Sumeina Masood* v. *IAT* [1992] Imm AR 69.

133 It is for this reason that in New Delhi Entry Clearance Officers have 'masterminded a system of an interrogation which is designed to get a man to say he wants to come to England which is bound to lead to a refusal'. *The Guardian* 27 January 1984.

134 Thus 'in one High Commission in the sub-continent . . . a list is posted showing how many applications for entry by husbands or fiancés have been granted or refused by each official. Its purpose is not clear, but the list was taken down during a visit by the Commission for Racial Equality.' *The Guardian*, 2 April 1984. Most officials continue to apply the instructions silently but 'a minority find their consciences strained because they think it offensive or morally wrong to ask what they regard as trivial and sordid questions'. *The Guardian, loc. cit.*

135 *Ibid.*

136 The decision in question is *R* v. *Immigration Appeal Tribunal, ex parte Bastiamillai* (1983) 2 All ER 844.

137 (1983–84) *Home Affairs Committee on Race Relations and Immigration* (6 Feb 1984), HC 224. at p. 12, para. 32.

138 (1983) *Statement of Changes in Immigration Rules* (9 February) HC 169, para. 52. During the meeting of the Home Affairs Sub-Committee on Race Relations and Immigration, the Assistant Secretary (Immigration and Nationality Dept) admitted that under the rules 'very few relatives qualify and this was deliberately tightly drawn.' See (1981–82) *Home Affairs Committee, Immigration from the Indian Sub-Continent* (26 July 1982), HC 90-II p. 30, Q.92.

139 In a letter to John Hunt MP, David Waddington said, 'I fully accept that guidance on the case should have been issued sooner to all Home Office staff and entry clearance officers overseas.' Fiona Mactaggart of the JCWI said that a number of applicants who should have been admitted were, many months later, winning their cases at appeal: see *The Guardian*, 29 March 1984.

140 Pannick, D. (1984) In Search of Just Immigration Laws. *The Guardian*, 4 June 1984.

141 Dummett, A. and Nicol, A. (1990) *Subjects, Citizens, Aliens and Others*, p. 256. London.

142 *Kumar* [1986] Imm AR 446, p. 455.

143 *Matwinder Singh* (23 March 1987, unreported). Subsequently see also *Hoque and Singh* [1988] Imm AR 216, and *Bashir* (15 March 1988, unreported) and *Khatab* [1989] Imm AR 313. Also see *Choudhary* [1990] Imm AR 211.

144 *Kandiya and Khan* [1990] Imm AR 377.

145 *Op. cit.* See note 128.

146 (1992) *Immigration and Nationality Law and Practice* 3(1), January 1992, p. 3.

147 *Op. cit.* note 132.

148 R v. *Immigration Appeal Tribunal and Another, ex parte Secretary of State for the Home Department* [1992] 3 All ER 798.

4

Freedom of Movement in Europe

'There is but one law for all, namely, that law which governs all law,
of our creator, the law of humanity, justice, equity – the law of nature,
and of nations.' – *Edmund Burke*

INTRODUCTION

It has become fashionable to assert that Britain can no longer afford to
have an open-door immigration policy. In the previous three chapters
we saw how the law has been used as an instrument to support this
theory and to progressively extend immigration control throughout
this century. In this chapter we hope to demonstrate that those who
espouse this notion fail to understand what can be meant by an open-
door or flexible immigration policy. As Vaughan Bevan explains:

> An open-door policy does not mean that aliens are
> unrestricted in what they can do once admitted or that they
> are free from the possibility of expulsion. Thus the grant of
> citizenship may be denied to them or carefully regulated,
> their economic activities may be circumscribed, e.g. by the
> payment of extra taxes, the denial of trading licences, an
> obligation to train local workers in their business; legal, civic
> and political rights may be withheld.[1]

The European Community (EC) is a uniform and unitary legal order.
But it is also totally autonomous and supranational. At first sight, it
may appear that national states can draw no lessons of value from it.
After all, it is a system that belongs neither to public international law
nor to municipal law. Its subjects are not states, as in international
law, but member states; nor are they individuals as in municipal law,
but nationals of those member states. Community law and national
law are two distinct legal orders independent of each other, one being
based on the Foundation Treaties, the other on a Constitution.
Indeed, the European Community as a system is probably *sui generis*.

Although there are other organizations in international law that possess their own institutions, affect the actions of their member states, and confer rights on individuals which can be enforced before national courts, the EC goes much further than most such obligations in developing the substantive powers, rights and obligations of its subjects, and in creating a system of remedies and procedures for their enforcement. This is largely the result of the very wide scope of the EEC Treaty. The extent to which autonomous institutions in the Community, such as the European Court of Justice, have been ceded power by national states to decide matters is also unique, as is the extent to which EC law penetrates the domestic legal order creating new legal rights and obligations that are enforceable within the domestic jurisdiction. Clearly the compelling impetus in this drive is the desire to limit national sovereignty.

Yet it may well be asked why individual governments in Europe would have wished to restrict their sovereign rights in this way and move towards an idea of a federal Europe with control over trade, money, security and related taxation being given over to a federal parliament, government and court,while retaining control over all other matters themselves. In *European Community: The Building of a Union*, J. Pinder gives the following explanation:

> World War II was a catastrophe that discredited the previous
> international order and, for many Europeans, the basic
> element in that order: the sovereign nation-state. In the
> Europe of such states, France and Germany had been at war
> three times in less than a century, twice at the centre of
> terrible world wars. Autarky and protection, fragmenting
> Europe's economy, had caused economic malaise and political
> antagonism. Fascist glorification of the nation-state had been
> revealed as a monstrosity; and many felt that insistence on its
> sovereignty, even without Fascist excess, distorted and ossified
> the political perspective.[2]

The European Community was thus not only an orgnization aimed at intergovernmental co-operation in free trade and the European economy, such as the GATT and EFTA treaties, but included a wide range of matters including those that were purely social. It is from this wider background and experience that national governments can draw their lessons in approaching their own problems.

To those who argue that the state always has an inalienable right to determine who may cross its borders, this experience indicates how a state may reduce, and how Britain has reduced, its rights by treaty. Thus the free movement provisions of EC law now embrace not only Britain, Belgium, Denmark, France, Greece, Ireland, Italy,

Luxembourg, Germany and The Netherlands but also Portugal and Spain from 1 January 1993. To those who argue that free movement means an open door for all, this experience demonstrates how full immigration rights may yet still be denied to individuals, for an association agreement with Turkey containing a programme of free movement rights has been held by the European Court not to be directly enforceable.[3] To those who argue that there is an overall loss of basic rights in the modern world, this experience, however, provides us with its most overwhelming lesson – that of the creation of the free movement provisions of the EC in that they bestow specific rights on the individual whilst restricting the powers of the state. The European Court of Justice has held these provisions to be a principal foundation of the European Community together with its free movement provisions for goods, services and capital.[4] Yet it is clear that even within this context there is much that can still be done in the coherent development of immigration rights. This chapter accordingly places the emphasis on two aspects: how the European Community has succeeded in enfranchising immigration rights, and how further improvements can still be made to this process in the conditions of the modern world. We begin by looking at the legal framework of EC law. Next, we look at how freedom of movement has been developed. We then look at the exceptions to this development. Our conclusion will be that these exceptions do not on the whole detract from, but on the contrary add to, the enfranchisement of immigration rights under EC law. Finally, we consider what lessons may be learnt for the future.

THE LEGAL FRAMEWORK OF EC LAW

The EEC Treaty and Its Institutions

The EEC Treaty – that is, the Treaty of Rome, signed in 1957 – brought into existence the European Economic Community at the beginning of 1958. It is basically a 'framework' treaty (*traité cadre*) in that it expresses broad principles of generality regarding its intended objectives, leaving its institutions to fill in the gaps by secondary legislation. There are four principal institutions set up by the Treaty. The first is the European Parliament, which is not a legislative but a purely advisory and supervisory body. Only since 1979, when MEPs began to be directly elected, has it begun to play a larger role in the legislative process, although its most important area of influence is still the Community Budget.[5] Secondly, there is the European Council,[6] made up of representatives, principally Foreign Ministers, of the 12 member states, and which aims to meet the objectives of the Treaty by co-ordinating the general economic policies of the member states. It is the Council that has the final say over much of secondary legislation, but most of its proposals have to come from the Commission. Member governments assume the Presidency of the Council in rotation every six months, Britain having held it in the second half of 1992. Thirdly, there is the European Commission,[7] which has 17 independent members who sit for four years, and where all important proposals are initiated. Once the Council has made a policy decision on a proposal, it falls to the Commission to implement that policy, often by further legislation, thereby bestowing this body with executive functions. It is the Commission also that acts as a watch-dog of the Community by seeking out infringements of EC law and if necessary bringing pro-ceedings against member states before the European Court. This brings us to the European Court of Justice,[8] which is the fourth and final major institution. Consisting of 13 judges appointed every six years, it was described by Lord Diplock in *R* v. *Henn* as giving effect 'to what it conceives to be the spirit rather than the letter of the Treaties; sometimes, indeed to an English judge, it may seem to the exclusion of the letter'.[9]

The importance of the role of these institutions has been height-ened by the Single European Act, signed in February 1986 and taking effect on 1 July 1987, which widened the Community's area of com-petence. The Act put European political co-operation onto a formal legal basis, rather than the intergovernmental agreements which had sufficed since 1970. Relations between institutions had to be changed by new rules. Voting by qualified majority, which means 54 votes out of a total of 76, was extended by the Council to a number of areas, so that two-thirds of the legislation necessary for the completion of the internal market may now be passed in this way.[10]

The Free Movement Provisions

The free movement provisions of the Treaty of Rome are contained in Articles 48 and 49, which allow for free movement of workers; Article 52, which allows for the right of establishment, defined to include the right to take up and pursue activities as self-employed persons; and Article 59, which aims to remove restrictions on freedom to provide services within the Community. All three provisions have their basis in the objective enshrined in Article 3(c), which is 'the abolition, as between member states, of obstacles to freedom of movement for per-sons'. How this is to be done is further explained in Article 7, which states that 'any discrimination on grounds of nationality shall be prohibited'.

At first sight, as Macdonald and Blake explain,[11] these provisions do not appear to be directly effective in the member states. They are framed as merely objectives to be achieved at certain stages and their language does not confer express rights on individuals. On closer examination, however, Articles 48, 52 and 59 reveal time limits within which the objectives must be achieved. According to the European Court, Treaty provisions that have not been put into effect by member states by their due date become directly effective,[12] and the European Court has also held that the fact that national governments may exclude people on grounds of public policy, public security or public health does not prevent these obligations from being directly effective.[13] This is on its face a surprising development. Article 189 of the Treaty provides only for a regulation to be 'binding in its entirety and directly applicable in all member states'. A Directive 'shall be binding, as to the result to be achieved', and a Decision 'shall be binding in its entirety upon those to whom it is addressed'. Does this make these provisions directly effective in member states, however? Presumably a provision has to be directly applicable before it can have direct effect. If so, this suggests that only Regulations, which are so defined, can have direct effect. The European Court has got around this limitation by saying, however, that any provision of EC law which is sufficiently clear and precise, and unconditional, and which gives a member state no discretion in its implementation, is directly effective. In this way all the basic principles regarding free movement of persons and goods, discrimination on grounds of nationality and sex, and competition law may be raised by individuals in their national courts.[14] In *Watson and Belmann*, indeed, the court explained that the binding effect of both the Treaty articles on free movement and the implementing Regulations and Directives resulted in conferring 'on persons whom they concern individual rights which the national courts must protect and take precedence over any national rule which might conflict with them'.[15]

The General Principles of Law

In reaching such a result, the European Court has clearly had regard to the general principles of law which may be invoked by the court as an aid to the interpretation of Community law.[16] In *Stauder* v. *City of Ulm*[17] the courts recognized fundamental human rights to be part of EC law, and in *Internationale Handelsgesellschaft* it declared such rights, which it found to be part of a common constitutional tradition in member states, to be an integral part of the general principles of law which the court would protect.[18] In *R* v. *Kirk* the court held the principle of non-retroactivity of penal measures enshrined in the International Convention for the Protection of Human Rights and

Fundamental Freedoms 1953[19] to be applicable so that the captain of a Danish fishing vessel could not be charged for fishing in British waters even though he had committed an offence under an EC Regulation.[20] The Court has also in the same way imported the principle of proportionality into EC law, which states that the means employed to attain a particular end in administrative law must be no more than what is necessary and required to attain that end. An administrative authority cannot just apply the test of reasonableness but must be able to justify the measures it employed in the context of possible alternatives. Thus when in *Watson and Belmann*[21] the Italian authorities sought to expel Mrs Watson, who was claiming rights of residence in Italy, for having failed to record and monitor her movements as required by Italian law, the Court held the penalty of deportation to be disproportionate to the desired end of such laws. Similarly, discrimination is outlawed under the general principle of equality. This decrees that unless a difference in treatment of persons in similar situations can be objectively justified, it should not be countenanced.[22] On this basis, the principle of equality has been applied, amongst other things, to sex discrimination[23] as well as to religious discrimination.[24]

Another general principle of great importance to individual rights is that of legal certainty.[25] This incorporates, firstly, the principle of legitimate expectations as derived from German law, meaning that the legitimate expectations of a person can only be ·abridged by Community measures on grounds of public interest;[26] secondly, it incorporates the principle of non-retroactivity which we saw earlier being applied in *R* v. *Kirk*.[27] Finally, the general principles of law contain the safeguard of procedural rights. These are implied whenever secondary legislation has failed to properly provide for them. Procedural rights mean the right to a fair hearing[28] as understood in English law, the duty to give reasons (since a person can only obtain legal redress if he knows of the reasons for the decision against him)[29] and the right to due process[30] (by which a person can challenge reasoned decisions). Without any of these general principles the judicial protection of individual rights would be hardly meaningful in a Treaty that is concerned so overwhelmingly with the economic security of member states. Yet the general principles derive their essence not from the Treaty itself but from the fundamental values and beliefs of individual countries where they have been so carefully fostered and nurtured. They apply to immigration rights within the Community, yet their universality is such that they could, and should, easily be applied as legal norms to all comers. Effective immigration control must not be at the expense of fairness, which must not only be applied but seen to be applied both by those within the Community and those without it.

THE IMMIGRATION RIGHTS IN EC LAW

The Worker and His Rights

The immigration rights giving free movement within the Community are most wide-ranging. They cover workers by giving them and their families the right of entry and residence in member states together with an equality of treatment in getting employment there. There is moreover full access to training in vocational schools as well as retraining for workers and their families. A 'worker' may therefore retire in a country in which he has been employed. The critical definition is, of course, that of a worker. Article 48 of the Treaty does not define the term but insists that 'Freedom of movement for workers shall be secured'. Workers have the right to: (a) accept offers of employment actually made; (b) move freely within the territory of member states for this purpose; (c) stay in a member state for the purpose of employment; and (d) remain in the territory of a member state after having been employed in that state.

It has been left to the European Court to construe the word 'worker', and this it has done generously. The definition in *Lawrie-Blum*[31] by the court was that of a person who 'performs services for or under direction of another in return for remuneration', as a national of a member state. That definition covers part-time workers provided that the work they do is 'real' work and not nominal or minimal. In *Levin*[32] a UK citizen accompanied her South African husband to The Netherlands and took part-time employment. The court considered her employment to be an effective and genuine one and disregarded her motives for going to The Netherlands, even though the effect of the decision was that an EC national could, by taking part-time employment, give her non-EC national husband an EC status. In *Kempf*[33] the court held that a German part-time teacher in The Netherlands teaching 12 hours a week could take advantage of Dutch law to supplement his income with supplementary benefit and obtain sickness benefit when he fell ill, since these benefits were available to Dutch nationals equally.

In order to make immigration a real right the definition of the 'family' of a worker has also been liberally construed.[34] In *Reed* whilst the court held that a cohabitee was not a 'spouse', nevertheless such a person could join a local national as his unmarried 'live-in' partner in The Netherlands since aliens had that right under Dutch law and to refuse it here would be in contravention of the non-discrimination provisions of EC law.[35] In *Diatta* it was held that a 'separated spouse' did not lose her rights of residence in Germany merely because she did not live under the same roof as her husband.[36] The position as to divorced spouses has yet to be decided but is no doubt less favourable.

The Right of Entry and Residence

Article 48 of the Treaty only gives the right of entry to workers who already have definite jobs to go to. Directive 68/360, however, gives a more general right of entry and residence. Article 2 of this Directive gives nationals and their families 'the right to leave their territory in order to take up activities as employed persons and to pursue such activities in the territory of another Member State'. In *Royer* the court held that this includes the right to enter in search for work. The UK immigration rules allow for a period of six months during which either an EC national should be issued with a residence permit or asked to leave. In *Antonissen*[37] a Belgian national was deported after six months and the court held that unless he could provide evidence that he was continuing to seek employment and had a genuine chance of succeeding, a member state was entitled to remove him. However, in *Pieck*[38] the court held that the UK requirement for leave to enter for EC nationals was unlawful and it has since been removed under the Immigration Act 1988.[39] A more interesting aspect of the law in this context is that illegal entry and residence, or legal entry followed by failure to comply with residence requirements, leaves one open to criminal sanctions but not to deportation, and the penalties must not be disproportionate or discriminatory in their application. The contrast with the position with regard to Commonwealth immigrants in Britain could not be more stark, in this respect, and it is a position that clearly needs reviewing.

The Right to Equality of Treatment

Freedom of movement for workers, however, cannot be fully realized just by generous rights of entry and residence. It must also, as Regulation 1612/68 requires, be followed up by equality of treatment in 'all matters relating to the actual pursuit of activities as employed persons'. There must also be the removal of 'obstacles to the mobility of workers' with a 'right to be joined by his family' as well as 'the integration of that family into the host country'. Again, these are principles which are not actively pursued, or even legally enshrined, in the domestic laws of the United Kingdom. Yet their pursuit is essential to demonstrate a serious commitment to human rights as well as to the maintenance of a stable society. Article 4 of this Regulation further states that a member state must not restrict by number or percentage the employment of foreign nationals in any undertaking or activity, and Article 5, that non-national applicants should be offered the same assistance in seeking employment as that which is on offer to a state's own nationals. Direct and indirect discrimination on grounds of nationality is moreover prohibited by Article 70.[40] It is, however, the social and tax advantage that 'packs perhaps the largest punch of all EC secondary legislation in this area'.[41]

The Right to Social and Tax Advantages

Article 7 (2) states quite simply that a worker 'shall enjoy the same social and tax advantages as national workers'. In an area such as immigration control where the social cost of new immigration is put at the highest premium, this provision is remarkable for its especially wide ambit that is free from all conditions. In *Even* the court read this to mean that social rights were available to workers 'by virtue of the mere fact of their residence on national territory'.[42] In *Castelli*[43] a guaranteed income which was given to all old people in Belgium was held to be equally available to an Italian mother who, on being widowed, went to live with her retired son in that country. In *Lebon*,[44] however, the court held that only those who are lawfully resident in a member state can claim full benefits and not those who have mere temporary residence rights. Even so, the position here must make the requirement in Britain that sponsors maintain and support their dependent relatives from non-EC countries seem harsh and unjustified.[45] In the same way, a worker who has lost or given up his job in a member state is entitled like the local nationals to training and retraining in vocational schools. The only restriction is that he must have migrated to the country genuinely in the capacity of a worker and not for any other purpose.[46] It is not only the worker who is entitled to install himself but also his family members, defined as his spouse and their dependants under 21 years of age and their dependent relatives in the ascending line, and they can then take up any activity as an employed person in the member state.[47]

Upon retirement all EC workers normally have two years in which to decide where they want to live.[48] They have the choice of going back to their own country, or of living in the country of which their spouse is a national, or where either of the two of them have been working before retirement.[49] These rules reveal the comprehensive coverage given to the proper determination and realization of immigration rights for EC nationals from the time that they enter a member state to their retirement. There is, unlike with respect to the immigration of non-EC nationals, a notable absence of executive discretion here. Clear guidelines are given.

The Right to Freedom of Establishment and Freedom to Provide Services

In completing this section of our discussion a few words need to be finally said about freedom of establishment (Article 52) and the freedom to provide services (Articles 59 and 60). These rights are accorded in the Treaty to EC nationals and to companies that are formed according to the law of one of the member states. If a company's management and place of business lies outside the community, it must be able to demonstrate an effective and continuous link with the economy of a member state in order to have the valuable access to Community markets. Both rights, however, can only be exercised in a member state 'under conditions laid down for its own nationals',[50] and non-nationals may very often not be able to meet these. The main conditions relate to having the requisite educational and training qualifications for the job and also being able to comply with the rules of professional conduct in a member state. These requirements have, however, been liberally applied. Even in the absence of a Directive being passed to ensure the mutual recognition of formal qualifications in a particular trade or profession, the European Court has held the refusal of permission to practice to someone whose qualifications have been recognized in some way as being equivalent to those of the relevant state to be discriminatory and in breach of Articles 52 or 59 and 60 and Article 7.[51] As regards the freedom to provide services, the court has similarly extended this in Article 59 and 60 to the freedom also to receive services.[52] Indeed, the law has been taken further still. Recipients of services, it has been held, can also have equal access to vocational training under the same conditions as local nationals, even where the course or training is financed as a matter of social policy by the member state.[53]

PUBLIC POLICY, PUBLIC SCRUTINY AND PUBLIC HEALTH

The expansive interpretation of free movement rights is limited only by the public policy proviso in Article 48(3) of the Treaty (repeated in Article 56(1) also). The ideal of non-discrimination still cannot be by-passed under any circumstances, but under this proviso freedom of movement for workers can be made 'subject to limitations justified on grounds of public policy, public security or public health'. This exception to free movement rights is implemented in detail by Directive 64/221,[54] the purpose of which is twofold. Firstly, it is to permit member states to exclude EC nationals on the said grounds and, secondly, it is to lay down stringent procedural safeguards which the expelling member state must abide by.

Unlike the free movement provisions of the Treaty the exceptions to it are not construed liberally, but most strictly. Macdonald and Blake state that this means that 'in contrast to UK immigration law, . . . the principle of free movement within the EEC is far more important than any exceptions to it'. Indeed, in their view, the 'early decisions of British courts on the applicability of the EEC provisions can no longer be relied on as . . . reliable . . .'.[55] The strict interpretation is dictated, in part at any rate, by the Directive itself. Article 2(2) of this prohibits a member state from invoking the public policy proviso to serve economic ends. Article 3(3) states that the expiry of the identity card or passport of a person shall not justify this expulsion, and Article 3(1) provides that measures taken on grounds of public policy or public scrutiny shall be based exclusively on the personal conduct of the individual concerned. How, then, are the member states to approach this question?

In *Van Duyn*,[56] the European Court, considering the claim of a member of the Church of Scientology under a general ban in the UK on the entry of scientologists, held that being a member of this organization was personal conduct by which a member state could justify an exclusion. However, as the requirements of public policy could vary from state to state, this standard could not be determined unilaterally. In *Rutili*,[57] involving the restriction of a noted Italian agitator to certain regions in France, the court held that this could be done by the French Government only if his presence constituted a 'genuine and sufficiently serious threat to public policy'. Clearly, therefore, the proportionality principle was required to be brought into play.

In *Bonsignore*[58] an Italian worker in Cologne accidentally shot his brother with a gun that he had illegally purchased. The German authorities wanted to provide a deterrent by making an example of him by deporting him, but the European Court found this factor to be extraneous to his personal conduct. In fact, Article 3(2) states that a person's 'previous criminal convictions shall not in themselves constitute grounds for taking of such measures'. No doubt this factor is also on its own extraneous to a person's personal conduct. The effect of this Article, as Macdonald and Blake explain, is that 'a country cannot apply a blanket rule excluding from their territory anyone with a criminal record, and certainly calls into question the applicability of the UK rule to this effect'.[59]

The leading case here is *Bouchereau*,[60] where an English court wished to deport a French national convicted of drug offences. The European Court held that the concept of public policy presupposes the existence 'of a genuine and sufficiently serious threat to the requirements of public policy affecting one of the fundamental interests of society'. A past criminal conviction can be taken into account, not just because it is serious, but because it constitutes 'a present threat to the requirements of public policy . . .'. What is important therefore is the tendency of a person to re-offend, not his conviction.

The Procedural Safeguards to the Public Policy Exception

The procedural safeguards in Directive 64/221 are also very important to the proper protection of immigration rights. Article 6 of this states that a person shall be informed of the grounds on which a decision has been taken against him unless this is contrary to the interests of the security of the state involved. In *Rutili*[61] the court said this meant giving such a person 'a precise and comprehensive statement of the grounds for the decision'. Article 7 states that the person concerned shall be officially notified of any decision to refuse the issue or renewal of a residence permit or to expel him. Article 8 gives the person concerned the same legal remedies as those that are available to local nationals. Article 9 effectively provides for a right of review of the merits of any adverse decision by an independent authority.[62]

Apart from these procedural safeguards, the other very notable feature of the Directive is the way in which it restricts the requirements of public health. Article 4 provides that the only diseases or disabilities justifying refusal of entry into a territory are those specified in the Annex to the Directive. These are basically infectious or contagious diseases requiring quarantine such as active tuberculosis and syphilis. However, public policy or public security may also be threatened by drug addiction and severe mental disturbance, which are listed as disease and disability. Clearly, what is being targeted here is a very extreme form of condition in an individual.

LESSONS FOR THE FUTURE

The creation of immigrants' rights in the individual examined at length in this chapter is singularly the product of a treaty that applies exclusively to EC nationals. Yet they give the lie to the widely held belief that Britain, with its empire gone, can no longer afford to operate an open-door immigration policy. Arguably, freedom of movement of the type discussed here can be countenanced with equanimity only if there is an economic parity between nations, otherwise one nation risks being subjected to a larger influx of migrants than the other. This view has considerable intuitive appeal but does not withstand closer scrutiny, if only because it overlooks the fact that there are in Europe large populations of non-EC nationals working in such countries as Britain, Germany, France, Belgium, The

Netherlands and Italy who nevertheless do not benefit from the free movement provisions of EC law.

Of course, in a planned immigration policy there is nothing stopping a better-off country from reaching agreement with another about its manpower needs, its economic requirements and its international obligations, in regulating its inflow. On current predictions, however, if anything, workers from Third World countries are likely to increase in number in the future to help sustain Europe's economic growth, as we saw in Chapter 1. But whether this happens or not, the truth is, that even the EC does not take a very cut and dried view of the immigration rights of its nationals despite what we have seen in the foregoing analysis, for although those rights are predominantly geared towards the attainment of stronger economies and a higher living standard in Europe, they do not eschew having to bear the social cost of immigration – as we have seen in this chapter.

This suggests that what ultimately helps underpin the immigration rights of EC nationals is not the mere belief in an economic value, but the belief in a value of much more universal application – of fundamental human rights, of non-discrimination and of equality, which are to be found in the general principles of law, and not the EEC Treaty. In fact, these principles could just as easily have come from such universally accepted human rights precepts as Article 1 of the Universal Declaration of Human Rights 1948, which states that: 'All human beings are born free and equal in dignity and rights. They are endowed with reason and conscience and should act towards one another in a spirit of brotherhood.' The judgments of the European Court could easily find their echo in the war-time English case of *ex parte Sacksteder*, when Pickford J, in extending protection to an alien, said: 'It is not a question of the liberty of a British subject; it is the question of the liberty of a person under the protection of our laws.'[63] It is these universal principles that are the essential bed-rock of the free movement ideals of EC law, and this has led various commentators to ask whether a more coherent framework of free movement rights could not yet be devised in Europe. There are two arguments here: firstly, that these rights should be extended to all comers in a spirit of brotherhood regardless of their nationality; and secondly, that they should only be extended to those non-nationals who can be said to have a connection with an EC country. Which one of these two options is more realistic has yet to be considered in Europe. However, let us consider the latter and easier option first.

Dummett and Nicol consider it perverse that the Commonwealth, with its long historic links with Britain, should now have to play second fiddle to Europe when it comes to the exercise of free movement rights. Britain is a member of the Commonwealth, and the

Commonwealth 'is supposed to be an association of equals, with an ideal of racial equality'. It is up to Britain to insist on a maintenance of those ties when it is negotiating on free movement rights in Europe.'

> It is clearly important for people in all Member States, concerned with what the Community policy will be after 1992, to set to work at once on various sets of possible proposals. Governments which are concerned to maintain special relations with countries outside Europe (as is Spain with the Latin American countries) have to be ready with clear policy proposals to argue.[64]

Failure by Britain to do so has meant, however, that it is the proposals of the Schengen Group (agreed by treaty in June 1990 between France, Germany, Belgium, Luxembourg and The Netherlands) that have now become the predominant model for immigration policy in the European Community. At Maastricht in December 1991, it was these proposals that were adopted in the draft External Frontiers Convention by the 12 member states for the purposes of negotiating and reaching agreements on immigration control. Also being followed is the Dublin Convention, which deals with asylum applications lodged in one country and the state's responsibility for examining this on behalf of all. What the 12 member states are doing is, whilst recognizing that the issues must be dealt with jointly, deciding to work through an informal intergovernmental treaty structure (similar to the one that preceded the Single European Act 1986 on political co-operation) and thereby keeping immigration outside the competence of the EC institutions. Decisions are made by the Ad-Hoc Immigration Group and the Trevi Group on security and counter terrorism. There is no democracy and accountability as there is no parliamentary discussion, and indeed, the draft Convention is a confidential document that is not in the public domain. The issues arising have been widely canvassed in the memoranda of interest groups to the Home Affairs Committee's 1992 *Report on Migration Control at External Borders of the European Community.*[65]

This is a primitive way of formulating policy. The European Community should be moving forward in the direction of openness and equality. It should be outward-looking, not inward-looking. The present position benefits neither the individual countries nor the Community at large. Take, for example, the two Conventions that we have just discussed. They do not have the proper enforcement mechanisms of international law, being outside the EC framework; nor do they necessarily serve the best interests of their signatories. The draft European Frontiers Convention contains major provisions for more policing of external borders; stricter controls of non-EC entrants; a common visa policy requiring some countries to have more visa nationals than hitherto; a requirement that asylum seekers can apply only once so that an application will be considered on the behalf of all countries at the same time; the introduction of passport stamping at an outer border; and a computerized database for exchanging information on immigrants between all countries. This Convention proved to be so controversial in The Netherlands that the Dutch Parliament had to refer it to the Dutch Council of State, which recommended against ratification on grounds of its incompatibility with national and international law. The Dublin Convention, although signed in June 1990, has similarly been ratified by only two countries to date, Denmark and Greece. Had these policies been openly considered by the European Commission not only would they have been able to address the needs of each individual country, but their acceptance in each country would have been easier.

Clearly, therefore, not only is there a 'democratic deficit' in the formulation of immigration policy in Europe, but there is a 'human rights deficit'. The draft External Frontiers Convention does not appear to contain in its preamble a recital of those binding international instruments that are normally to be found in conventions of this type. All member states are signatories to the following instruments, a reference to which is absent in the draft Convention: the Universal Declaration of Human Rights; the International Covenant on Civil and Political Rights; the European Convention on Human Rights; the various ILO Migrant Conventions, particularly 97 and 143; the Helsinki Final Act and the Paris Charter; and the Council of Europe Social Charter.[66] Undoubtedly these would have been mentioned in some way had the matter been formally dealt with by the European Community. There is, moreover, no mention of the new UN Convention on the Legal Status of Migrant Workers and their families, which follows the approach of ILO Convention 143, but which Britain has so far not signed. This states that since there is a negative effect on both the labour market and the workers themselves, illegal immigration and irregular employment should be stemmed. Its preamble, sponsored by Mediterranean and Scandinavian countries, further expresses the hope that 'recourse to the employment of migrant workers who are in irregular situations will also be discouraged if the fundamental human rights of all migrant workers are more widely recognized'. Again, this is a philosophy that might well have been properly included in a more formal proposal from the European Community, but which is noticeably absent now.

The European Commission must bring immigration within its jurisdiction. In its memorandum to the Home Affairs Committee in

1992, the Immigration Law Practitioners Association[67] explained how the present procedure leads to unnecessary duplication, waste, expensive co-ordination, lack of enforcement, and lack of uniformity of application between member states. Were Community institutions to extend their jurisdiction into immigration control, there would be at least four areas of potential advantage. Firstly, the European Commission would take over, and is ideally suited for, investigating, comparing and drafting legislation for the 12 member states. Already, Directorate General V of the Commission of the European Communities has undertaken an inquiry into the legal provisions and social policy relating to third-country nationals in the 12 states. Enforcement under the Treaty of Rome would be easier, and the European Court of Justice would ensure uniformity of application of legislative provisions, which it presently cannot. Secondly, there would be no secrecy, since Community procedures provide for the publication of draft legislation at an early stage in the *Official Journal*. Debates by the European Parliament would, moreover, be undertaken in open sessions. Thirdly, there would be consistency in the drafting of legislation that is suited to the needs of all 12 member states with their differing legal systems. It is in the best position to undertake considered and in-depth research on the substantive provisions of the immigration systems of the 12 member states because it has permanent, dedicated personnel, office space, and support staff. Finally, the risk of such countries as Britain being consistently exposed to *de facto* human rights violations would be reduced as the European Court of Justice has many times held human rights to be an integral part of the general principles of Community law.

There are other important questions of free movement that must be immediately addressed. Only the Community institutions can bring the urgency to bear on these that they undoubtedly deserve. For example, the Single European Act (in a new Article 8A of the Treaty of Rome) provides that 'the internal market shall comprise an area without internal frontiers' by 31 December 1992. The reference is to an *area*, and not to people, where there would be only an external (but no internal) frontier. However, the estimated seven million residents of the Community who do not have citizenship of a Community country cannot, say, travel from Germany to France with total freedom. Unless these nationals of third countries, most of whom are legitimately settled and have been living in a Community country for several years, can also travel freely across borders, their current situation will potentially drive a coach and horses though the free movement provisions of EC law. In a recent paper, 'Freedom of Movement Rights of Community Nationals', Dr Christopher Vincenzi has argued that there should be 'minimum substantive rights with equality for treatment' for EC nationals; so that entry and residence rights should not be dependent on employment, and that there should be equal access to political and public service, to legal advice and representation, and to non-contributory benefits.[68] The problem is that this, he argues, will then widen the gap between EC nationals and non-nationals in Europe. As a result, as the Community is committed to eschewing racism and xenophobia, it will then be necessary to upgrade the rights of non-national minorities as well, especially in view of the fact that these minorities will not now be joined by further third-country immigrants. This leads us on naturally to consider our second option: whether the EC rights of free movement can be extended to all comers. There are at least two reasons why this question should be seriously considered.

Firstly, it would appear that in developing an immigration policy for the nationals of Third World countries, the Community is not going to disregard its human rights norms willy-nilly. The European Court of Justice has held that the European Convention on Human Rights is part of the body of Community law (see, for example, Case No. C/49/88) and must be regarded as such by the court. At Maastricht, moreover, a *Statement on Racism and Xenophobia* was appended to the draft Treaty which requires anti-discrimination practices to be effected in such areas as immigration procedures, employment, education and training opportunities, and the treatment of immigrants by the police. Also mentioned are rights to family reunion, which implies that common rules here should be drafted consistently with the respect for family and private life that is enshrined in Article 8 of the European Convention on Human Rights and Article 19 (6) of the Council of Europe Social Charter (signed by an EC member state). The European Commission has also repeatedly emphasized that immigration controls would only be respected and effective if accompanied by a concerted effort directed at ensuring that the cultural and economic rights of the resident ethnic minority populations are officially protected and did not in themselves threaten these minorities.[69]

Secondly, an attempt to plan an overall Community immigration policy will need to consider the number of workers that may be required in the next five to ten years and from where they might come. Declining birthrates in many Community countries point to the need for additional manpower from other countries. The Joint Council for the Welfare of Immigrants, in its Memorandum to the Home Affairs Committee in 1992, stated that the Community should not just focus on the short-term problems of any new migrants thus attracted into Western Europe: it should focus on the medium and long-term benefits of immigration.[70] Instead, the draft External

Frontiers Convention has now reduced immigration to a mere policing matter. The reality, however, is that the French National Institute of Demographic Studies has reported that the declining birthrate will cause France by the end of the 1990s to need over 100,000 immigrant workers a year. In Germany, the Institute of Economic Research in Rhineland-Westphalia has calculated that since 1988 100,000 new jobs have been created in the economy by firms employing cheap migrant labour. Without the tax and social contributions of these workers, estimated at DM 29 billion in 1991, German nationals would have had to pay 40 per cent more tax for the same level of service provision.[71] The Institute of German Economy believes that the number of young people below the age of 15 will drop from 13.7 million in 1990 to 10 million in 2010, and that Germany will need 300,000 immigrants annually just to fill the gap in its labour market.[72] In Britain, the first of two reports prepared for the Carnegie Inquiry into 'The Third Age' states that Britain's policy-makers should start preparing now for a demographic 'time-bomb'. Government, employers and the trade unions, it says, should look beyond the recession when 'third-agers', people aged between 50 and 74, will withdraw from the workforce and yet remain healthy. They will then burden the economy and affect the chances of a long-term recovery because the number of younger people in the national workforce will by then also have fallen and they will be unable to sustain those who are out of work.[73] The answer seems to be more workers. Surveys in Germany, Belgium and Sweden have already demonstrated that immigrants are necessary to maintain the welfare state and the workforce. In Germany it has been proved that while migrant workers have contributed DM 57 billion to the Welfare State, they have had only DM 16 billion spent on them. In Belgium it has been shown that if immigration had been any lower the overall aging of the population would have proceeded at twice the actual rate.

There is, however, a more general argument of wider accessibility to the European Community, not necessarily grounded in arguments of economic needs. Unless this right is recognized in some form, then as the Council of Churches for Britain and Ireland said to the Home Affairs Committee:

> the accusations of the countries of Western Europe creating a
> 'Fortress Europe' possessing an excess of wealth over and
> against the poorer countries of the world, and refusing access
> to their citizens, will prove justified.[74]

Similarly, Dr Claire Palley, in her Hamlyn Lectures on *The United Kingdom and Human Rights*, has observed that:

There is difficulty in practice of separating internal minorities issues, immigration and refugee questions. To Third World eyes the United Kingdom does not appear humane. Instead, it appears hypocritical when United Kingdom emigration of the poor to the underdeveloped world in the nineteenth and early twentieth centuries is contrasted with current attempts of the poor in Asia and Africa to emigrate to the developed world. Recent United Kingdom Governments' treatment of immigrants and those seeking political asylum is particularly criticised.[75]

Stronger criticism still comes from Geoffrey Robertson QC, in his *Freedom, the Individual and the Law*. Although the brunt of his criticism is directed at Britain, it is submitted that it can just as well be applied to the current machinations in Europe:

Britain's current record in considering claims to refugee status is the worst of any country in Western Europe. It accepts only a few hundred asylum-seekers each year, intimidating airlines and shipping companies from carrying them by heavy fines. . . . What makes this treatment so unconscionable is that refugee status is a legal right, which all civilized nations have a duty to recognize. . . . The position is made the more untenable by the fact that claims on our compassion are so minimal compared with the burden shouldered by other and poorer nations: Pakistan is home to 3 million refugees, Jordan has 800,000, and Somalia and Malawi give sanctuary to 600,000.[76]

It is beyond the scope of this book to examine these questions in any great depth. Suffice it to say that the experts' report of the European Commission on 'Policies on Immigration and the Social Integration of Migrants' in September 1990 declared that:

One of the positive aspects of immigration is that migrants are tenacious and flexible people, who, in order to improve their lot, are prepared to up-root themselves, face the drawbacks and risks of travelling and settling into a new place, work hard in difficult conditions, learn a new language and take on different cultures and environments.[77]

The study of immigration rights is still in its infancy. This is no doubt because most countries in Europe have been more concerned to exclude people than to admit them. The enfranchisement of immigration rights is only beginning to unfold in a practical and realistic way after 1992. It is more likely to be seen now as a fundamental human right than a privilege extended to individuals by sovereign states.

NOTES AND REFERENCES

This chapter is an extended version of a paper delivered by the author at the First Conference of the Commonwealth Legal Education Association, held at the National Law School of India University, Bangalore, in June 1993.

1 Bevan, V. (1987) *The Development of British Immigration Law*, p. 29. London.
2 Pinder, J. (1991) *European Community: The Building of a Union*, pp. 1–6. Oxford.
3 See Case 12/86: *Demirel* v. *Stadt Schwabisch Gmund* [1987] ECR 3719, [1989] 1 CMLR 421. It should be noted, however, that limited rights of free movement agreed by Resolution of the Council of Association under the Association Agreement may be indirectly enforceable: see Case 192/89: *Sevince* v. *Staatsecretaris van Justitie* (20 September 1989, unreported).
4 Case 167/73: *Re French Merchant-Seamen EC Commission* v. *France* [1974] ECR 359, [1974] 2 CMLR 216.
5 Articles 137–144. In its advisory role the European Parliament has to be consulted for any legislative proposals by the Council of Ministers, whilst in its supervising role it has a direct political control over the Commission, which has to satisfy the European Parliament in its general report and answers to questions asked: see *Roquette Frères SA* v. *Council* [1980] ECR 3333, and *Maizena BmbH* v. *Council* [1980] 3393.
6 Articles 145–154.
7 Articles 155–163.
8 Articles 164–168.
9 [1981] AC 850.
10 Article 100A of EEC Treaty as introduced by SEA.
11 Macdonald, I. and Blake, N. (1991) *Immigration Law and Practice*, 3rd edition, p.142. London.
12 *Reyners* v. *Belgian State* [1974] ECR 631. Also see *Van Binsbergen Bestuur van de Bedriffsvereniging voorde Metaalnijverheid* [1975] 1 CMLR 298; *Van Gend en Loos* v. *Nederlandse Administratie de Belastingen* [1963] ECR 1; *Alfons Lutticke GmbH* v. *Haaptzollamt Saarlouis* [1966] ECR 205.
13 *Van Duyn* v. *Home Office* [1974] ECR 1337.
14 *Grad* v. *Finanzamt Traustein* [1970] ECR 825 and *Verbond van Nederlandse Ondernemingen* v. *Inspector der Invoerrechten en Accijnzen* [1977] ECR 113. Note, however, that a Directive cannot be directly effective if its time limit has not expired: *Pubblico Ministero* v. *Ratti* [1979] ECR 1629.
15 [1976] ECR 1185. See also *Rutili* v. *Minister of the Interior* [1975] ECR 1219.
16 See Articles 173 and 215(2), for instance.
17 [1969] ECR 419.
18 [1970] ECR 1125; [1972] CMLR 255. Also see *Nold Ka* v. *Commission* [1974] 491; [1974] 2 CMLR 338.
19 Article 7.
20 See *R* v. *Kirk* [1984] ECR 2689, [1984] 3 CMLR 522, [1985] 1 All ER 453.
21 [1976] ECR 1185, [1976] 2 CMLR 552.

22 *Royal Scholton-Honig Holdings Ltd* v. *Intervention Board for Agriculture Produce* [1978] ECR 2037, [1979] 1 CMLR 675.

23 *Airola* [1975] ECR 221.

24 *Prais* [1976] ECR 1589, [1976] 2 CMLR 708.

25 *Defrenne* v. *Sabena* [1976] ECR 445; [1976] 2 CMLR 98.

26 *August Topfer & Co. GmbH* v. *Commission* [1978] ECR 1019.

27 *Supra.* note 20.

28 *Hoffman-La Roche & Co. AG* v. *Commission* [1979] ECR 461, [1979] 3 CMLR 211.

29 *UNECTEF* v. *Heyleus, The Times,* 26 October 1987.

30 *Johnston* v. *Chief Constable of the Royal Ulster Constabulary* [1986] 3 CMLR 240.

31 [1987] 3 CMLR 389.

32 [19821 ECR 1035.

33 [1987] 1 CMLR 764.

34 Families are defined in Regulation 1612/68 (Article 10(1)) as a worker's 'spouse and their descendants who are under the age of 21 years or are dependants' and 'dependent relations in the ascending line of the worker and his spouse'.

35 [1987] 2 CMLR 448. See Articles 7 and 48 of the EEC Treaty and Article 7(2) of Regulation 1612/68.

36 [1986] 2 CMLR 164.

37 *R* v. *IAT ex parte Antonissen* [1991] 2 CMLR 373.

38 *R* v. *Pieck* [1981] 1 QB 571, [1981] 3 All ER 46.

39 See Section 12(3) and (4).

40 See here *Ugliola* [1969] ECR 363, [1970] CMLR 194 and *Sotgiu* [1974] ECR 165.

41 Steiner, J. (1990) *Textbook on EEC Law,* p. 172. London.

42 [1979] ECR 2019, [1980] 2 CMLR 71. See also *Fiorini* [1975] ECR 1085, [1976] CMLR 573; and *Reina* [1982] ECR 33, [1982] 1 CMLR 744.

43 [1984] ECR 3199, [1987] 1 CMLR 465.

44 [1989] 1 CMLR 337.

45 See (1990) *Statement of Changes in Immigration Rules* (23 March), HC 251, para. 56.

46 See *Lair* [1989] 3 CMLR 545; and *Brown* [1988] 3 CMLR 403.

47 See Articles 10–12 and *Güll* [1987] 1 CMLR 501.

48 See Regulation 1251/70 of Article 5.

49 See Article 2.

50 See Articles 52(2) and 60(3).

51 In *Thieffry* ([1977] ECR 765, [1977] 2 CMLR 373) the French Bar Council could not prevent a Belgian national with a Belgian degree from practising in France, and an English architect in *Patrick* ([1977] ECR 1199, [1977] 2 CMLR 523) could practise his profession in France.

52 In *Watson and Belmann* ([1976] ECR 1185, [1976] 2 CMLR 552) the ECJ said that receiving services is a necessary corollary to providing them, so that tourists, persons receiving medical treatment and those who travelled for the purposes of education and business were recipients of services.

53 See *Gravier* v. *City of Liège* [1985] ECR 593, [1985] 3 CMLR 1.

54 Also see Directive 72/194 and Directive 75/35.

55 Macdonald and Blake, *op. cit.* p. 174.

56 *Van Duyn* v. *Home Office* (No. 2) [1975] Ch 358, [1975] ECR 1337.

57 [1975] ECR 1219, [1976] 1 CMLR 140.

58 [1975] ECR 297, [1975] 1 CMLR 472.

59 Macdonald and Blake, *op. cit.* p. 175.

60 [1978] QB 732, [1977] ECR 1999.

61 [1975] ECR 1219, [1976] 1 CMLR 140.

62 See *R* v. *Secretary of State for the Home Department*, *ex parte Santillo* [1980] ECR 1585, [1980] 2 CMLR 308, [1981] 2 All ER 897. Also see *R* v. *Secretary of State for the Home Department*, *ex parte Dannenberg* [1948] QB 766.

63 See *R* v. *Chiswick Police Station Superintendent*, *ex parte Sacksteder* [1918] 1 KB 578, pp. 585–6.

64 Dummett, A. and Nicol, A. (1990) *Subjects, Citizens, Aliens and Others*, p. 258. London.

65 (1992) *Migration Control at External Borders of the European Community*, HC 215 i, ii and iii.

66 *Ibid*, see Memorandum by INTERIGHTS, p. 78.

67 *Ibid*, pp. 89–91.

68 Quoted in Weatherill, S. (1992) *Cases and Materials on EEC Law*, pp. 295–6. London.

69 See Memorandum by INTERIGHTS, *op. cit.* p. 80.

70 See *Migration Control at External Borders of the European Community*, *op. cit.* pp. 71–7.

71 *Ibid.*, pp. 71–2.

72 See *The Guardian*, 4 February 1992.

73 (1992) *Income: Pensions, Earnings and Savings in the Third Age*. Folkestone. Also see *The Guardian*, 16 September 1992.

74 See *Migration Control at External Borders of the European Community*, *op. cit.* p. 87.

75 Palley, C. *op. cit.* p. 134.

76 Robertson, G. *op. cit.* pp. 331–2.

77 See *Migration Control at External Borders of the European Community*, *op. cit.* p. 86.

5

Immigration Control and the Legal Process

(1) The Administrative System and Personnel

'If there is one virtue that our books of authority claim for the Common Law more positively than another, it is that of being reasonable.'
– Sir Fredrick Pollock

The previous chapters have shown how the absence of a rational and properly thought out immigration policy in Britain accounts for the slap-dash way in which specific issues in immigration law have been determined. The experience of the European Community is different, but only within its particular context. Outside this context and in relation to immigration from Third World countries, informal decision-making and secrecy prevails, and the abolition of internal border controls is quite meaningless. In the final two chapters of this work we examine the informality that characterizes the structure of immigration appeals. We first in this chapter examine the administrative structure that defines the apparatus of immigration control. We then in the next chapter consider the nature of the legal and administrative rules that keep this structure oiled and working. Both these aspects are timely ones to examine today, for it is more than 25 years now since the United Kingdom's modern immigration administrative system was first set up.

THE REPORT OF THE WILSON COMMITTEE

The present system of immigration control has its origins in the report of the Wilson Committee in 1967.[1] This led to the passing of the Immigration Appeals Act 1969, which created a framework for statutory rights of appeal against immigration decisions. Before 1969, the Aliens Act of 1905 had indeed allowed for an appeal against refusal of leave to land by an alien to be brought to an Immigration Board, but the war-time provisions of the Aliens Restriction Act 1914 had swept this away. Since then various administrative measures had been instituted[2] but these fell far short of providing a legally established right for an alien to call into question the correctness of a decision made against him. The Wilson Committee, set up in February 1966, was a Government-appointed body under the chairmanship of Sir Roy Wilson QC, whose task was 'to consider whether any, and if so what, rights of appeal or other remedies should be available to aliens and to Commonwealth citizens who are refused admission to, or are required to leave the country'. In 1957 the Franks Report on *Administrative Tribunal and Inquiries*[3] had already set the tone and standard for administrative adjudications in public law. J.M. Evans explains this well when he writes that by the time of Wilson, there was 'a changed climate of thought about administrative law' for the 'desirability of statutory appeals to administrative tribunals had become since the Franks Report, part of the accepted wisdom about the appropriate machinery for resolving disputes between the individual and the state'.[4] It was against this background that the Wilson Committee was asked to look at immigration control.[5]

That Committee looked first at the existing system of immigration control. It considered the evidence of representative organizations before it; heard oral evidence from individual witnesses; and it drew comparisons and took guidance from the immigration control systems in the United States and in Canada. Only after all this did it conclude that a statutory system of immigration appeals was necessary in cases of exclusion. However, the Wilson Committee's conclusion in this respect raises more questions than it answers. Was a right of appeal to be given in recognition of an immigrant's substantive rights under law? Are not procedural rights in any case dependent on the recognition of substantive rights? Or was this rather an exercise in form – of aesthetics? No clear answers emerge from the Report of the Wilson Committee. The Committee's support for a statutory right of appeal is ambivalent and paradoxical. It said that it had been argued before it by witnesses that many decisions under existing conditions resulted in the improper exclusion of intending immigrants, that the operation of the present method of control could be arbitrary and capricious, and that an applicant's case often did not receive the full attention that it deserved.[6] Remarkably, the Committee rejected these arguments even though they have been consistently and continuously raised for the past 25 years. They have even been raised by the courts, which have over the years become increasingly impatient with the repeated failure by officials to apply proper standards of law and practice to the nature of decision-making in immigration law. They, the immigration appellate authorities, and the Home Affairs Committee on Immigration and Nationality have persistently had to remind officials about the proper standard of proof to apply,[7] about how they should approach witnesses when asking them questions,[8] and about how they should write their reports following a decision afterwards.[9] None of this, apparently, was considered to be sufficiently important by the Wilson Committee.

Instead the Committee opted for what it considered to be an argument of more 'basic principle' that

> however well administered the present control may be, it is fundamentally wrong and inconsistent with the rule of law that power to take decisions affecting a man's whole future should be vested in officers of the executive, from whose findings there is no appeal. In our opinion these critics have reached the heart of the matter. Even if generally speaking, justice is being done under the present system, it is not apparent that this is the case.

Manifestly, therefore, the Committee was not perturbed by the substantive aspect of decision-making, in which it expressed full confidence:

> It is one thing for us, after a protracted inquiry, to express our confidence that the power of final decision entrusted to officers of the Immigration Service is being exercised fairly; it is another to expect a newly arrived immigrant, and his relatives and friends at the other side of the barrier, to feel the same confidence. The evidence we have received strongly suggests that among the communities of Commonwealth immigrants in this country, and among people specially concerned with their welfare, there is a widespread belief that the Immigration Service deals with claims of Commonwealth citizens seeking admission in an arbitrary and prejudicial way. We doubt whether it will be possible to dispel the belief so long as there is no ready way of having decisions in such cases subjected to an impartial review.[10]

The Committee's pre-eminent concern therefore was to dispel a 'widespread belief' that immigration decisions were made in an 'arbitrary and prejudicial way', and not with securing substantive justice for beleaguered immigrants. Nevertheless, the Committee's proposals for procedural reform of immigration were very positive:

> In many other fields of public law – such as that relating to national insurance – there are now well-established methods of resolving disputes between a private individual and the administration under a procedure requiring *a clear statement of the administration's case; an opportunity for the person affected to put his case in opposition and support it with*

evidence, and a decision by an authority independent of the Department interest in the matter.[11] (emphasis added).

These observations by the Wilson Committee constitute the first attempt in the United Kingdom to apply, at governmental instigation, the basic principles of administrative law to a system of immigration control. Its main recommendations consisted of the setting up of a two-tier structure of a central tribunal and of subordinate judicial officers to be designated 'adjudicators'. The central tribunal would be called the Immigration Appeal Tribunal and it would sit in divisions comprising not fewer than three members each. It would have a president, and certain other members would be authorized to preside as Chairman over the full tribunal in the president's absence, or over other divisions of the tribunal. Only the central tribunal and those members who were authorized to act as Chairman would need to be legally qualified and to serve full-time. The adjudicators did not have to be legally qualified:

> The primary qualification for appointment as an adjudicator should be the ability to conduct hearings impartially and in a judicial spirit, with due regard both to the law and policy which it is his duty to apply and to the right of an appellant to full consideration of his case.[12]

The President and the Chairman would be appointed by the Lord Chancellor. The other members, including the adjudicators, should be appointed by the Home Secretary. This did not mean, in the Committee's opinion, that the independence of those adjudicators and tribunal members would be any less complete.[13] As far as the procedure was concerned, an immigration officer who decided to refuse entry would give notice to that effect to the person concerned, stating briefly the reasons for the decision and informing him of his right of appeal and the sources from which he might seek advice. The person concerned would then give notice of appeal to an immigration officer whose duty it would be to ensure that the appeal was brought before an adjudicator as soon as possible. The adjudicator, in considering the appeal, would consider the evidence of both parties. The aggrieved party would have a right to appear personally before the adjudicator. 'At the end of the hearing', the Committee stated, 'the adjudicator would give a *reasoned decision* allowing or dismissing the appeal'.[14] If the case went a stage further and reached the Tribunal, the Tribunal would decide it on consideration of the adjudicator's findings. Here again, 'the decisions of the Tribunal, like those of an adjudicator, should be *reasoned decisions* . . .'.[15]

It was further recommended that the appellate authorities be brought within the scope of the Tribunals and Inquiries Act, 1958. This would give the Council on Tribunals the jurisdiction to keep under review the constitution and working of the immigration appellate authorities and to report on these matters from time to time, which would further result in their becoming obliged, once more, to give reasons for their decisions.[16]

Some Shortcomings of the Wilson Committee

The basic difficulty with the Wilson Committee is that it is not known how it came about. The notion that it presaged the extension of administrative law into the murky waters of immigration control because it was 'part of the accepted wisdom' to do so affords only part of the explanation. The Queen's Speech in 1965 outlined[17] in serious terms the Government's intention of strengthening controls to restrict further Commonwealth immigration.[18] The debate on the Queen's Speech, however, saw the Prime Minister speak of 'the need to ensure that the individual concerned has a due and fair opportunity to state his case'. Accordingly, 'a small independent Committee' would be set up to look into this.[19] Quite how and when the transmutation took place is an enigma which can only be fathomed when someone goes to the trouble of examining the relevant government papers on this matter.

It is not clear what the Government's own intention was behind the setting up of an inquiry. The Committee itself implicitly rejected the notion of better safeguards for the protection of substantive rights, preferring to base its recommendations for the creation of an appeals system on the need to allay the fears of the immigrant communities. According to some critics, therefore, the reason why fairness and justice is still so much in issue is because it was never fully tackled by Wilson in the first place.[20] The Runnymede Trust has observed how the Wilson Committee dismissed claims that the system was arbitrary and unfair.[21] The Committee's impression was that 'immigration officers act with fairness and respect for the rights and feelings of the people with whom they . . . deal'.[22] Its view was that 'generally speaking, justice is being done under the present system'. The only difficulty was that 'it is not apparent that this is the case'. Small wonder then that today, 25 years later, the Home Affairs Committee is still having to address problems of 'bureaucratic delay', that the Immigration and Nationality Department (IND) is being used as 'an instrument of control' and that 'a poor quality of service' is being provided by that Department.[23] Setting up an appeals system in 1967 was, in the Wilson Committee's own words, nothing more than 'a kind of reassurance' so that today in the words of the Runnymede

Trust, 'In general the conduct of appeal hearings is to some extent a reflection of the intention behind the establishment of the system which . . . was primarily "a need to reassure appellants".'[24] This view of the work of the Wilson Committee is not novel and has been canvassed by others.[25]

The more interesting question, however, is why the more positive aspects of procedural reform recommended by Wilson have not taken root in the administration of immigration control. The fact is that immigration officers still do not give proper 'reasons for the decision'.[26] Many hearings have still not been conducted 'impartially and in a judicial spirit'.[27] For many years after Wilson, moreover, determination of the IAT still did not take the form of 'reasoned decisions' in any probative sense.[28] The answer to this question must in a large part lie in the absence of substantive rights that Wilson failed to seek protection for. Procedural rights are after all parasitic upon substantive rights. If Wilson did not advocate these rights, and Acts of Parliament and the immigration rules did not either for the most part, then what was it that the new system was striving to achieve? Reginald Maudling, when Home Secretary, once candidly explained the attractions of such a system from officialdom's point of view:

I have never seen the sense of administrative law in our country, because it is only someone else taking the Government's decision for them. I cannot see that [tribunals] are better qualified if it is not a legal but a practical matter.[29]

The Inadequacy of Wilson

Further inadequacies can be specifically attributed to the Wilson Committee. Its basic problem has been one of insufficient sagacity. Firstly, the Committee failed to foresee how technical and unwieldy immigration law would become both as a result of the new litigation procedures that it recommended and the general character of the law in this area. Secondly, its view of appeals was simplistic. The Committee envisaged that most appeals would be instantly determined following a refusal at a port. It held this view because under its recommendations immigrants would have been allowed to remain in the United Kingdom to contest an adverse decision[30] but also because they would not have been required to go through entry clearance procedures before embarking for the United Kingdom.[31] Thirdly, it underestimated the difficulty of determining disputed questions of fact in the absence of the appellant. This difficulty is exacerbated today as appeals against refusal of entry are nearly always lodged from overseas. Fourthly, it did not envisage the developing importance and growth (now curtailed) of representations to the Minister, often in cases that have already been through the formal appeals structure.[32]

IMMIGRATION APPEALS

Since the inception of the immigration appeals system very many more appeals by the Home Office have been allowed by the Immigration Appeal Tribunal than by an immigrant appellant. The trend has been constant from the early years of the appeals system. During the four years ending 31 December 1978 adjudicators allowed only 15.7 per cent (5527) of appeals heard whilst the tribunal allowed 22.2 per cent (221). In 1979 the number of appeals upheld by adjudicators was 11.5 per cent of all appeals heard whilst the tribunal allowed 14.8 per cent (46) of all appeals. The largest number of appeals to adjudicators is for refusal of entry clearance. This also represents the highest category of appeals for immigrants, being over 18 per cent in 1979. Appeals against exclusion on deportation succeeded in only 4 per cent of the cases at this time. By contrast the Home Office success rate in appeals against an adjudicator's decision was 58 per cent in 1979.[33] This pattern continues today. In 1981 the 2234 appeals allowed by adjudicators represented 12 per cent of all disposals and 16 per cent of all those which went to a hearing, exactly the same proportions as in 1980. Even accepting that a large number of 'hopeless' appeals are heard by adjudicators, in part because representatives are unaware that the function of adjudicators is to establish whether the acting authority has acted in accordance with the immigration rules, there is a notable differential here. This can be combined with the fact that the tribunal refuses many more applications for leave to appeal by an immigrant appellant than by the Home Office. Of those that get through to be heard by the tribunal only 18 per cent of immigrants' appeals are successful compared to 58 per cent of the Home Office appeals.[34]

The Wilson Committee also recommended informality of proceedings.[35] This was after all in line with the findings of the Franks Committee on Tribunals.[36] But the Wilson Committee failed to foresee how inscrutable the system would become. Complex primary legislation has been combined with awesome subordinate legislation and a mounting pile of case-law, which means that difficult questions of fact and law have to be dealt with in a system which lacks the formality of the law courts both on procedure and evidence. Informality is by no means a good thing in every case now. The effect is that some adjudicators behave like judges whilst others remain true to the Wilson recommendation by adopting a more inquisitorial approach. The Head of the IND, in his evidence to the Home Affairs Committee in 1990, accepted that the current appeals system 'is probably of a more legalistic nature now than was originally anticipated' and that it was the constant preoccupation of the IND to streamline procedures.[37] Moreover the number of cases going through the appellate process has also meant that the appellate authorities have a say in the shaping of British immigration policy since they interpret and apply the immigration rules to innumerable factual situations.[38]

In April 1981, the Home Office published a discussion document proposing to reform the immigration appeals system.[39] Its background was that the Government was concerned about delays in the appeals system.[40] The delays arose from three sources: in the time taken for an appeal to take place once notice has been lodged by the appellant; in the time taken for the Home Office to produce an explanatory statement; and, once the appeal had been heard, in the time taken for decision. The Home Office had two objectives: to reduce expenditure and to ensure that those who have no prospect of being allowed to remain in Britain do not spin out their stay by making 'hopeless' appeals.[41] Nothing came of this discussion document, however. In 1990 the Home Affairs Committee itself had to refer to the growth in the backlog of immigration appeals. In ten years things had gone from bad to worse: 'At the end of 1989 over 21,000 cases were outstanding, almost as many cases as were considered by the adjudicators in that year.' But it sang a different tune. It said that an appeals system provides 'a vital safeguard against alleged tightening of immigration control or unfair decisions by those enforcing the immigration rules'. The Chairman of the United Kingdom Immigrants Advisory Service thought, however, that the present situation made the right of appeal 'nugatory' and 'a mockery has been made of the system'. In these circumstances, the Home Affairs Committee found it necessary to make three recommendations:

> (a) the officials who are working on changes in appeals procedure should complete their work urgently, so that proposals can be put forward for the full public discussion which has been promised and which is vital to secure the consent of all concerned; (b) the backlog of appeals should not be used as an excuse for reducing rights of appeal; (c) any options which would streamline and simplify the appeals procedure should be actively considered.[42]

ADMINISTRATION

Immigration policy and its application is the responsibility of the Home Office under which the Immigration and Nationality

Department and the Immigration Service carry out their work. The Home Office is assisted by the Foreign and Commonwealth Office which administers control at posts overseas and which controls Entry Clearance Officers and the procedures to which they are subject. The policy aspect and the power of final decision, however, remain in the hands of the Home Office. The Work Permit Scheme is managed by the Department of Employment, but this is likely to change now. If permanent settlement is to be granted to those who have been in approved employment for four years, this decision is made by the Home Office again. Illegal immigration is investigated by the Immigration Service and the police, whilst the Department of Health and Social Security is responsible for the work of the port medical inspectors in health checks, etc. Immigration officers at ports of entry in the United Kingdom are responsible for giving leave to enter with or without conditions, to those arriving at sea and air ports. They are concerned basically with the entry, control and policing of illegal immigrants, although in *Oladehinde* the House of Lords held that they could also take the decision to deport on behalf of the Secretary of State.[43]

The duties and functions of individuals and departments outlined above are in principle clear-cut but as *Oladehinde* demonstrates, the strains on the Home Office have begun to show.[44] In its memorandum to the Home Affairs Committee on immigration from the Indian sub-continent in 1982, the Home Office stated: 'There is a close consultation between the two Departments [i.e. the Home Office and the Foreign and Commonwealth Office] in the formulation of policy and procedure'.[45] As one member of the Home Affairs Committee pointed out, however, 'the Foreign Office do not have the right to determine policy in relation to any single case or any group of cases' and they have 'no right to decide an individual case'.[46] This would appear to be correct, and the Immigration Tribunal itself has accepted that the 'Immigration Officer is an agent of the Home Secretary',[47] not of the Foreign Office. The responsibility in the final analysis in all cases should therefore lie with the Home Office.

PERSONNEL

There is increasing concern that the personnel involved in the various aspects of immigration control and representation are inadequately trained, monitored and funded.

The IAT and Adjudicators

The creation and function of the IAT and the adjudicators in the immigration process have already been discussed above. Many lawyers regard the work of adjudicators and the IAT as being low grade. Legally and socially the same significance is not attached to their work as, for example, the Social Security and industrial tribunals. There is a difference, indeed, in status and salary. The training of adjudicators also is modest and insubstantial. During the 1980s they were no longer given a full set of Immigration Appeals Reports. The result was that hearings were often adjourned leading to both delay and considerable expense while the adjudicator found and acquainted himself with the relevant law in previous decisions. Adjudicators were also criticized for not having a proper understanding of the areas on which they were required to give decisions.[48] Not only were most of them unfamiliar with the indigenous culture of applicants but the handling of legal issues by some was very unsatisfactory. Both these points have been illustrated in the case of *Ghulam Sughre*. Here the adjudicator refused the appeal of the principal appellant, *inter alia*, because there was 'considerable inconsistency as to who arranged [her] marriage'. The principal appellant's representatives argued before the tribunal that 'as many people are involved in arranging a marriage', it was a mistake to view this as a discrepancy. On the legal side, the adjudicator proceeded wrongly with regard to the question of whether the sponsor had acquired a new domicile by leaving Pakistan and going to England. He said:

> I am of the opinion that the sponsor had acquired an English domicile of choice at least by 1968. He said in evidence, 'From my first arrival I was considering applying for British nationality' and this he did in 1971. Again he said that 'in 1966 I only visited to see my parents; I intended to return to the UK'.[49]

It is well established, however, that a domicile of origin is not easily shaken off. Also, as it connotes one's permanent home it is quite different from citizenship.[50] In the recent case of *Saftar* the Court criticized an adjudicator for his 'surprising' decision.[51] It seems that most adjudicators who have been to the sub-continent did so during the British Raj, and this colonial experience has often shown itself to be harmful as many have been reluctant to accept a view of life in the sub-continent, proffered by witnesses, which does not coincide with their own.[52] Of the majority who do not have any experience at all of the Indian sub-continent, the tendency is naturally to prefer the interpretation of an Entry Clearance Officer to that of the appellant. This is because once it is accepted that Entry Clearance Officers are hard worked and do a difficult job the inclination is to say, 'Well, we have got to balance between his view and that of the sponsor. The sponsor is pretty inarticulate. He does not speak English very well. I think the

Entry Clearance Officer has probably got the right answer.'[53] Only a more extensive training programme for adjudicators can help them to empathize with the situation of the immigrant, especially as the Joint Council for the Welfare of Immigrants told the Home Affairs Committee in 1990: 'new staff are not always adequately trained before they take on their duties . . . Staff morale is low, and staff turnover high, because the volume of casework produces little job satisfaction', a fact to which the trade union at the IND readily acceded.[54]

No amount of training, however, can help an adjudicator who is inveterately unsympathetic. In 1977 the adjudicator for Scotland, Leslie Aitcheson, told a private meeting of the Glasgow Juridical Society that there was a 'bottomless pit of immigrants waiting to flood into Britain and that if every Pakistani was allowed to come here you would very soon be in a minority'. He criticized MPs who took up immigration cases, suggesting that they did so only to score political points and that he himself had urged William Whitelaw MP to ask 'a series of awkward questions of the government on immigration'.[55] In the actual conduct and hearing of appeals the bias of some adjudicators is often betrayed. In *Qeemat Bibi*, for example, the adjudicator granted the Home Office leave to appeal against a decision, in the absence of the applicant's representative. The applicant's representative was prevented therefore from making representations to the adjudicator. He claimed that

> he was present with the Appellant's representative when the determination was read. The Adjudicator had then retired and he then left the hearing room. The first time he knew that leave to appeal had been granted was when he had received the papers relating to the appeal.[56]

Some adjudicators have also glossed over the more favourable aspects of an applicant's appeal. Thus in *Shafait Bi*, the adjudicator in his determination only referred to matters which were adverse to the applicant and the sponsor. There was no mention, for instance, of the income tax allowances and remittances by the sponsor to the appellant over a period of time, which suggested that he might have a wife in Pakistan.[57] In *Tula Bibi*, decided in 1982, the adjudicator said that only a handful of remittances were produced at the hearing as proof that the sponsor was sending money to a wife in Bangladesh. In fact, there were 38 such remittances and they dated as far back as 1969.[58] There is also evidence that some adjudicators are not prepared to accept the testimony of witnesses. Thus in *Sarwar Jan*, where the issue was whether the appellant was married to the sponsor here, the adjudicator refused the appeal, saying, 'I have had before me four witnesses all of whom, in greater or lesser degree, had an interest in the appellants' succeeding in their appeal.'[59] In *Zarina Jan*, a case quoted above, the adjudicator said of the witness that he had 'little doubt' that the witness felt 'unable to stray from the brief he had received from the sponsor'.[60]

Nevertheless, there are a number of adjudicators who are determined to do their utmost in ensuring that appeals are conducted fairly. Indeed, one adjudicator, Malcolm Hurwitt, resigned his post in November 1978 because he found it impossible to operate fairly 'within an inherently unjust system'.[61]

Entry Clearance and Immigration Officers

The delays in the hearing of appeals for dependants of people settled in the United Kingdom have doubled since 1977. The criticism of the entry clearance procedures is therefore that more resources ought to become available. Entry Clearance Officers are not only hard worked but they have been reduced in number in the past at posts overseas, particularly in New Delhi and in Pakistan.[62] Even today there are gross variations in waiting times between posts. In Bangkok the average waiting time for an interview for those seeking entry clearance for settlement is 8 weeks, in Manila it is 16 weeks, and in Kingston, Jamaica, it is 20 weeks. But it is the delays in the Indian sub-continent which are the worst. A re-applicant in Karachi interviewed in 1989 had to wait, on average, 4 months for an interview, and one in Islamabad had to wait a staggering 23 months. The Home Affairs Committee in 1990 recommended that 'greater efforts' should be made 'to improve the conditions in which ECOs work and applicants queue' and that the Government should redeploy ECOs and employ more ECOs to help with the situation.[63] Because of their limited number ECOs are also unable to undertake field visits into villages to ascertain whether an applicant is related as he claims. It is now established that a number of genuine applicants have been refused who would not have been refused if the question of their relationship could have been more extensively pursued.[64] In this sense, indeed, the role of Entry Clearance Officers is crucial in getting at the truth. Thus in *Khadaja Bi* the adjudicator regretted that the Entry Clearance Officer did not investigate further the existence and marital status of the principal appellant and her son. The tribunal went along with this, drawing a distinction between the function of immigication officers and Entry Clearance Officers. Immigration officers 'could merely stand at the bench and wait for what the intending immigrant had to say'[65] but the Tribunal regarded 'the obligations on entry clearance officers to investigate matters in such circumstances as greater than those of immigration officers'.[66]

It also appears that the practice of monitoring individual Entry Clearance Officers to see if they are doing their job well has ceased,[67] although the Government told the Home Affairs Committee in 1990 that in relation to the slow preparation of explanatory statements 'action was being taken to remedy the situation' where necessary.[68] The number of immigration officers is also limited. Occasionally, an Entry Clearance Officer refers a case to London so that the sponsor can be interviewed; but there is a delay of many months before this happens. One reason for this is that the immigration officers, whose number is limited, are tied to the ports of entry, particularly during the summer months because of the very heavy flow of traffic during this time. In addition, the allegation is once again made against these officers of bias and unfairness. Immigration officers are directed in confidential instructions that 'references to the tendency of immigrants of particular national origins to evade immigration control should be avoided' in their decisions. The argument is that the very fact that such instructions are deemed necessary is confirmation that such preconceptions and prejudices are recognized by the Home Office to exist in the Immigration Service.[69] A Commission for Racial Equality research project published in February 1985 has found evidence to this effect at posts overseas. It states:

> ECO's file notes and correspondence on files also, in a number of instances, do reflect attitudes other than a detached objective view of their duties. In one case, for example, the ECO wrote: 'I want to do this reinterview myself. Hands off. This must be this year's strongest refusal.' Notes occasionally implied a reluctance to issue entry certificates even where the ECO appeared to recognize explicitly that he had no grounds for doing otherwise, and were expressed in such terms as: 'I may have to issue in this case.'[70]

Other Officers

Few presenting officers before the appellate authorities can cope with the prolix law and practice in this area. Access to tribunal decisions is difficult and those who work for such representative bodies as the United Kingdom Immigrants Advisory Service (hereafter UKIAS) do not always follow their internal instructions and often fail to draw the tribunal's attention to an important case. UKIAS is funded by the Government. Its staff vary in competence and quality and are mostly underpaid. Resources again are severely limited and there is no legal aid available for litigants. Lack of resources also means that complex cases cannot be subject to detailed preparation. There is little doubt that some preparation and presentation of immigrants' cases at hearings is not good. Inevitably, this must take its toll in the ultimate refusal of cases. In one case this is what an adjudicator had to say before dismissing the appeal:

> I must say a word about the conduct of Mr Qamar, the appellant's representative. At the hearing on 9.7.82 he arrived 40 minutes late. He knew well the correct time of the hearing, having been advised of it by the Clerk to the Adjudicator. That hearing had to be adjourned after evidence in chief until today, 1 October 1982 at 10.30 hours. At the appointed time Mr Qamar did not appear nor had he given any advanced warning to the appellate authorities. Consequently, a whole day's hearing time was wasted and interpreter's fees unnecessarily incurred. At 11.23 hours Mr Qamar telephoned to say he was not appearing and asked for the case to be decided on the papers. I regard Mr Qamar's conduct as grossly discourteous and will not give him leave to appear before me in future.[71]

In *Inayat Begum* the tribunal again dismissed the appeal, adding that both it and the respondent 'had the greatest difficulty in understanding the arguments and submissions put forward in support of the appellant's case' because the appellant's representative did not speak English well.[72]

THE HOME OFFICE

The Home Office, and not the immigration appellate authorities, wields the maximum influence over the conduct of immigration appeals. Service of notice of appeal by an appellant is to the Home Office, which then informs the adjudicator or the tribunal that an appeal has been lodged.[73] It is the appellant's opponent, the Home Office, therefore that decides the order in which appeals are heard. It is extremely difficult to come to any agreements about pending appeals with the Home Office. For one thing, the Home Office cannot be easily contacted by telephone. For another, presenting officers who are approached cannot make a deal without reference back to the Home Office. The appellate authorities themselves cannot do anything until and unless they are approached by the Home Office. The Home Office is also required to produce an 'Explanatory Statement' at hearings.[74] It is required to 'prepare a written statement of facts relating to the decision in question and the reason therefor . . .'.[75] But the Home Office is not bound to produce such a statement if it takes the view that it has insufficient time to do so before the hearing.[76]

The importance of the Explanatory Statement where it is produced in appeals cannot be over-stated. Usually it embodies the whole of the immigration authorities' case. It must be a 'written statement of facts', which means that it must include all the relevant facts. Thus a Home Office official has stated that 'entry clearance officers are under formal written instructions in writing the appeal statements that they must bring out the points made by the appellant, and this is part of the art of writing the appeal statement'.[77] But as Entry Clearance Officers are not monitored any more it is difficult to enforce compliance with this requirement. The result is that an explanatory statement is, invariably, the most slanted recital of the case before adjudicators and the tribunal.[78] This is because it is really only an account, on the Home Office's side, of the reasons for refusal of application. Thus only discrepancies and matters prejudicial to the case of the immigrant are mentioned. It is by definition, therefore, a one-sided account of the case. As one Director of UKIAS has stated, 'the explanatory statement appears to be drafted for the one purpose of justifying the refusal' and that what is necessary is 'a much fuller statement of the interview so that not only the negative points appear in the explanatory statement as to what happened, but also the positive points'.[79] For example, statements have concentrated on areas of disagreements between the interviewees but have left out a much greater area of agreement between them, thereby conveying a false impression. One adjudicator, in a case, has referred to the

> declining standard of objectivity by the Dacca Office in assessing the reality or otherwise of family relationships. It seems to me that the search for 'kitchen sink' discrepancies is becoming almost an obsession . . .[80]

Most statements are based on the original notes of an Entry Clearance Officer taken at the time of the interview. The original notes are obtainable at the direction of the adjudicator for a hearing. Most of these, it has emerged, are hand-written using certain abbreviations marked with varieties of coloured pencils signifying agreement or disagreement between the interviewees. These marks, when photocopied and submitted to an appellant's representative, are totally incomprehensible. Often explanatory statements are prepared in the United Kingdom from notes written by another Entry Clearance Officer abroad. There have been cases when statements were written up over two years after the actual interview.[81] Adjudicators and the tribunal have expressed some concern over this. In a letter to the author the Acting Chief Administrator Mr T.D. Healy, confirmed this situation:

> From the inception of the system the adjudicators were concerned by the delays on the part of Entry Clearance Officers and the Home Office in writing up explanatory statements. The provision of the Immigration Appeals Procedure Rules were not being followed but, as they were not regarded as mandatory, there was little one could do except to keep the problem constantly before the authorities concerned.

He accepted that 'it is, of course, a fact, particularly on the Indian sub-continent, that explanatory statements are not written for many months'.[82] In fact, delays can now amount to over a year, as the Home Affairs Committee explained in 1990:

> A simple statement for an appeal concerning variation of leave to remain in this country will now take over a year before it is prepared, although the work itself takes little time. . . . A particularly disturbing element . . . is that straightforward cases now take longer to prepare than more complex cases. This is because insufficient staff have been allocated to deal with the straightforward cases, where most of the increase has come. The backlog in less complex cases increased markedly during 1988 where there was a high turnover of staff and difficulty in finding replacements.[83]

The Joint Council for the Welfare of Immigrants (JCWI) gave evidence that throughout the appeals process appellants are required to comply with strict time limits, but that the IND has to comply with none in preparing its statements. At its behest the Home Affairs Committee recommended as an 'effective discipline upon the IND' that it prepare all statements within 15 weeks.[84]

Another problem with an explanatory statement is, however, that it comprises, contrary to the Immigration Appeals Procedure Rules, much else besides a mere statement of facts. It is a motley of assertion, law, hearsay, evidence, argument and fact. It is also not subject to the normal tests of verification in civil litigation. Thus discovery of documents, interrogatories and cross-examination of witnesses is very much more restricted in immigration appeals than is usually the case in civil litigation. This is particularly problematic as the Divisional Court has now made it clear that explanatory statements have the status of evidence. Yet it is extraordinary that there is no way of verifying its authenticity.[85]

A number of suggestions have been made recently on reforming the drafting of these statements, and are worth mentioning here. It has been suggested that interviews should be tape-recorded and played back by the adjudicator for the full story.[86] The format of an explanatory statement should be such that it discloses full details, i.e. each and every question asked and each and every question recorded, leading questions should not be asked, and that an independent observer should be present at all interviews. The objection raised here is that at no other first instance stage of government decision-making is there such a provision. But this objection is misconceived because in all other spheres an appeal against a decision can be attended by all the parties concerned whereas in entry clearance appeals the appellant is not present (as he is applying to enter).[87] This is a fundamental matter of natural justice that should be addressed immediately.

REPRESENTATIVE AND VOLUNTARY ORGANIZATIONS

The bulk of the cases are handled by UKIAS, the Joint Council for the Welfare of Immigrants (JCWI), and the Tower Hamlets Law Centre. In 1974 after discussions with the British Embassy in Islamabad and the Government of Pakistan, an Immigrants Advice Centre of Pakistan was formed which works closely with UKIAS. UKIAS was set up during Harold Wilson's second administration in 1970. From its ten offices in London, Glasgow, Manchester, Birmingham, Leeds and Cardiff, it provides advice and legal representation for about 2000 families a month on an annual Government grant of £1.5 million. However, UKIAS has come close to the brink of collapse. This was induced by the Government's decision in July 1991 to force the service to expand and become the monopoly supplier of legal assistance for immigrants and asylum seekers. This decision by the Home Secretary, Kenneth Baker, may have been influenced by the way in which independent solicitors succeeded on more than one occasion in embarrassing the Home Secretary in judicial review proceedings. It was decided to withdraw the 'green form' legal aid system of public funding from all independent solicitors. UKIAS, however, which had not been consulted about these changes, refused to accept a monopoly, whereupon in a letter of 7 October 1991, the Home Office warned the service that 'this must throw a question mark over the funding you already receive'. Mr David Pannick (now Queen's Counsel), as a Treasury Junior to the Crown, with considerable experience of immigration cases, wrote that the government is proposing to confer on that satellite body a monopoly of legal services for one of the most vulnerable groups in our society. That is a philosophy totally at variance with the competition policies of the government in the legal context and generally.[88]

In fact, UKIAS had problems of its own of which the Government was not completely unaware. With ever more restrictive laws, an increasing amount of the rising workload of UKIAS was being devoted to asylum seekers from non-Commonwealth countries, and the body was under pressure to bring members of other ethnic communities onto its general council. In January 1992, after it failed to agree a new constitution, the Home Office stripped the service of its asylum work, hiving off that work to another body, and set a three-month deadline for reform, failing which it 'would be obliged to terminate the grant paid to UKIAS and transfer all its services to a new organization'.[89] The deadline ended in April 1992, but the situation had still not been made any clearer by the Government by the end of the year. In the House of Lords, however, Earl Ferrers, the Home Office Minister, announced the Government's intention to abandon its proposals to withdraw legal aid from solicitors during the second reading of the abortive Asylum Bill.[90] Such had been the widespread criticism of the Government in this matter from the legal profession and other advice groups.

Unlike UKIAS, JCWI does not seek or accept Government funding, being financially dependent on grants from private trusts and other donations. It was the first national voluntary organization, founded in 1967, on the initiative of immigrant and multi-racial organizations. It was thus already in existence before the report of the Wilson Committee. It has a single office in London and a staff of about ten that works closely with law centres and other advice agencies. The General Secretary of JCWI, Anne Owers, recently explained to the Home Affairs Committee that the JCWI has 'never as an organization, advocated the abolition of immigration controls', but what it wanted to see was 'a control which was more firmly based on principles of rights, which gave more rights to those people on the other side of the control'.[91] Finally, the Tower Hamlets Law Centre deals with about 100 cases at any given time. It is situated in the East End of London, which has a large local Bengali community. The majority of its cases, therefore, relate to the decisions made by the Dacca post of the British High Commission.[92]

THE REPORTING OF IMMIGRATION CASES

Because immigration law, generally speaking, is not highly regarded, it is not a subject that arouses any great general public interest.[93] A leading immigration law expert once lamented that for access to important cases it is not enough to rely on general publishers alone because:

> the general series of law reports have not always identified the most important precedents and, somewhat curiously, *The Times*, that instant bible of the busy lawyer, has taken to curtailing its reports of immigration cases at the same time as expanding usefully its coverage of other judgments.[94]

Access to appeal determinations became limited some years ago after closure of the library at Thanet House, where immigration appeals are heard. A journal of the *Immigration Appeal Reports* now publishes some selected cases quarterly. The quality of editing of these reports is high, meticulous care being taken over annotation and head notes. However, Macdonald and Blake argue that the balance of reported cases has perhaps shifted too much in favour of High Court cases and away from tribunal decisions 'which give valuable guidance on the working of particular Immigration Rules'. As a result, '[T]oo many such cases cited in this edition can only be found in manuscript form in the Supreme Court Library'.[95] Of the cases reported, moreover, many have been heard up to a year previously. It is not unusual for decisions to come to the appellant's representative for the first time when they are cited by the Home Office presenting officer. There was an interval of two and a half years between the publication of the 1978 volume and the 1979–80 volume. Lawyers who form JCWI's Advisory Legal Committee wrote to the Home Office then requesting a meeting to discuss ways in which access to cases could be improved for practitioners. The Home Office replied that its responsibility to appellants 'is recognized by the provision . . . of UKIAS' and that copies of appeal cases are sent to UKIAS, JCWI, the Law Society, the Royal Courts Library and the Press Association.[96]

Clearly, then, the problem is not accorded a very high priority by the Government. In 1983 the 1981 edition of the *Immigration Appeal Reports* was published. Until this was published in the summer of 1983 the most recent immigration appeal determination was heard in October 1980. It transpired that the delay had been caused by the Home Office's requirement that it be printed in prison in order to save money. The books turned out to be shoddy and did not meet the standard of HMSO, whereupon they had to be reprinted, which only added to the delay and cost.[97]

CONCLUSIONS

What this chapter demonstrates more than anything else is that a right of appeal can never serve as an antidote for a wrong decision if the spectrum in which the resolution of disputes is conducted is not first grounded in the basic principles of fairness. A right of appeal will impose a surcharge on the exercise of official discretion. It will delay for a time an adverse decision from taking its effect. It will even help to cushion an individual from the harsher realities of immigration control by acting as a 'kind of reassurance'. It cannot, however, on its own hope to affect the essential content of those adverse decisions, or protect the substantive rights of individuals affected by those decisions, if in its essence the system continues to function in a way that is oblivious to an appeals procedure, and all that such a procedure implies. To a large extent, the problem is due to officials acting in the context of their own culture, induced by the expectations of the job that they are doing. Such an insular approach is not in itself far removed from the overall absence of a well thought out immigration policy that would serve to underpin the exercise of administrative discretion in all such cases – a situation induced by insularity itself. The fact is that decision-makers at present do not actually benefit from the adoption of such an unstructured and incoherent approach to immigration control buttressed by bureaucratic delays. For example, the Home Affairs Committee in 1990 was itself critical of this approach when it referred to delays of over a year in the preparation of explanatory statements, particularly in view of the six-month time-limit recently imposed on visitors to Britain. While the statements are being written up, it said:

> the appellant has a right to stay in this country, even though in 95 per cent of after-entry appeals they will lose their case. Many people might see this as undermining the notion of control implied by the imposition of a six month limit on visit visas.[98]

This is what happens when an activity is not considered serious enough; when its administration is starved of public funds; and when its personnel suffer from low morale. It is submitted that policymakers in Parliament and the bureaucracy must now seek out a more coherent and effectual strategy for dealing with this particular area of public administration. They must, as we have said in earlier chapters, ask themselves what it is that they are setting out to do, why they are doing it, and whether or not there may not be an alternative and a better way of doing it. For an even clearer elucidation of this thesis, however, we must turn to our next and final chapter.

NOTES AND REFERENCES

1 (1967) Report of the Committee on Immigration Appeals (the 'Wilson Committee'). Cmnd 3387.

2 A number of administrative concessions were given as, for example, in 1919 when an advisory committee was set up to recommend to the Home Secretary that a former enemy alien should not be deported. This system ended in 1939. From 1956 aliens were allowed to put their case against deportation before the Chief Magistrate if they had been resident in the United Kingdom two years prior to receiving notification of deportation. However, the recommendations were not binding on the Home Secretary.

3 (1957) *Administrative Tribunals and Inquiries*. Cmnd 218.

4 Thus in prescribing the procedures that an adjudicator should follow, the Wilson Committee said (p. 55, para. 168), 'We recommend that an adjudicator should have the power to enforce the attendance of witnesses; that he should have power to administer the Oath . . ., that he should be empowered to accept any form of credible evidence, without being bound by the rules of evidence that are binding on courts of law.' These recommendations were consistent with those made by the Franks Committee (at paras 90–92) in relation to tribunals generally.

5 Evans, J.M. (1983) *Immigration Law*, p. 329. London.

6 Wilson Report, *op. cit.* p. 27.

7 See Stephenson LJ in *R* v. *IAT*, *ex parte Alam Bi* [1979–80] Imm AR 146, CA; Glidewell J in *R* v. *IAT*, *ex parte Motahir Ali* (1981) 29 January (unreported) QBD; Woolf J in *R* v. *IAT*, *ex parte Zaman* (1982) Imm AR 61, QBD. For a discussion of these cases see Juss S. (1992) Review and Appeal in Administrative Law – What Is Happening to the Right of Appeal in Immigration Law? *Legal Studies* 12(3), 364–76.

8 See *Mohammed Saftar*, *op. cit.* Chapter 3, note 128. Also see *Ali* v *Secretary of State for the Home Department* [1988] Imm AR 274, CA.

9 (1990) *Administrative Delays in the Immigration and Nationality Department*, HC 319, p. xv.

10 Wilson Committee, *op. cit.* pp. 27–8. The Committee's confident assertion that 'the power of final decision' is 'being exercised fairly' is difficult to accept. It is a view that is reiterated with equal confidence in the subsequent reports of the Home Affairs Sub-Committee on Race Relations and Immigration. It is not, however, for want of evidence that the Wilson Committee and the Home Affairs Sub-Committee has declined to state that immigration control has been known to be unfair, and even unlawful at times. Giving evidence to the Wilson Committee in 1967, Dr Paul O'Higgins drew its attention to how British immigration officials abroad collaborated unlawfully with foreign police and immigration authorities for the apprehension and removal of certain individuals. The evidence is not, however, mentioned in the body of the report and plainly contradicts the conclusions drawn by Wilson.

11 Wilson Committee, *op. cit.* p. 28.

12 *Op. cit.* p. 52.

13 Nevertheless, as late as 1981–82 the Council on Tribunals in its annual report

recommended that the Home Secretary should not choose any tribunal members or adjudicators.

14 Wilson Committee, *op. cit.* p. 37.

15 Wilson Committee, *op. cit.* p. 55.

16 Tribunal and Inquiries Act 1958 sections 1 and 12.

17 Evans, *op. cit.* p. 329.

18 See Queen's Speech, HL Deb, Vol. 270, col. 5 (9 November 1965).

19 Debate on the Queen's Speech, HC Deb Vol. 720, cols 49–50, 59–149 (9 November 1965).

20 Thus it is curious that the Wilson Committee, notwithstanding its preoccupation with arguments of 'basic principle' and the 'rule of law', should have gone on to recommend that adjudicators could be appointed by the Home Office from members of the Immigration Service: see Wilson Committee, p. 52, para. 154.

21 (1981) *The Pivot of the System. Briefing Paper on Immigration Appeals*, p. 6. London.

22 Wilson Committee, *op. cit.* pp. 19–20, para. 62.

23 (1990) *Administrative Delays in the Immigration and Nationality Department*, HC 319, p. xxi.

24 *The Pivot of the System*, *op. cit.* p. 22.

25 C. Blake says of the Wilson Committee that 'The focus was upon reassurance of immigrants and . . . not upon the possibility that errors, bias, even prejudice could enter into the decision making process: see Blake (1983) Immigration Appeals: The Need for Reform, unpublished paper presented at the AGIN Conference on the Reform of British Immigration Law and Its Administration. He does accept, however, that its proposals were 'a positive step' (see pp. 1 and 2). See also Watkins (1971) A Strange Death for Liberal England, *New Statesman* 81 (15 January), p. 67.

26 For example, in *Kumar* Entry Clearance Officers were criticized for having 'scratched around' for evidence to disprove the existence of a genuine marriage. See the Master of the Rolls in *R* v. *IAT ex parte Kumar* [1986] Imm AR 446. Also see similar criticism in *Mohd. Saftar* referred to in Chapter 3. In *Savita Rani* v. *ECO, New Delhi*, TH/62675/92, d. 22-1-93, an ECO recorded events in his statement that had not even taken place.

27 See, for example, *R* v. *IAT, ex parte Mohd. Amin* [1992] Imm AR 367, QBD. Howover, the most striking example of recent years is the specially constituted Appeal Tribunal decision in *Vinod Bhatia* referred to in Chapter 3.

28 See *Marion Khatun* v. *ECO, Dacca* (1666) (d. 5.12.79, unreported) and *Tula Bibi* v. *ECO, Dacca* (2310) (d. 18.3.82, unreported).

29 HC Deb., Standing Committee B, col. 1508 (15 May 1971).

30 Under the Immigration Appeals Act 1969 this would have been possible but this proposal was never brought into effect or implemented.

31 Contrary to the express proposals of the Wilson Committee the Government introduced a mandatory entry clearance requirement for everyone going for settlement in the final stages of the Immigration Appeals Act 1969. The result is that in a system ridden with delays, appeals by someone from abroad take, by their very nature, three or four times as long as appeals by someone present here.

32 Thus, an immigration officer's suspicion that a person is not a bona fide student is sufficient for him to refuse entry and there is no right of appeal before removal

within the appeals system. In such an event representations were made to the Minister through an MP to instruct the immigration officer to delay the person's removal from the UK in order to give time to those acting on his behalf to establish his entitlement. Representations to the Minister have now been restricted.

33　*The Pivot of the System*, *op. cit.* p. 15. Also see Table 2 on p. 16. These figures are also to be found in the publication of *Immigration Statistics* for the relevant years. This is a publication by the Home Office which regularly puts out statistics of immigration in quarterly statistical bulletins and, in more detail, in the annual Command Paper (e.g. Cmnd 8199 for 1980).

34　(1982–83) *JCWI Annual Report*, p. 11.

35　It said: 'Our hope would be that the proceedings should be as informal as is consistent with preserving the general "feel" of a judicial hearing', partly because it believed that adjudicators 'should be empowered to accept any form of credible evidence, without being bound by the rules of evidence that are binding on courts of law'. *Report of the Committee on Immigration Appeals*, *op. cit.* p. 55, para. 188.

36　(1957) *Administrative Tribunal and Inquiries*, Cmnd 218, paras 90–92.

37　(1990) *Administrative Delays in the Immigration and Nationality Department*, HC 319, p. xvi.

38　The 'primary-purpose' marriage cases as seen in Chapter 3 are the best example of this.

39　(1981) *Review of Appeals under the Immigration Act 1971*.

40　The Council on Tribunals has hinted that the delay in the time that it took for a case to appear before an adjudicator 'continued to be a source of concern': (1982–83) Annual Report.

41　(1982–83) *UKIAS Annual Report*, p. 8.

42　(1990) *Administrative Delays in the Immigration and Nationality Department*, *op. cit.* p. xiii, xvi.

43　*R* v. *Secretary of State for the Home Department, ex parte Oladehinde* [1991] AC 254.

44　See Juss, S. (1993) Administrative Convenience and the Carltona Principle, *Oxford Journal of Legal Studies* 13 (1), pp. 142–5.

45　(1981–82) *Immigration from the Indian Sub-Continent: First Report from the Home Affairs Committee*, 1981–82, HC 90-II, p. 1.

46　*Ibid.* p. 31, Q. 108 and p. 32 Q. 112 (Mr Lyon MP).

47　*Parveen Begum* v. *Visa Officer, Islamabad* TH/20235/77 (1419) d. 8.1.79 (unreported).

48　(1982) *Immigration from the Indian Sub-Continent*: Fifth Report from the Home Affairs Committee 1981–82, HC 90-II, p. 114 (Q. 325).

49　*Ghulam Sughre* v. *Visa Officer, Islamabad* TH/96117/82 (2974) d. 28.11.83 (unreported) at pp. 3–4.

50　*Halsbury's Laws of England* states that, 'A change of domicile is a serious matter, not to be lightly inferred and it must be clearly and unequivocally proved. . . . The task of proving the change of domicile is particularly onerous when the domicile alleged to be displaced is one of origin as opposed to one of choice' (see (1974) *Halsbury's Laws of England*, 4th edn, Vol. 8, para. 432). In the case of *Khatoon* (1683) the Tribunal declared, 'Domicile is different from citizenship, a change of citizenship does not necessarily involve a change of domicile, though it may be some evidence to demonstrate such a change'. Quoted in *Sufia Khatoon* v. *Eco Dacca* TH/89275/82 (2793) d. 13.7.83. (unreported).

51 *Mohd. Saftar* v. *Secretary of State for the Home Department* [1992] Imm AR 1, p. 12.

52 *Ibid.* p. 114, Q. 325 (John Ennals, UKIAS, Director). It seems that by 1982 only two adjudicators had ever been to Bangladesh from whence the bulk of the family reunion cases came: see (1982) *Immigration from the Indian Sub-Continent, op. cit.* p. 114, Q. 326 (Mr Lyon MP).

53 *Ibid.* p. 114, Q. 326 (John Ennals). In its annual report for 1977–78 UKIAS said that adjudicators are 'called upon to give their decisions in a high proportion of cases where a sound knowledge of the customs, cultures, religions and way of life of the peoples of the sub-continent is essential if the justice is to be done, but how many of them possess that knowledge . . . ?'

54 (1990) *Administrative Delays in the Immigration and Nationality Department, op. cit.* p. xix.

55 *The Pivot of the System, op. cit.* p. 26. In another case three Chilean refugees who were members of the Chilean Socialist Party were described by an adjudicator as being 'communist agitators' and advised to go back to Cuba (*loc. cit.*).

56 *Eco Islamabad* v. *Qeemat Bibi* TH/1655/74 (450) d. 8.4.74 (unreported) at p. 2.

57 *Shafait Bi* v. *Eco Islamabad* TH/2900/73 (627) d. 16.3.76 (unreported) at p 2.

58 *Tula Bibi* v. *Eco Dacca* TH/48214/79 (2310) d. 10.3.82 (unreported) at p. 2.

59 *Sarwar Jan* v. *Visa Officer, Islamabad* TH/22706/77 (1757) d. 25.3.80 (unreported) at p. 3.

60 *Visa Officer, Islamabad* v. *Zarina Jan* TH/53001/79 (2300) d. 2.2.82 (unreported) at p. 2.

61 *The Pivot of the System, op. cit.* at p. 26.

62 (1982) *Immigration from the Indian Sub-Continent, op. cit.* p. 142, Q. 483–88 (Mr Partridge, Head of Migration and Visa Department).

63 (1990) *Administrative Delays in the Immigration and Nationality Department, op. cit.* pp. xii, x, xiii.

64 (1982) *Immigration from the Indian Sub-Continent, op. cit.* p. 143, Q. 497 (Mr Gardner MP).

65 *Safira Begum, The Times*, 28 May 1976.

66 *Visa Officer, Islamabad* v. *Khadaja Bi* TH/26083/78 (1571) d. 10.7.79 (unreported) at p. 3. Note, however, that in *Aziz Fatima* the tribunal made a complete *volte face*. Here the ECO, it appears, had not given the interviewees the opportunity to resolve the discrepancies by commenting upon each other's evidence. The adjudicator said: 'I would agree that, generally speaking, it is both helpful and desirable to ensure that interviewees are given an opportunity to resolve such discrepancies. . . . Some officers invariably do so. Others are content to let the evidence speak for itself. I do not consider that an omission of this kind is, of itself, a ground for criticism.' The tribunal concurred in this: see *Aziz Fatima* v. *Visa Officers, Islamabad* TH/76822/81 (2994) d. 20.7.83 (unreported) at pp. 2–3.

67 (1982) *Immigration from the Indian Sub-Continent, op. cit.* pp. 47–8, Q.187–192 (Mr Partridge).

68 (1990) *Administrative Delays in the Immigration and Nationality Department, op. cit.* p. xi.

69 (1982) *Immigration from the Indian Sub-Continent, op. cit.* p. 145, Q. 497 (Mr Raison). See also Memorandum submitted by JCWI at p. 86. Reference may also be made to the 39 immigration officers at Heathrow who signed a petition to support Mr Enoch Powell's famous 'rivers of blood' speech in 1969: see *Crossman Diaries, op. cit.* Vol. 3, p. 26.

70 See the four-year research by the Commission for Racial Equality on the operation of the entry clearance system published in February 1985: (1985) *Immigration Control Procedures: Report of a Formal Investigation*, p. 55. London.

71 *Fatima Bibi* v. *Visa Officer, Islamabad* TH/82357/81 (2641) d. 5.4.83 (unreported) at pp. 1–2.

72 *Inayat Begum* v. *Visa Officer, Islamabad* TH/43561/79 (2338) d. 16.4.82 (unreported) at p. 2.

73 Immigration Appeals (Procedure) Rules 1984, SI No. 2041, see r. 6 and r. 7.

74 We have already seen this in Chapter 3 (see note 77).

75 Immigration Appeals (Procedure) Rules, *op. cit.* r. 8.

76 *Ibid.* r. 8(2). In this event, it must inform both the appellate authorities and the appellant of this and confirm that an oral statement will be given at the hearing. In most cases, however, it is rare for the Explanatory Statement to be dispensed with.

77 (1982) *Immigration from the Indian Sub-Continent, op. cit.* Q. 490 (Shirley Littler, Asst Under-Secretary, Immigration and Nat. Dept).

78 *Ibid.* Memorandum by JCWI (at p. 59) and by Tower Hamlets Law Centre (at pp. 60–1).

79 (1982) *Immigration from the Indian Sub-Continent, op. cit.* p. 133, Q. 322 (John Ennals). Mr Ennals stated that 'It is very difficult for an appellant to persuade an adjudicator to overturn a decision taken by an ECO. The adjudicator knows the ECO has a difficult job to do. We know that . . .' and 'to overturn that in the absence of the appellant and in the absence of the wording of what happened in the inquiry . . . does create a very difficult problem . . .' (*ibid.* p. 113 at Q. 323). The Runnymede Trust has argued that the difficulty lies in the fact that 'the rules of procedure do not require a Home Office view of the fact prepared by a party to the appeal' (*The Pivot of the System, op. cit.* p. 22). This statement is then officially accepted as being true.

80 Air Vice-Marshal Richard Ayling, CB, MBE, quoted in (1982) *Split Families* (UKIAS RESEARCH PROJECT) at p. 5 (*footnote*). Similarly, the explanatory statement in *Aziz Fatima* (TH/76822/81 (2794) d. 20.7.83) was most inadequate as it did not disclose whether the ECO had sought to resolve the discrepancies in the evidence by seeking the comments of both interviewees. For an even more up-to-date example, see *Ilsey* v. *ECO, Manila* Appeal No. TH/20190/1991.

81 In *Qeemat Bibi* TH/1655/74 (450) d. 8.4.75 (unreported) two interviewees were conducted by different officers whose notes were then used by a third officer in preparing an Explanatory Statement. Also see (1982) *Split Families* (UKIAS Research Project), *op. cit.* p. 5.

82 Letter to the author written 13 June 1984.

83 (1990) *Administrative Delays in the Immigration and Nationality Department, op. cit.* p. xv.

84 *Ibid.* p. xvi.

85 (1982–83) UKIAS, *Annual Report*, p. 9.

86 (1982) *Immigration from the Indian Sub-Continent, op. cit.* Q. 322 (Mr John Ennals).
87 *Ibid.* Memorandum by the Tower Hamlets Law Centre, p. 61.
88 Pannick, D. (1992) A Monopoly in Life and Death Decisions. *The Times*, 23 July 1992.
89 *The Guardian*, 13 May 1992.
90 *The Times*, 11 February 1992 and *The Guardian*, 11 February 1992.
91 (1992) *Migration at External Borders of the European Community, op. cit.* p.49, Q. 296, 297.
92 *Ibid.* Memorandum by the Tower Hamlets Law Centre, p. 61.
93 Beloff, M. (1984) *Public Law* (Spring edn), p. 170.
94 *Loc. cit.*
95 Macdonald and Blake, *op. cit.* p. viii.
96 (1981–82) *JCWI Annual Report*, p. 11.
97 (1982–83) *JCWI Annual Report*, pp. 13–14.
98 (1990) *Administrative Delays in the Immigration and Nationality Department, op. cit.* p. xv.

6

Immigration Control and the Legal Process

(2) The Immigration Rules and Their Application

'Government, even in its best state, is but a necessary evil; in its worst state, an intolerable one.' – *Thomas Paine*

Writing in 1936 in the *Yale Law Journal*, L.L. Fuller and W.R. Perdue in a seminal article on contract law expressed a sentiment that is today all too applicable to immigration law. They wrote:

> We are still all too willing to embrace the conceit that it is possible to manipulate legal concepts without the orientation which comes from the simple inquiry: toward what end is this activity directed? Nietzsche's observation, that the most common stupidity consists in forgetting what one is trying to do, retains a discomforting relevance to legal science.[1]

The legal regulation of immigration control in the United Kingdom is based on a confusing *mélange* of statute law, administrative rules and ministerial discretions. This regime can be ranked hierarchically where each tier, properly speaking, should have its own specific regulatory objectives. The first tier comprises primary legislation in the form of a statute, the Immigration Act 1971, which bestows upon the Secretary of State the power and responsibility to determine the conduct and practice of immigration control. The second tier comprises administrative rules, in the form of the immigration rules, which are made and published by the Home Secretary under the 1971 Act, and which concern the exercise of discretion by subordinate officers. The third tier, in so far as it comprises rules, consists of 'house rules' made by the Home Office but which are not published.

In terms of their objectives, it is clear that only the first and the second tiers exist for the benefit of the broader public in so far as they inform them of the basic principles of immigration control. But they also (particularly the second tier) help officers to facilitate enforcement of official immigration policy. Only the third tier, to which the public is not privy, aims to control officials in the exercise of their bureaucratic discretions. The second tier, more than the first, can provide a basis for negotiation between controllers and the controlled by providing more detail to both enforcement officials and to regulatees on what they should be doing. Yet the overall picture remains unsatisfactory from the point of view of both controllers and the controlled because administrators have not asked or have forgotten, as Fuller and Perdue warned them, what exactly it is that they are setting out to do in every particular case. In a very careful and important analysis, Robert Baldwin has pointed to the existence of at least four prerequisites of effective rule-making. Depending on what it is that it is promulgated to do, a rule should have the necessary degree of *specificity* or *precision*, its *extent* should be appropriate to the purposes for which it is employed, it should be readily *accessible* and *intelligible* to those who would seek to rely on it, and its *status* and *force* should be clear so that proper weight can be given to it.[2]

This chapter aims to demonstrate that in the administration of immigration control the present system of legal regulation can have unhappy consequences for both regulators and regulatees. The focus is on the immigration rules, because it is these, and not the Immigration Act 1971, which are the linchpin of the modern system of control, although discretionary control is also considered as this aspect is also important. In so doing this chapter fulfils two ancillary aims: it allows the broader implications of the use of rules and discretion to be explored, and it enables some specific reforms to be suggested in this particular regulatory context. This is done by considering (1) the genesis and history of the immigration rules; (2) the rules in Parliament; (3) alternative approaches to drafting the rules; (4) the binding effects of the rules; (5) their interpretation; and (6) extra-statutory decision-making in immigration law.

GENESIS AND HISTORY OF THE RULES THAT REGULATE THE SYSTEM OF IMMIGRATION

'A people without history/is not redeemed from time', wrote T.S. Eliot, 'for history is a pattern/of timeless moments'.[3] And certainly no one analysing the immigration rules can ignore their history. Traditionally, the immigration rules have not been well understood. The Court of Appeal once described them as 'a curious amalgam of information and description of executive procedures' and as being 'in a class of their own'.[4] Academic and other analysts, troubled by the growing use of departmental rules to effect important matters of governmental policy without due regard to the proper interests of a parliamentary democracy,[5] have on the whole tended to view them as a species of 'informal rules'. The term informal rules is used interchangeably with administrative quasi-legislation (a phrase coined by Mr Megarry in 1944) or with administrative rules. All these terms connote the idea of a sub-delegated legislation; that is, a subordinate-form departmental legislation that is not made formally by statutory instrument as the Statutory Instruments Act 1946 prescribes that it should be by all departments. However, describing the immigration rules as only one of the better-known examples of informal rules may be sometimes convenient but is not always helpful, since informal rules come in a variety of forms and have differing legal effects.[6] Moreover, many of their characteristics may well be shared with more formal rules, especially *formal* directions which have the force of law but are not laid before Parliament. If all such rules are conflated under the appellation 'informal rules', it may well be asked exactly what characteristics distinguish informal rules from other rules. Therefore, careful detailed analysis of the regulatory context may be necessary if one is to reveal the balance between rules and discretion in each particular case.[7]

Rules as a technique have not been a very happy method for effecting immigration control because traditionally the matter has been dealt with by the Home Secretary through the exercise of the Royal Prerogative to the exclusion of formal statutory criteria.[8] As administrative law developed in the twentieth century governments were forced to follow rules, or were called upon to confine, structure and check 'unnecessary' bureaucratic discretions.[9] They chose the medium of administrative rule-making rather than the formal flexibility of an Act of Parliament as this did not leave them with as much discretion.[10] What is more interesting is why they did not always choose delegated legislation as this was the prescribed method of departmental rule-making under the Statutory Instruments Act 1946 after the Second World War. That Act provided a formal approach to legislative rule-making and so did not cater for the creation of more informal rules in the way that its predecessor, the Rules Publication Act 1893, did. In the 1946 Act form took priority over substance, but governments still tended to prefer informal rules as these had the advantages of quickly and inexpensively structuring the discretion of untrained officials through the flexible and non-technical use of language. This is amply demonstrated today by the use of such rules in planning, housing, picketing, the stop, search and detention powers under the Police and Criminal Evidence Act, and parole policy – to name but a few areas.

In immigration control itself, administrative rule-making as a technique goes back nearly a hundred years. Despite this history, rules were developed very slowly by administrators because the existence of ministerial discretion led to a traditional reluctance to structure discretion through the adoption of more formal criteria. This is evident if we examine the origin of the immigration rules. Under the Aliens Act 1905 the Home Secretary issued guide-lines to immigration officers on how to carry out their duties. Those guide-lines were not, at the time, known as rules but as 'instructions', as the 'rules' terminology was adopted only in the Immigration Act 1971. The instructions advised immigration officers about the scope of their duties and informed them about the rights of intending immigrants so that, for example, under the Aliens Order of 1920 and 1953 authority to admit without permits certain categories of workers such as doctors was given by the Home Secretary in his 'General Instructions'. By 1967 the 'General Instructions' ran to a loose-leaf volume of 400 pages.[11] The importance of retaining ministerial discretionary control was demonstrated by the fact that these instructions were not published by the Home Secretary. It was not until a sharp rise in New Commonwealth immigration occurred in the late 1950s and early 1960s that the Home Secretary, R.A. Butler, announced during the Committee stage of the Commonwealth Immigrants Bill in 1962 that the instructions to immigration officers would be published.[12] It is important to note that at this stage there was no specific duty upon the Home Secretary to publish the rules or indeed even to make them because all that section 16(3) of the 1962 Act provided was that the instructions *may* be given by the Secretary of State.[13] The setting up of the Wilson Committee and the subsequent passing of the Immigration Appeals Act 1969 did not result in the mandatory publication of the rules, even though the 1969 Act established an immigration appeals structure in which individual cases could be tested against relevant primary and subsidiary legislation. It was only the Immigration Act 1971 which first made publication of the rules mandatory.

Nevertheless, the tradition of informality of approach together with a commitment to official administrative discretion has influenced the subsequent development of the immigration rules.

PARLIAMENT AND THE RULES

Parliamentary control of rule-making, whatever form it takes, is important because it requires that the validation of rules of legislative character comes from Parliament and not from administrators. The first question to ask, therefore, is whether a statute has anything to say about this in relation to the rule in question. If the rule is made under powers conferred by a statute then the manner of its control and precise legal effects can be properly gauged from the statute.

Parliamentary control of the immigration rules is laid down in section 3(2) of the Immigration Act 1971:

> The Secretary of State shall from time to time (and as soon as may be) *lay before Parliament statements of the rules*, or of any changes in the rules, laid down by him as to the practice to be followed *in the administration of the Act* for regulating the entry into and stay in the United Kingdom of persons required by the Act to have leave to enter . . .
>
> If a statement laid before either *House of Parliament* under this subsection is disapproved by a resolution of that House passed within the *period of forty days* beginning with the date of laying . . . then the Secretary of State shall, as soon as may be make such changes or further changes in the rules as appear to him to be required in the circumstances, so that the statement of those changes be laid before Parliament at the latest by the end of the period of forty days, beginning with the date of the resolution. (emphasis added)

This section indicates the following: First, it is clear that the rules are not expressed to be exercisable by a statutory instrument[14] but are merely required to be laid before Parliament from time to time. It is possible for a statement of the immigration rules to be incorporated in a statutory instrument or to be approved by a statutory instrument and then be subject to a negative resolution of the House if the Act so prescribes. This is a technique used, for example, in the Pollution Act 1974, but it is not used here.[15] Secondly, the rules are subject to a negative resolution of either House within a period of 40 days, an illustration of the fact that the rules do not have to be made by statutory instrument to be subject to parliamentary procedure. Thirdly, there is no procedure for annulling the rules as distinct from annulling a 'statement' of the rules. This point is all too easy for commentators to overlook,[16] but what it means is that section 3(2) only lays down a negative procedure for annulment of the statement of the rules, so that the rules themselves remain perfectly valid until a new set is placed before Parliament.[17] Disapproval of a statement of the immigration rules by either House does not mean that the rules are thereby nullified: '[I]t merely becomes necessary for the Secretary of State to devise such fresh rules as appear to him to be required in the circumstances.[18] The *obiter* statement by Stephenson LJ in *Pearson* v. *IAT*[19] that 'Parliament must look at them and not disapprove them before they can have effect' would therefore appear to be a mistaken view.[20]

The important question is, however, why the rules are not made by statutory instrument as formally required by the Act of 1946. Flexibility and the opportunity to experiment are often cited as reasons, but these advantages are shared equally[21] with statutory instruments as is well illustrated by the rules for the criminal injuries compensation scheme. The real reason, and the one on which we must now focus, is, firstly, the informality of language used and, secondly, the lack of direct legal effect which such quasi-legal rules have compared with those in statutory instruments.

The informality of language is in fact traceable to the essential form and style of the rules prior to the Immigration Act 1971 and the days when they were referred to as 'General Instructions' as described earlier. In the 1971 Act this style of the rules has been preserved intact and has influenced the approach which the courts have taken to their interpretation. As Lord Bridge said in the House of Lords in *Bakhtaur Singh*, the rules

> are discursive in style, in part merely explanatory and, on their face, frequently offer no more than broad guidance as to how discretion is to be exercised in different typical situations. In so far as they lay down principles to be applied, they generally do so in loose and imprecise terms.[22]

Thus, like the 'General Instructions', the immigration rules do not set out to establish clear-cut individual rights. Rights are not framed in absolute terms but are invariably subject to the general provision that 'account is to be taken of all the relevant facts' and that mere compliance with formal requirements is not conclusively in favour of an individual.[23] Commentators generally agree that the effect of a variable terminology is also unsettling. They are really 'each a hotchpotch of different kinds of rule – some prescriptive, some advisory, some expressing discretionary powers'.[24] By this it is meant that some rules provide that 'those who satisfy the stated criteria *will normally be admitted*', whilst others provide that a person who falls within a category *'may be admitted'*.[25] The use of 'the language of exhortation and advice'[26] makes many rules non-normative, for it has been argued that many are 'couched in descriptive not normative language, and designated merely as "principles" to be followed in the exercise of discretion'.[27]

The informality of language used to imply a lack of direct legal effect means that despite the passage of the 1971 Act the discretionary powers of the executive remain largely unchanged from what they were in the 'General Instructions'.[28] There may be a desire here to preserve the traditional and historical position of the Home Secretary, but if so, it is at the expense of parliamentary control. Thus the deportation rules inform the Minister that 'in considering whether deportation is the right course on the merits, the public interest will be balanced against any compassionate circumstances of the case'.[29]

Here, because the decision-maker must make value judgments about what is in the 'public interest' and what are the 'compassionate circumstances' and then proceed to balance them out, the width of the choice before him is enormous, for 'public interest' and 'compassionate circumstances' can mean different things to different people. This important point is again addressed below when the binding effects and interpretation of the immigration rules are considered.

ALTERNATIVE APPROACHES TO DRAFTING THE RULES

This issue about how discretion is to be exercised under the rules in different situations can only be resolved satisfactorily if legislators and administrators avowedly use a specific form of rule-making for a specific kind of rule. This can be done by the adoption of clear principles and objectives.

First, mandatory and normative rules should be put into statutory instruments to allow the courts to apply the normal *ultra vires* principles with ease. Immigration legislation should make it clear that these rules are made by the Home Secretary under delegated authority and are intended to have specific legal effects in relation to specific people. This would require a whole host of the current immigration rules ranging from 'au pairs'[30] to refugees,[31] to visitors,[32] and to large parts of the deportation rules[33] to be made by statutory instrument.

Secondly, proper guidance should be given by the Home Secretary in relation to other rules to give them a purposive construction, so that the almost gratuitous use of lax language can be avoided. Take, for example, the rule in section 3(5)(c) of the Immigration Act 1971 regarding the statutory liability of the wife or child to deportation as a member of a family.[34] What is any person or court to make of rule 170 of the current immigration rules:

> 170: Where the wife has qualified for settlement in the
> United Kingdom in her own right, for example, following
> 4 years in approved employment, she has a valid claim to
> remain notwithstanding the expulsion of her husband and
> her deportation will not normally be contemplated. Where
> the wife has been living apart from the principal deportee it
> will *not normally* be right to include her, or any children
> with her, in the deportation order. (emphasis added)

If the wife has 'qualified for settlement' in 'her own right' and has a 'valid claim to remain' as this rule suggests, what is the purpose and intent of 'normally' in this rule? It seems that there is none. If there is a purpose and intent, surely it ought to be clearly spelt out, otherwise there is a very real danger that what looks very much like a normative rule will be vitiated by an unstructured administrative discretion.

The same point can be made in relation to the deportation of older children aged 18. Under rule 171 their removal 'will *not normally* be contemplated if they have spent some years in the United Kingdom and are near that age. Nor will deportation *normally* be *appropriate* if the child left the family home on taking employment and has established himself on an independent basis . . .' (emphasis added). Are there any cases where a married child, no longer part of the principal deportee's household, has been deported in the circumstances envisaged by rule 171? Can there indeed be such cases? And if so, how will they differ from the general run of ordinary cases for which rule 171 was designed? Again, it seems that there are no such cases, but if the Home Office contends that there are, then this should surely be specifically spelt out.

Detailed guidance is necessary if these rules are to be given a more purposive construction otherwise a rule becomes 'so opaque that its application deprives a person of 'due process of law'.[35] Words such as 'normally' in the examples above should be avoided as they are positively unhelpful and even misleading. In deportation cases, which involve such an awesome use of executive power, such ambiguity has particularly serious consequences.

Thirdly, non-mandatory, descriptive and permissive rules should be dealt with separately from those discussed above and which could be made by statutory instrument. The rule dealing with deportation on 'conducive to the public good'[36] grounds is possibly the best example of such a rule, and it cannot be made by statutory instrument and probably not even by delegated authority. It states that 'General rules about the circumstances in which deportation is justified on these grounds cannot be laid down, and each case will be considered carefully in the light of the relevant circumstances.' Such a rule reminds one of the dissenting judgment of Judge Freedman in the American case of *Ameeriar* v. *Immigration and Nationality Service* where he referred to the American immigration service's exercise of discretion as

> an utterly unguided and unpredictable undertaking. Only the inevitable necessity of disposing of the case is specified, like a result without a case. What is the desired goal and what guides should channel the course to it to receive no recognition.[37]

Therefore, the rule 'on conducive grounds' is more likely to be a rule of practice in the sense that section 3(2) of the Immigration Act 1971 envisages, and given that the Act leaves the Home Secretary with a residual discretion to make detailed supplementary rules to effect immigration control, this view has added plausibility.[38] The rule here is employed both with complete informality and is intended to have no legal effects.

Finally, it should be said that choosing an informal approach over the adoption of more formal statutory criteria should not be done lightly. The benefits of making such a choice are bound to be minimal for both regulators and regulatees and are likely today to be out-weighed by the general interest in the law, which requires legal rules to be characterized by clarity and precision. As one uniter has said, 'One would naturally expect the concept of rule precision to occupy a central place in any coherent philosophy of law' and that a rational rule-maker will use words with 'well-defined and universally accepted meanings'.[39] The rules so far discussed have been neither very precise nor have well-defined and accepted meanings.

BINDING EFFECTS OF THE IMMIGRATION RULES

Given that the immigration rules are not made by statutory instrument under authority delegated by Parliament, are they binding on those whom they may affect? This is a question that has often taxed the minds of immigration practitioners and the courts, and once again it is a question that is inextricably linked with the historical development of the rules and the preservation of official discretionary power today. This is a different question from how a rule is to be interpreted, which requires a consideration of its language, nature and form in order to determine whether it is prescriptive of a power or duty vested in the immigration authorities or merely descriptive. Here, once again, we have to look to the statute to provide us with the answer. The Immigration Act 1971 contains specific rules describing the position of adjudicators and the Immigration Appeal Tribunal but none regarding the effect of the immigration rules on immigration officers and the Home Secretary. Thus we are told that under section 19(1) an adjudicator must allow an appeal 'if he considers that the decision or action against which the appeal is brought was not in accordance with the law or with any immigration rules applicable . . .'. This means that adjudicators are duty bound to observe the rules and apply them.[40] It is because the rules are binding on adjudicators and the Tribunal that their decisions are open to review by a superior court for error of law on the face of the record or for excess of jurisdiction.[41]

The position of the Secretary of State for the Home Department is, however, rather different for he is not bound by the rules in exactly the same way. Clearly, if he fails to follow a rule, his action may be reviewable by the courts if it infringes a right that emerges by legitimate expectation.[42] If he actually purports to follow the rules, his action may still be reviewable, as we have seen, if, for example, he misinterprets them.[43] But it is equally clear that the Home Secretary may decide not to follow a rule by waiving its requirements for the benefit of an applicant. The applicant will not wish to appeal because he will have received a benefit to which he was not entitled under the rule. Indeed, even if there is a rule providing that an extension of stay 'should be refused' the Minister is entitled to make specific exceptions to it.[44] For the Home Secretary, therefore, the rules seem to be more like the rules of 'practice' that Parliament enjoins him to enact under section 3(2) of the Act. This particular aspect of the Minister's power is not, however, free from difficulties. Section 3(2) states that the Secretary of State must 'lay before Parliament a statement of the rules as to the practice to be followed in the administration of the Act'. If only some of the rules are to be laid before Parliament, then there is clearly an element of the administrative rules and the exercise of discretion which is undisclosed by the Home Office. This must undermine the authority of Parliament and the primacy of the Immigration Act 1971 as the legal basis for control.

INTERPRETATION OF THE IMMIGRATION RULES

The interpretation of an immigration rule is dependent on its language, nature and form, which may or may not be shared with other rules in the same statement of the rules. This means that it may be misleading to refer collectively to the rules as having the same legal effect. It may even be misleading to refer to an immigration rule as having the same legal effect on every occasion.[45]

The first proposition is demonstrated by the case of *Nisa*.[46] There it was held that the rule on dependent 'widowed' mothers could not be extended to apply to dependent 'divorced' mothers, to whom no immigration rule was applicable given that the position of both was stigmatized in the Muslim society of Pakistan. The Tribunal rejected the argument that, following *Hosenball*, the rules could be interpreted in the way that best gave effect to their intention.[47]

The second proposition is demonstrated in the cases on deportation. Where the court recommends deportation following conviction, the Minister must take into account 'every relevant factor known to him . . .'.[48] Depending on how much weight a decision-maker wishes to give to the 'relevant factors' he could reach different decisions in different cases. Similarly, another deportation rule says that deportation will 'normally be the proper course' where a person contravenes a condition attached to his stay or remains without authorization but that 'full account is to be taken of all the relevant circumstances'.[49] There is a large element of subjective discretion here also, so that in 1977, 1978 and 1979 deportations under this rule numbered 403, 619 and 544 people respectively, whilst in 1980, 1981 and 1982 the numbers rose to 1553, 1345 and 1389 respectively.[50] The Immigration Appeals Tribunal has, however, begun to give careful and detailed guidance on the weight to be given to each of the 'relevant circumstances' after the case of *Muhammed Idrish* in 1985.[51] This is surely right, for as Lord Denning MR said in *GEC* v. *Price Commission*:

> The courts will ensure that the body acts in accordance with the law. If a question arises on the interpretation of words, the courts will decide it by declaring what is the correct interpretation.[52]

Thus depending on the language used, the courts will decide whether a particular rule is prescriptive or descriptive and whether it should be interpreted strictly or liberally. Arguably, a rule such as the one on 'au pairs' can only be applied strictly.[53] But because most immigration rules are deliberately phrased in non-normative language, the courts have more recently inclined towards a broad common-sense approach giving them a purposive construction.[54] Accordingly, in *ex parte Manshoora Begum*, Simon Brown J said that the decided cases indicate that

> the rules should be approached in essentially the same way as the construction of legislation save only less strictly: the fullest rein should be given to the proposition that the more unreasonable the result of giving the phrase its natural and ordinary meaning, the readier would the court be (a) to find the phrase capable of bearing another meaning, and (b) to prefer such other meaning if, contrasted to the meaning first suggested, that other meaning was substantially further from the literal and grammatical sense of the phrase.

In appropriate cases, however, the strict statutory approach could be the right one, taking priority over the common-sense approach:

> But that was not to say if the words were wholly ambiguous that they would be given some other meaning, even in order to accommodate the demands of fairness and reasonableness.[55]

The extent, however, to which the courts are today prepared to go in demanding appropriate standards of reasonableness and common sense from officialdom is seen in the fact that in this case the court took the novel step of severing a part of the rule which said that a dependent relative could be admitted for settlement only if he could establish that he had a standard of living substantially below the average of his own country, because such a rule plainly, the court said, offended against common sense.

CONCLUSIONS

Rules such as the immigration rules are characterized by an informality of approach on grounds that they perform an indispensable function which requires flexibility and ease of use in difficult areas of law and policy. This flexibility is not, however, an unmixed blessing. 'The ability to choose among several methods of policy formulation carries with it the responsibility for choosing wisely . . .'[56]. It must not be forgotten that the courts also have a difficult function to perform. It has not previously been uncommon for them to look at the precision of an administrative rule in order to decide how to review the legality of an action based on it.[57] But even after the great changes heralded by the GCHQ[58] case the words of one leading commentator still ring true:

> What they need to discharge that function is neither philosophizing nor model-making, but hardheaded guidelines for adjudicating disputes between the government and the public. When is a rule so opaque that its application denies a person 'due process of law'? When is it an 'abuse of discretion' to ground actions on an accretion of an *ad hoc* rationale rather than a more comprehensive directive? When does the application of a rule become so mechanistic that it denies an individualized hearing guaranteed by Statute? At what point does its application to borderline cases become arbitrary and capricious or deny equal protection of the law?[59]

Addressing such questions specifically tells us more about the immigration rules than simply classifying them as informal rules. Accordingly, the following conclusions may be drawn from the foregoing analysis.

First, it is clear that the form and content of the rules need to be defined more precisely. Once this is done it should be possible to hive off a sizeable portion of the immigration rules into statutory instruments under the Immigration Act. After all, the immigration appellate system has now been working with the rules for over twenty years, during which time not only the appellate system and those appearing before it have gained in experience and expertise, but new principles and standards of law have been developed. It is important that these are now formally consolidated. The present rules are a clear improvement on the previous rules,[60] but continued reliance upon the

Government department for the rules could mean that further specific details will be slow to emerge. The Immigration Appeals Tribunal has tried to give explicit guidance on the interpretation of certain key phrases, but so long as they remain wholly dependent on a Government department for the formulation of these rules, they will be faced with the unsatisfactory situation where the broad sweep of language confers unstructured discretion on the decision-maker.

Secondly, the Immigration Act itself should contain greater detail and substance. As Christopher McCrudden says, 'Any advances made through code-making should be secured and legitimated by explicit primary legislation', otherwise 'the absence of explicit parliamentary authority in legislation is likely to undermine the legitimacy of the gain'.[61] Certainly, the Immigration Act, and not the rules, should now provide the detailed guidance on how the Minister's discretionary powers are to be exercised.

Thirdly, Parliament should be given more control over the immigration rules by requiring that the rules are specifically approved before they take effect. The present position whereby control is only over a Statement through a negative resolution of either House is unsatisfactory because it means that the rules can continue to have effect even when rejected until such time that a new Statement is placed before Parliament.[62]

Most importantly, it needs to be asked whether the concerns of the Wilson Committee that the immigration system in 1967 was 'fundamentally wrong and inconsistent with the rule of law' are just as real today as they were then, in spite of more than two decades of the purported application of due process to it. Immigration is a difficult issue. In America also, 'immigration law as it has developed over the past one hundred years . . . represents an aberrational form of the typical relationship between statutory interpretation and constitutional law'.[63] In fact, an American judge once despaired. 'We are in the never-never land of the Immigration and Nationality Act, where plain words do not always mean what they say.'[64] He could have added, however, that perhaps the problem is that the words are not always so plain. This is because ultimately there is an attempt by rule-makers to leave in the hands of the decision-maker as much unstructured discretion as possible. This is a matter to which we must now turn in the form of extra-statutory decision-making.

EXTRA-STATUTORY DECISION-MAKING IN IMMIGRATION LAW

The existence of extra-statutory decision-making is recognized by statute under section 19(2) of the Immigration Act 1971. This states that an immigration appeals adjudicator or tribunal[65] in appeal proceedings before it:

> may review any determination of a question of fact on which the decision or action was based; and . . . *no decision or action which is in accordance with the immigration rules shall be treated as having involved the exercise of a discretion by the Secretary of State* by reason only of the fact that he has been requested by or on behalf of the appellant *to depart*, or to authorize an officer *to depart, from the rules and has refused to do so.* (emphasis added)

The reference to departing 'from the rules' recognizes that a decision may be taken outside the immigration rules and is to that extent an important statement of general immigration policy in that it points to the existence of discretion that is unstructured by the published immigration rules. However, what is the nature of this Home Office discretion? It is of two kinds. There is, firstly, the exercise of ministerial discretion in respect of specific applications made exceptionally to the Minister by individuals. Here there do not appear to be any rules, published or unpublished. Secondly, there are the unpublished informal instructions issued by the Minister to immigration personnel to supplement the immigration rules. Here there are rules but they are undisclosed to the public. It is necessary for us to consider both these aspects.

Ministerial Discretion

The Minister's exercise of discretion outside the immigration rules may be based on statute, or it may derive from the Royal Prerogative. For example, the discretion to give or vary leave is governed specifically by statute under section 4(1) of the Immigration Act 1971, which provides that:

> The power under this Act to give or refuse leave to enter the United Kingdom shall be exercised by immigration officers, and to give leave to remain in the United Kingdom, or to vary leave under section 3(3)(a) (whether as regards duration or condition), shall be exercised, by the Secretary of State.

However, where the statute is silent the position is governed more generally by the Royal Prerogative. Glidewell LJ in *ex parte Rajinder Kaur and Others*, described it thus:

> immigration was formerly covered by the royal prerogative and it was a matter which lay entirely within the exercise of

that prerogative. Much of the prerogative powers vested in the Crown in this field have now been superseded by statute but there remains – and this is what the royal prerogative is – a residual power in the Crown through her Majesty's Secretary of State for Home Affairs, to exercise such residual powers as is necessary for the proper control of immigration. In my view the exercise of discretion in relation to leave to enter the realm is an exercise of the remaining part of that prerogative power.[66]

In fact, the Immigration Act 1971, whilst putting the law on a formal basis, expressly recognizes the exercise of prerogative power in this way. Section 33(5) says that 'any power exercisable by Her Majesty in relation to aliens' by virtue of her prerogative 'is to be preserved'.[67] Thus together with section 19(2) cited earlier, section 33(5) shows that there is ample provision within the statutory framework of the Immigration Act 1971 for the exercise of discretionary decision making by the Minister.

The use of ministerial discretion remains an unsatisfactory device nevertheless. At common law this power related specifically to aliens only so that the authority of section 33(5) cannot be said to extend to control of Commonwealth immigration. Indeed, even as regards aliens the precise scope of this power was not always clear.[68] A distinction nevertheless was traditionally maintained between aliens and Commonwealth citizens. Thus, the rules for the admission and treatment of aliens have never been published yet have always been given by the Home Secretary to immigration officers;[69] whereas the rules on Commonwealth citizens were published after 1962 when the first Commonwealth Immigrants Act of that year was passed.[70] Publication here was finally put on a statutory basis under section 3 of the Immigration Act 1971 but the position in relation to the admission of aliens has never been changed. The circumstantial and historical evidence in favour of confining the exercise of the Royal Prerogative to aliens only is therefore compelling and any exercise of ministerial discretionary power that is designed to control Commonwealth immigration is unlawful, and it has been so held by the Court of Appeal in *R v. IAT, ex parte Secretary of State.*[71] In fact in *ex parte Swati*, Watkins J even denied the existence of prerogative powers in relation to friendly aliens.[72]

Ministerial discretion in this area is itself of two kinds. The first kind can be divided into either a case where the rules are drafted so as to exclude an applicant, or into a case where there is simply no rule existing in relation to the type of application being considered. In the first type of case the appellate authorities would have no jurisdiction on the merits[73] but could make a recommendation to the Minister that he act in the applicant's favour by exercising his discretion outside the rules.[74] In the second type of case, however, they would have substantive jurisdiction.[75] The second kind of case is where the effect of the published rules themselves may appear to the Minister to be unjust in a particular case or class of cases and to that extent require the exercise of discretion outside the rules. In such a case, the Minister may, of his own accord, follow a more liberal policy without officially saying so. A well-known case is where the published rules state that children of single parents resident in the United Kingdom are to be refused entry unless there are considerations 'which make exclusion undesirable'.[76] In reality, the Home Office has decided to allow all cases of children under 12 years of age even though this is contrary to official policy and is not mentioned in the published rules. It also appears that after martial law was declared in Poland in 1987, the Home Secretary decided, contrary to the rules, not to return over-stayers to Poland for a time.[77] On 14 June 1989 the Home Secretary announced that many previously unsuccessful applicants for admission who could many years later prove their relationship to their parents settled here, because of DNA genetic tests, may now be admitted. Such applicants were no longer children, being now over 18 years of age, but the Home Secretary would 'consider waiving the requirements of the Rules in certain circumstances'.[78] However, the best example of ministerial discretion is perhaps the grant of 'exceptional leave' by the Secretary of State to refugees who failed to satisfy the requirements of the Geneva Convention.[79] Thus if it is exercised at all, ministerial discretion outside the rules is invariably exercised in favour of individuals and not against them.

Be that as it may, this area is not free from difficulty. The whole area of discretionary concessions is anathema to the legal purist. In the field of revenue law Lord Parker CJ once castigated extra-statutory concessions as 'the word of the Minister outweighing the law of the land'.[80] One question for the purist is whether ministerial discretion is so important to immigration control that it cannot be done away with altogether. The trend in central government nowadays is towards structuring discretion through statutory rules rather than by internal rules. However, one argument against the complete elimination of discretion is that if discretion is replaced by statutory rules, these rules would be more readily amenable to political control and extensive judicial scrutiny which regulators may not welcome. In the case of immigration control, the elimination of governmental discretion is further likely to be politically unacceptable, as it affects considerations of national sovereignty and national interest. In the United States, a study by Professor Abraham Sofaer on the American Immigration and Nationality Service in 1972 recognized this when it concluded that 'discretionary denials were considerably more susceptible to political intervention and administrative reversals then denials based on the more explicit statutory criteria'.[81] In 1984 a secret instruction was issued by the Home Secretary to exclude the American black power advocate, Stokeley Carmichael, even though the instruction was contrary to the published rules.[82] Absolute political control may therefore be a luxury difficult for a government to give up. But against this, it can just as easily be said that in a free and open democracy discretion should be retained for reasons other than merely those of political expediency. This is the view of Dr Vincenzi, who has written that 'often in extra-statutory leave cases the criteria for grant or refusal are never fully known. The objective of an open system that is subject to the rule of law is lost.'[83]

Unpublished Informal Instructions

Unpublished informal instructions are also a well-established technique for the structuring of official administrative discretion. Their relationship to the more formal rules, such as the immigration rules, is described as follows by Diver:

> Administrative rule-makers typically promulgate two kinds of rules: 'external' rules addressed to persons charged with the enforcement of the 'internal rules'. There is often a substantial difference in the context of the two types of rules. Sometimes an internal rule directly contradicts an external rule. More commonly, internal rules seek to establish priorities for the allocation of resources to the enforcement of facially absolute commands.[84]

As with ministerial discretion more generally, unpublished informal instructions cannot be accepted with equanimity. 'Secret law', K.C. Davis once wrote, 'whether in the form of precedents or in the form of rules, has no place in any decent system of justice.'[85] In 1969, the *Report of the Committee on Immigration Appeals*, whilst paradoxically setting out to establish a system of immigration appeals in this area, had 'no objection to the issue of supplementary unpublished instructions or advice on matters of administrative detail and procedure',[86] which were quite separate from the 'General Instructions' that were more formally given. The Immigration Act 1971 was rather more specific about it. Under Schedule 2, paragraph 1(3) any (unpublished) instructions were required to be 'not inconsistent with the immigration rules'. This stipulation recognizes the existence of such instructions under modern immigration legislation, which has led Marrington, a former immigration officer, to observe that there is:

concealed behind the statutory endorsed rules a system of instructions, circulars and practices which may truly be called the 'hidden agenda' for the control of immigration. This not only confines, structures and checks the discretion left open within the immigration rules (and exercised by subordinate officials) but also embraces policy-making at the highest level for the regulation of these categories of would-be immigrants who fall outside the provisions of the rules.[87]

What is more disconcerting, however, is the existence of instructions in the past which, contrary to Schedule 2, paragraph 1(3) of the 1971 Act, have had the appearance of being inconsistent with the immigration rules. It is here that discretionary activity outside the rules has caused particular concern.

This may be illustrated by reference to the admission of children. Under the Commonwealth Immigrants Act 1962, when immigration control was first applied to Commonwealth citizens, the right of their children to join them in the UK was expressly preserved by statute.[88] But in 1968 the second Commonwealth Immigrants Act severely restricted this right so that children joining one parent had to show that that parent had had sole responsibility in their upbringing or that family or other special considerations made exclusion undesirable – for example, where the other parent is physically or mentally incapable of looking after the child.[89] This reflected the fact that most cases arose from the West Indies, where children were frequently cared for by relatives or even friends before seeking to join a parent here. In 1970 accordingly, the rules substituted 'family or other considerations'.[90] But it was the Immigration Appeals Tribunal (at that time even more executive-minded than the executive) that added the gloss 'serious and compelling'[91] family or other considerations which the 1980 rules were later drafted to reflect and which has been incorporated in the rules ever since.[92]

As far as age was concerned, under the 1970 rules, all dependent children, whether married or not, could be admitted for settlement.[93] In 1978, however, the Select Committee on Immigration proposed that 'the admission . . . of a child . . . should normally be *limited* to children under 12 years of age' (emphasis added). Unpublished instructions from the Foreign and Commonwealth Office in 1978 (now out of date) then appeared to be carrying forward the policy of the Select Committee by focusing on children under 12 years:

8.12.8. Children aged 12 or over *will not qualify* for admission as dependants to join a single parent unless there are *exceptional compassionate circumstances* which make exclusion undesirable. There must be evidence that the child is suffering from conditions which make the continuance of its current mode of life *intolerable*. (emphasis added).

However, the rules in 1980[94] stipulated for the first time the age of majority as the relevant threshold: 'if the requirements of paragraph 52 are satisfied, children under 18, provided that they are unmarried, *are to be admitted for settlement*' (emphasis added). It could be argued that there is no inconsistency here between the 'external' and 'internal' rules, that the effect of the instructions overall is to benefit children under 12 rather than create hardship for those over 12. However, it is respectfully submitted that there is a distinct difference in emphasis in the internal unpublished instructions to immigration officers which will undoubtedly affect the balance of decision-making by them. Indeed, in the words of Vaughan Bevan, this particular provision 'is an excellent example of the extent to which internal guidance can modify the rules'.[95]

The inconsistency is, in fact, symptomatic of the conflicts between the demands of official and unofficial policy in immigration control. Take, for example, the test of 'sole responsibility' that we have mentioned above. How is a child to satisfy this? The Home Secretary has not given any guidance in the immigration rules on this, so the appellate authorities have naturally tried to formulate their own workable definitions, with the result that in *Emmanuel* it was said that 'sole responsibility' must not be strictly construed because:

> there must be in nearly all cases some form of responsibility of the relative or grandmother with whom the child lives. . . . We do not therefore think the literal or absolute sole responsibility of the parent in the UK could ever be established.[96]

The unpublished 1978 instructions interpret 'sole responsibility' in a different manner altogether:

> 5.12.3. The phrase 'sole responsibility' is intended to carry the idea that the sponsoring parent's responsibility should have been *exclusive from the outset*. . . . If the responsibility . . . falls *entirely on the shoulders* of one parent, then there are good grounds for permitting the child to enter . . . (emphasis added)

The instructions continue:

> 8.12.6. The parents claiming to have had 'sole responsibility' should be expected to produce evidence that he or she has been responsible for the child for a period of some years and has *consistently supported* the child, either by *direct personal*

care or by regular and substantial financial remittances. . . .
If, for example, a mother applies for a child to join her and
it emerges that the father lives nearby and takes an active
interest in the child's welfare, the application should normally
be refused. (emphasis added)

This extensive guidance which the Minister or the Government of
the day gives to its officials is not given to the appellate authorities,
who are presumably not aware of it, but who ultimately have to
adjudicate on the merits of an application before them. Inevitably,
the officials will apply one standard of eligibility and the appellate
authorities will apply another. Even when the adjudicating authorities
resolve this conflict by giving a determination of the appropriate standard at the hearing, can it realistically be assumed that this will be
acceptable to the officials, who have their own instructions to heed?
The result is quite likely to cause very considerable confusion to applicants. Happily, the philosophy in *Emmanuel* has now, however, been
approved by the High Court.[97]

Finally, it may be noted that unpublished instructions are likely to
be less precise in their formulation than the more formal 'external'
rules. Diver states that 'since they are addressed to different audiences
and serve different functions, the two types of rules would be expected
to have a different degree of precision'.[98] In fact, even as a body the
unpublished rules, like the immigration rules, can be of varying precision. In the case of the 1978 instructions, the precision appears to be
less where the instructions are intended to benefit the applicant. For
example, the unofficial Home Office policy of admitting all children
under 12 outside the immigration rules is couched in the following
terms:

8.12.9. The application of the 'under 12' rules may give rise
to difficulty where there are two or more children, one over
12 and one under 12. It is not possible to lay down general
rules for those cases, but the principle underlying the rules of
the control is to *preserve the unity* of families. (emphasis
added)

This can be construed either as allowing two or more children to enter
or as refusing them leave to enter on the basis that the stipulated principle of family unity is thereby maintained. It is submitted that if
secret instructions are to become the norm in the field of government
and administration, they will have to achieve a higher degree of rule
precision than this if they are to properly convey their import to the
officials to whom they are addressed.

CONCLUSIONS

Can discretion 'outside the rules' be eliminated from the immigration process? In 1969 K.C. Davis revolutionized thinking on administrative law when, by focusing on discretionary powers, he called for the confining, structuring and checking of 'unnecessary'[99] bureaucratic discretions. It is submitted that the first part of ministerial discretion that we discussed above could not, and should not, be removed since it is not an 'unnecessary' discretion. The Minister's exercise of discretion here is, more often than not, for the benefit of the applicant. Moreover, the context in which it operates, where considerations of national interest and security loom large, would suggest that its removal would be difficult.

The more important question is whether discretionary decisions are subject to review by the immigration appellate authorities, who (rather than the Courts) get to hear the vast majority of immigration cases. The answer to this question lies in section 19(1)(a)(i) of the Immigration Act 1971 which states that an appeal shall be allowed if 'the decision or action against which the appeal is brought *was not in accordance with the law* . . .' (emphasis added). The reference to 'the law' refers to English law in general whatever its source,[100] so that to the extent that a principle declared generally applicable by the High Court is expressly or impliedly applicable to immigration decisions, the appellate authorities are bound by section 19(1)(a)(i) to recognize that application.[101] However, section 19(2) still excludes from appellate jurisdiction a decision by the Secretary of State not to depart from the immigration rules – that is, not to exercise a discretion outside the rules in favour of the applicant. Such a decision would, on a narrow construction, be 'in accordance with the law' because it complies with the rules, so the appellate authorities cannot say that the discretion ought to have been exercised differently here.[102]

The part of our discussion on unpublished informal instructions gives cause for much greater concern, however. Much of this guidance can properly be put in the published immigration rules, so that the informal rules can to a great extent be eliminated. Davis had said that discretion could be structured through 'more elaborate administrative rule-making'. However, this discussion suggests that if administrative rules are to be promulgated this must be done with clarity and precision and always with the needs of open government and democratic principle in mind. Ultimately, as this book has shown, all problems of immigration control can only be resolved from this perspective – or we stand to witness further human hardship.

NOTES AND REFERENCES

A substantial part of this chapter was first published by the author in his article (1992) Rule-Making and the Immigration Rules – A Retreat from Law? *Statute Law Review* 13(2), pp. 150–64. The text is reproduced by permission of Oxford University Press.

1 Fuller, L.L. and Perdue, W.R. (1936–37) The Reliance Interest in Contract Damages. *Yale Law Journal* 46, p. 52.
2 Baldwin, R. (1990) Why Rules Don't Work. *Modern Law Review* 53 (pp. 321–37), p. 321.
3 (1943) Eliot, T.S. 'Little Gidding'; from *Four Quartets*. London.
4 Per Cumming-Bruce LJ in *R* v. *Secretary of State for the Home Department, ex parte Hosenball* [1977] 3 All ER, 452 CA, pp. 465–6.
5 See especially Baldwin and Houghton (1986) Circular Arguments: The Status and Legitimacy of Administrative Rules. *Public Law*, p. 239: Baldwin (1990) Why Rules Don't Work. *Modern Law Review*, pp. 321–37; Ganz, G. (1987) *Quasi-legislation*. London; McCrudden, C. (1988) Codes in a Cold Climate: Administrative Rule-Making by the Commission for Racial Equality. *Modern Law Review*, p. 409; Drabble, R. and Lynes, T. (1989) The Social Fund: Discretion or Control? *Public Law*, pp. 297–322; Lord Campbell of Alloway (1985) Codes of Practice as an Alternative to Legislation. *Statute Law Review*, pp. 127–32. Other works include: Allen, C.K. (1965) *Law and Orders*. London; Beatson, J. (1979) Legislative Control of Administrative Rulemaking: Lessons from the British Experience. *Cornell International Law Journal* 12, p. 199; Beatson (1981) A British View of Vermont Yankee. *Tulane Law Review* 55, p. 435. Some American writers should also be considered, including Diver, C.S. (1983) The Optimal Precision of Administrative Rules. *Yale Law Journal* 93, p. 65; Shapiro, D.S. (1965) The Choice of Rulemaking or Adjudication in the Development of Administrative Policy. *Harvard Law Review* 78, p. 921.
6 See particularly the works by Baldwin and Houghton and by Ganz, note 5 *supra*.
7 Although such detailed analysis of regulatory context has on the whole been lacking, some excellent discussions do, however, exist in the general works. See, for example, Legomsky, S. (1987) *Immigration and the Judiciary*, pp. 50–71. Oxford; Macdonald, I. and Blake, N. (1991) *Immigration Law and Practice*. London; Bevan, V. (1987) *The Development of British Immigration Law*, pp. 13–14. London; Harlow, C. and Rawlings, R. (1984) *Law and Administration*, 510–17. London; Turpin, C. (1990) *British Government and the Constitution*, pp. 400–1. London. Recently the more specific works have been Vincenzi, C. and Marrington, D. (1992) *Immigration Law: The Rules Explained*. London; and Vincenzi, C. (1992) Extra-statutory Ministerial Discretion in Immigration Law. *Public Law*, pp. 300–21. Both of these provide an invaluable insight into this area.
8 See Glidewell LJ's dictum in *R* v. *Secretary of State for the Home Department, ex parte Rajinder Kaur* (1987) Imm AR 278, at p. 291.
9 The words are those of K.C. Davis: see Davis, K.C. (1969) *Discretionary Justice: A Preliminary Inquiry*, 217, at p. 219.
10 For example, Reginald Maudling, the Home Secretary, even argued against an

affirmative procedure in Parliament for the immigration rules in case he had 'to act quickly and could not' because Parliament was not sitting: HC Deb., Vol. 819, cols. 482-3 (16 June 1971).

11 Wilson Committee Report Cmnd 3387, p. 5, para. 15.

12 HC Deb., Vol. 633, col. 319 (6 February 1962).

13 See *Visa Officer, Islamabad* v. *Saeedan* (1983) Imm AR 131.

14 See the Statutory Instruments Act 1946, s. 1(1)(b).

15 The Pollution Act 1974, s. 71, so provides in the case of codes of practice for minimizing noise and makes the statutory instruments subject to a negative resolution.

16 See, for example, Ganz, note 5 above, at p. 29.

17 In *R* v. *Immigration Appeal Tribunal, ex parte Joyles* (1972)

18 See (1983) *Statement of Changes in Immigration Rules*, HC 169. See also Mr Davis, HC Deb., Vol. 823, col. 591 (19 October 1971).

19 (1978) Imm AR 212.

20 This point about ineffective parliamentary control of the rules is not always appreciated because on a number of occasions since 1971 the immigration rules have caught the attention of the House – sometimes in the most dramatic circumstances. Take, for example, the very first instance that this happened in November 1972, during the Parliament of 1970–74, and leading to the Government suffering its most important defeat in post-war parliamentary history. This defeat was, until 1976, the most significant suffered by a government on the floor of the House, the first Government defeat in this era where a three-line whip had been issued, and one with important constitutional implications in so far as it dispelled a widely held view that a government defeated on a three-line whip is required to resign. (See Norton, P. (1976) Intra-party Dissent in the House of Commons: A Case Study. The Immigration Rules 1972, *Parliamentary Affairs* 29 (pp. 404–17) at p. 404). The immigration rules proposed by the Heath Government were felt necessary on account of Britain's accession to the European Communities, but when it was suggested that EC nationals should be more favourably treated than non-patrial Commonwealth citizens, who were mostly from the Old Commonwealth, backbenchers revolted. (See *The Economist*, 25 November 1972 at p. 23). Similarly, Mrs Thatcher's first defeat, during her first administration of 1979–83, came when her Government proposed stricter rules over 'foreign spouses'. See HC Deb. Vol. 29, col. 282 (22 October 1982). The *Proposals for Revision of Immigration Rules*, Cmnd 8683, were then debated for a full day before the Home Secretary could lay a statement of the rules before the House (see above, Vol. 31, cols. 692–755). In all such cases, it was the statement of the rules which had been annulled, but the rules continued to take effect without amendment, until a new set was placed before Parliament.

21 See Ganz, note 5 above, at p. 97.

22 *R* v. *Immigration Appeal Tribunal, ex parte Bakhtaur Singh* (1986) 1 WLR 910 at 917. Quoted also by McNeil in *R* v. *Immigration Appeal Tribunal ex parte Takeo and Takeo* (1987) Imm AR 522 QBD.

23 E.g. see the previous rules; see (1983) *Statement of Changes in Immigration Rules*, HC 169, para. 97 before the current ones were placed before Parliament on 23 March 1990 (see (1990) *Statements of Changes in Immigration Rules*, HC 251).

24 Baldwin and Houghton, note 5 above, at p. 263.

25 *Ibid*. For example, in the current rules see para. 34 (work permit holders); para. 23 (visits for the purpose of obtaining private medical treatment); para. 39 (permit-free categories of employment).

26 Ganz, note 5 above, at p. 98.

27 Baldwin and Houghton, note 5 above, at p. 263. E.g. in the previous rules see para. 62 regarding 'children born in the United Kingdom who are not British citizens'. The point has also been made by Lord Bridge in *R* v. *Immigration Appeal Tribunal, ex parte Bakhtaur Singh* (1986) 1 WLR 910.

28 Per Stephenson LJ in *Pearson* v. *IAT* (1978) Imm Ar 212, CA at p. 225.

29 See para. 162 of the current rules.

30 Para. 33 of the current rules on au pairs states that 'A girl admitted under an *au pair* agreement has no claim to stay in the United Kingdom in some other capacity.' There is no reason why this rule could not be made by statutory instrument.

31 Para. 21 of the current rules, which states that 'Nothing in these rules is to be construed as requiring action contrary to the United Kingdom's obligations' under the 'Convention and Protocol relating to the status of Refugees'. This is an important statement of principle which should not be consigned to the shadowy realm of quasi-legislation.

32 Para. 22 of the current rules, which state that a visitor 'is to be admitted if he satisfied the immigration officer that he is genuinely seeking entry for the period of the visit as stated by him and that for that period he will maintain and accommodate himself and any dependants . . . without working or recourse to public funds, and can meet the cost of the return or onward journey'.

33 The deportation rules, including the power to deport, the rights of appeal, deportation following a conviction and the procedure to be followed could also all quite easily be put into statutory instrument. (See paras 155, 157, 164 of the current rules.)

34 Section 3(5) of the 1971 Act introduced the specific power to deport the family of a deportee up to eight weeks after the deportee had left the UK. Most cases here are those of deportation following the husband's conviction and deportation thereafter or following his breach of conditions of stay.

35 See Diver, note 5 above at p. 106.

36 This is under s. 3(5)(b) of the Immigration Act 1971, and the formulation 'if the Secretary of State deems . . .' indicates the amplitude of discretionary power in the parent statute itself, where the Secretary of State may act to deport someone for reasons of political nature or national security or for considerations of public good. Bevan says that 'At worst, it epitomizes the ultimate discretionary power which the Crown has always claimed as the sole arbiter of the expulsion of aliens.' See note 7 above at p. 308.

37 438 F. 2nd 1028 (1971).

38 Under Sched. 2, para. 1(3) of the Immigration Act 1971 any (unpublished) instructions given to the Secretary of State are required to be 'not inconsistent with the immigration rules'. This recognizes the existence of supplementary instructions.

39 Diver, note 5 above at p. 67.

40 The power is extended to the Immigration Appeals Tribunal under s. 19(4) and

20(1). At the risk of oversimplification, judges have sometimes sought to make this point through the language of legal effects. Thus in the well-known case of *Hosenball*, where an American journalist was deported for allegedly publishing information harmful to national security, the Court of Appeal (Geoffrey Lane, Cumming-Bruce, and Lord Denning LJ) unanimously held that the rules are in a broad sense 'rules of practice and not delegated legislation amounting to strict rules of law' (see *R* v. *Secretary of State for the Home Department, ex parte Hosenball* [1977] 1 WLR 766 at p. 788). The majority view expressed by Cumming-Bruce LJ was that the rules have 'legal effect in the field of the appellate process to the adjudicator or the tribunal' because s. 19 requires the appellate authorities to enforce them (at p. 788).

41 See *R* v. *Immigration Appeal Tribunal, ex parte Joseph* (1977) Imm AR 70 at p. 73. Also see *R* v. *Immigration Appeal Tribunal, ex parte Alexander* [1982] 1 WLR 1076.

42 As for example in *ex parte Khan*, where the Home Secretary's decision in an adoption case was not based on an adoption circular which he had himself issued. *R* v. *Secretary of State for the Home Department, ex parte Khan* (1984) 1 WLR 1337.

43 In one well-known case the Home Secretary was held to have construed the rules too strictly: see *R* v. *Immigration Appeal Tribunal, ex parte Shaikh* (1987) 1 WLR 1107.

44 In *Pearson* v. *Immigration Appeal Tribunal* (1978) Imm AR 212 at pp. 224–5, Stephenson LJ said in the Court of Appeal that the immigration rules do not lay down 'an inevitable rule admitting to no exceptions or departures'.

45 As Ganz has said, the rules habitually use 'the language of exhortion and advice' and such advice may differ for each particular set of facts. See Ganz, note 5 above at p. 98. Stephenson LJ was closer to the truth when he said that the immigration rules 'mark out guidelines some more rigid than others, and declare the policy which regulates the control of immigration more firmly in some cases than others'. See Pearson, *ibid*. p. 224. The Court of Appeal previously appears to have erred in this respect in the two well-known cases of *R* v. *Chief Immigration Officer, Heathrow Airport, ex parte Salamat Bibi* (1976) 2 WLR 979 and *Hosenball*, note 40 above.

46 *Nisa* v. *Secretary of State for the Home Department* (1979–80) Imm AR 90.

47 The same strict approach was taken in *R* v. *Immigration Appeal Tribunal, ex parte A.K. Ali* (1979–80) Imm AR 195, where the rules for control after entry had made no provision for the status of 'returning resident' to be claimed by a visitor, but the control on entry rules did. The Tribunal did not allow a cross-fertilization between the two to cater for this situation and so the divorced wife of a man settled in the UK was refused the status of a 'returning resident' and refused entry. Other cases of a similar nature are *ex parte Ram* (1979) 1 WLR 148 QBD, *ex parte Kharrazi* (1980) 1 WLR 1396, *ex parte Nathwani* (1979–80) Imm AR 9, and *Gurdev Singh* (1988) Imm AR 510. According to some observers this is of the essence of an administrative rule. Their very informality 'demonstrates the utility of such rules to administrators. The courts are reluctant to construe them in a manner that creates due process rights in individuals . . .' and yet 'challenges to the legality of such rules can . . . be deflected with some ease by

attributing informal status to them'. See Baldwin and Houghton, note 5 above, at pp. 251–2.

48 The rule in full says: 'every reluctant factor known to him, including: age, length of residence in the United Kingdom; personal history, including character, conduct and employment record, domestic circumstances; the nature of the offences of which the person was convicted; previous criminal record; compassionate circumstances; any representations received on the person's behalf' (see rule 164 of the current rules).

49 Rule 166 of the current rules.

50 *Control of Immigration Statistics* (Cmnd 9844), Table 16.

51 The tribunal held that the decision to deport must specifically indicate how it was reached. In this case, 'The Chief Adjudicator did not refer to the possibility that the public interest may vary depending on the *length* and *nature* of the overstay, nor did he consider in his conclusion the precise context of the decision to deport in his case' (emphasis added). See *Muhammed Idrish* v. *Secretary of State for the Home Department* (1985) Imm AR 155 at pp. 173, 176. Different criteria are, however, employed by the High Court in the exercise of its *Wednesbury* jurisdiction where it will only look at the the the reasonableness of the decision-maker's decision, so that where in *Sohnia Malhi*, the appellant argued that there was only 'a bland reference' in the notice of deportation to the 'relevant factors', Popplewell J held that it was not necessary to set out each and every factor to show that it had been considered. See *R* v. *Sohnia Mahli* (1989) QBD d. 1 September 1989 Co/936/89. See now also *Sohnia Malhi* v. *Secretary of State for the Home Department* [1990] 2 Imm AR 275.

52 ICR (1975) 1 at 12. Lord Scarman said in a similar case, *HTV* v. *Price Commission*, that 'the interpretation of statutory language (including the language of delegated legislation) is a matter of law' and that 'it is for the courts to determine the meaning'. See ICR (1976) 170 at pp. 188–9.

53 Para. 33, note 30 above.

54 *Alexander* v. *Immigration Appeal Tribunal* (1982) 1 WLR 1080. Also see *R* v. *Immigration Appeal Tribunal, ex parte Bakhtaur Singh* (1986) 1 WLR 910.

55 *R* v. *Immigration Appeal Tribunal, ex parte Manshoora Begum* (1986) Imm AR 385. Other more recent cases include *ex parte Mohammed Shayequr Rahman* (1987) Imm AR 313 CA at pp. 322–3, *Mamon* (1988) Imm AR 364 at p. 368, *Sayana Khatun* [1989] 1 All ER 482, and *Mario Joseph* [1988] Imm AR 329.

56 See Shapiro above, note 5.

57 Prime examples here are the cases of *Salamat Bibi* and *Hosenball*, above, at note 45.

58 As is well known, this case established beyond doubt that immigration decisions made through the exercise of ministerial prerogative power are reviewable, on the basis that provided the subject-matter of a prerogative power is *justiciable* so as not to involve, for example, questions of national security (i.e. a matter on which the court can adjudicate), judicial review is possible on the grounds of illegality, irrationality, and procedural impropriety. See *Council for Civil Service Unions* v. *Minister for the Civil Service* (1985) 1 AC 374 at pp. 410–11 and p. 417.

59 Diver above, note 5 at pp. 106–7.

60 For example, notes 28 and 32. The current rules do not, for instance, suggest that

mere compliance with formal requirements is not conclusively in favour of an individual or designate rules as merely 'principles' to be followed, in the way that the previous rules did. Manifestly, therefore, the language of the rules can be improved.

61 McCrudden above, note 1 at p. 436.

62 The 40-day annulment period is more noted for the way in which it favours the administration. It leaves insufficient time for parliamentary debate. Members are not always aware of what the rules say or mean and the Home Department is often reluctant to alter completed instruments. In 1977 Mr Alex Lyon, a former immigration Minister, failed to move a prayer to annul a new statement of the rules within the 40 days. When eventually he did succeed in raising the matter in Parliament, he was prevented from proceeding with his motion because the Government had pre-empted his action by tabling its own motion to take note of the intended amendment, see HC Deb., Vol 932, cols. 1333-34 (24 May 1977). Similarly, see Mr Davis, HC Deb., Vol. 823, col. 592 (19 October 1971) after the changes made to the rules in 1971 by the Home Secretary which were not discussed in Parliament.

63 See Motomura, H. (1990) Immigration Law after a Century of Plenary Power: Phantom Constitutional Norms and Statutory Interpretation, Yale LJ 3, pp. 545–613 at p. 549. See also Gilbey (1991) Deciding Who Gets In: Decision-Making by Immigration Inspectors. *Law and Society Review*, 25, pp. 571–99, and Schuck (1984) The Transformation of Immigration Law. *Columbia Law Review*, 84, pp. 1–90.

64 *Yuen Sang Low* v. *Attorney-General*, 479 F. 2d 820, 821 (1973).

65 Section 20(1) states that in appeals from an adjudicator to the Tribunal 'the Tribunal may affirm the determination or make any other observation which could have been made by the adjudicator'.

66 *R* v. *Secretary of State for the Home Department, ex parte Rajinder Kaur* (1987) Imm AR 278 at p. 291.

67 In Parliament also it has been well recognized that 'The exercise of immigration control is the exercise of a prerogative under the discretion of [The Home Secretary]. The rules are a guidance to the officials and the tribunal about how they should operate, but there is still a reserve discretion which all Governments use': See HC Deb. Vol. 905, col. 599 (12 February 1976).

68 See Thornberry (1963) Dr Soblen and the Alien Law of the United Kingdom, 12 ICLQ 414 at pp. 422–8.

69 See Aliens Order 1953 (No. 1671) reg. 30(2).

70 Cmnd 3387 para. 65.

71 [1990] 1 WLR 1138.

72 *R* v. *Secretary of State, ex parte Swati* [1986] 1 WLR 477. Also see *R* v. *Secretary of State, ex parte Kaygusuz* [1991] Imm AR 300, 301. Earlier, however, the courts appear to have assumed the existence of this power. In *ex parte Prajapati* the scope of prerogative power was automatically assumed to cover Commonwealth citizens by Forbes LJ in the High Court. In *ex parte Firat* Simon Brown J in the same court held that the Secretary of State had 'an overriding discretion' arising from the prerogative 'to authorise the admission of persons in the United Kingdom and to authorise persons already in the United Kingdom to remain'.

The Court of Appeal too earlier said that the Home Secretary has a common law power to this effect. See the following authorities respectively for these propositions: *R* v. *Immigration Appeal Tribunal, ex parte Prajapati* (1981) Imm AR 199; *R* v. *Immigration Appeal Tribunal, ex parte Firat*, 12 January 1983 (unreported); *R* v. *Secretary of State for the Home Department, ex parte Khan* (1984) 1 WLR 1337 at p. 1344 (per Parker LJ).

73 Section 19(2) of the Immigration Act 1971 prohibits this. It lays down that an 'adjudicator [or Tribunal] may review any determination of a question of fact on which the decision or action was based . . .' *but that 'no decision or action which is in accordance with the immigration rules shall be treated as having involved the exercise of a discretion by the Secretary of State* by reason only of the fact that he has been requested by or on behalf of the appellant to depart, or to authorize an officer to *depart, from the rules and has refused to do so'*. (emphasis added).

74 See, for example, *Kalvinder Singh* v. *Secretary of State for the Home Department*. TH/51354/79 (2012) d. 21.4.91 (unreported).

75 This is because under section 19(1)(ii) the appellate authorities are required to allow an appeal if they consider 'where the decision or action involved the *exercise of a discretion by the Secretary of State* or an officer that the discretion should have been exercised differently' (emphasis added).

76 See the current rules: (1990) *Statement of Changes in Immigration Rules*, HC 251 at para. 53 (f).

77 See *Secretary of State for the Home Department* v. *Bialek* TH/89418/82 (2476) d. 20.10.82 (unreported).

78 HC Deb., Vol. 154, col. 462 (14 June 1989).

79 See further, p. 318 of Vincenzi, *supra*.

80 *R* v. *Commrs of Customs & Excise, ex parte Cooke and Stephenson* (1970) 1 All ER 1068 at p. 1072.

81 Quoted from Diver, C.S. (1983) The Optimal Precision of Administrative Rules (1983) 93 Yale LJ, 65 at p. 93 as Sofaer (1972) The Change of Status Adjudication: A Case Study of the Informal Agency Process. 1. *J. Legal Stud.* 349, pp. 365–93.

82 *The Guardian*, 9 February 1984.

83 Vincenzi, *op. cit.* p. 319.

84 Diver, *supra* at p. 76.

85 Davis, K.C. (1972) *Discretionary Justice*, p. 110. Baton Rouge, LA.

86 *Report of the Committee on Immigration Appeals* (August 1967). Cmnd 3387 at p. 511, para. 65.

87 Marrington, D.K. (1987) Commitment and Contradiction in Immigration Law *Legal Stud.*, pp. 272–91 at p. 274.

88 See section 2(2) of the 1962 Act and the rules made under that Act: (1966) Commonwealth Immigrants Act 1962 (Instructions to Immigration Officers) Cmnd 3064, para. 26.

89 (1968) Commonwealth Immigrants Act 1962 and 1968 (Instructions to Immigration Officers); Cmnd 3566, paras 1 and 2.

90 (1978) Commonwealth Immigrants Act 1962 and 1968, Instructions to Immigration Officers Cmnd 4298, para. 40. Subsequently, see (1973) *Statement of*

Immigration Rules for Control on Entry (Commonwealth Citizens); HC 79, para. 43. Also see (1973) *Statement of Immigration Rules for Control on Entry* (EEC and Other Non-Commonwealth Nationals); HC 81, para. 38.

91 See, for example, *Campbell* [1972] Imm AR 115, *Howard* [1972] Imm AR 115, *Ravat* [1974] Imm AR 79.

92 *Statement of Changes in Immigration Rules* (23 March 1990) HC 251, para. 53(f).

93 Cf. (1970) Commonwealth Immigrants Act 1962 and 1968. *Instructions for Immigration Officers*, Cmnd 4298, para. 40.

94 (1980) Statement of Changes in Immigration Rules HC 394, para. 45.

95 Bevan, *op. cit.* p. 256.

96 *Emmanuel* v. *Secretary of State for the Home Department* (1972) Imm AR 69.

97 *R* v. *IAT, ex parte Sajid Mohammed* [1988] Imm AR 121.

98 Diver, *op. cit.* p. 76.

99 See his book *Discretionary Justice, op. cit.* p. 110.

100 *Dawood Mohd. Patel* v. *Secretary of State for the Home Department* [1990] Imm AR 479.

101 *Aujla* (unreported) (6459) and *Sohnia Malhi* v. *Secretary of State for the Home Department* [1990] Im AR 275; [1990] 2 WLR 92.

102 *Dawood Mohd. Patel, op. cit.* Also see *Somasundaram* v. *ECO, Columbo* [1990] Imm AR 16.

Appendix

The following tables relate to the processing, in three cities of the Indian sub-continent, of applications for settlement made during the mid-1970s by wives and children seeking to join their husbands and fathers, respectively, settled in the UK.

When Alex Lyon became Minister of State for Immigration in February 1974 he changed the instructions to immigration officers, as explained on p. 88. In June 1976 he was dismissed from his position. The tables suggest that, as a result of the new instructions, the proportion of applications granted rose during 1975; however, they fell back again in the second half of 1976.

Source of tables: Adapted from minutes of evidence taken before the Select Committee on Race Relations and Immigration, 21 April 1977.

Islamabad (Pakistan)

Year	Applications refused (%)	Applications referred/deferred for enquiries (%)	Applications granted (%)
1974, 1st quarter	8	48	44
1974, 2nd quarter	10	47	43
1974, 3rd quarter	18	46	36
1974, 4th quarter	16	41	43
1975, 1st quarter	15	28	57
1975, 2nd quarter	13	27	60
1975, 3rd quarter	13	28	59
1975, 4th quarter	10	22	68
1976, 1st quarter	9	25	66
1976, 2nd quarter	14	31	56
1976, 3rd quarter	24	34	42
1976, 4th quarter	22	30	48

New Delhi (India)

Year	Applications refused (%)	Applications referred/deferred for enquiries (%)	Applications granted (%)
1974, 1st quarter	12	33	55
1974, 2nd quarter	16	20	64
1974, 3rd quarter	11	26	63
1974, 4th quarter	11	33	56
1975, 1st quarter	7	25	69
1975, 2nd quarter	3	24	72
1975, 3rd quarter	7	25	68
1975, 4th quarter	4	21	75
1976, 1st quarter	5	28	67
1976, 2nd quarter	1	22	77
1976, 3rd quarter	8	26	66
1976, 4th quarter	12	29	59

Dacca (Bangladesh)

Year	Applications refused (%)	Applications referred/deferred for enquiries (%)	Applications granted (%)
1974, 1st quarter	19	65	16
1974, 2nd quarter	22	53	25
1974, 3rd quarter	12	61	27
1974, 4th quarter	6	70	24
1975, 1st quarter	5	50	45
1975, 2nd quarter	5	44	51
1975, 3rd quarter	6	43	51
1975, 4th quarter	9	42	49
1976, 1st quarter	10	48	42
1976, 2nd quarter	10	51	39
1976, 3rd quarter	22	54	24
1976, 4th quarter	25	53	22

Select Bibliography

BOOKS

Allen, C.K. (1965) *Law and Orders*. London.

Anderson, N. (1978) *Liberty, Law and Justice*. London.

Anwar, M. (1979) *The Myth of Return: Pakistanis in Britain*. London.

Anwar, M. (1980) *Votes and Policies: Ethnic Minorities and the General Election of 1979*. London.

Bevan, V. (1987) *The Development of British Immigration Law*. London.

Blackstone, W. (1965) *Commentaries*. London.

Castles, S. and Kosack, G. (1973) *Immigrant Workers and Class Structures in Western Europe*. Oxford.

Coke, E. (1788) *The First Part of the Institutes of the Laws of England* (ed. by F. Hargrave and C. Butler). London.

Crossman, R. (1975) *Diaries of a Cabinet Minister*, Vol. 1. London.

Cunningham, W. (1969) *Alien Immigrants to England*. London.

Davis, K.C. (1972) *Discretionary Justice*. Baton Rouge, LA.

Deakin, N. (1970) *Colour, Citizenship and British Society*. London.

Dicey, A.V. (1910) *The Law of the Constitution*. London.

Dummett, A. (1973) *A New Immigration Policy*. London.

Dummett, A. and Nicol, A. (1990) *Subjects, Citizens, Aliens and Others*. London.

Dummett, M. (1978) *Immigration: Where the Debate Goes Wrong*. London.

Evans, J.M. (1983) *Immigration Law*. London.

Foot, P. (1965) *Immigration and Race in British Politics*. Harmondsworth.

Fransman, L. (1989) *British Nationality Law*. London.

181

Freeman, G. (1979) *Immigrant Labour and Racial Conflict in Industrial Societies 1945–1975*. Princeton, NJ.

Fryer, P. (1984) *Staying Power*. London.

Gainer, B. (1972) *The Alien Invasion*. London.

Ganz, G. (1974) *Administrative Procedures*. London.

Ganz, G. (1987) *Quasi-legislation: Recent Developments in Secondary Legislation*. London.

Garrard, J.A. (1971) *The English and Immigration, 1880–1910*. Oxford.

Gartner, L.P. (1971) *The Jewish Immigrant in England, 1908–1914*. London.

Geipel, J. (1969) *The Europeans: An Ethnological Survey*. London.

George, M.D. (1965) *London Life in the Eighteenth Century*. London.

Goodwin-Gill, G.S. (1978) *International Law and the Movement of Persons between States*. Oxford.

Gordon, P. (1981) *Passport Raids and Checks*. London.

Grant, L. and Martin, I. (1982) *Immigration Law and Practice*. London.

Griffith, J.A.G. (1960) *Coloured Immigrants in Britain*. Oxford.

Hammar, T. (1985) *European Immigration Policy*. Cambridge.

Hall, W.E. (1924) *A Treatise on International Law*. Oxford.

Harlow, C. and Rawlings, R. (1984) *Law and Administration*. London.

Hartley, T.C. (1978) *EEC Immigration Law*. London.

Henriques, H.S.Q. (1906) *The Law of Aliens and Naturalization*. London.

Holmes, C. (1978) *Immigrants and Minorities in British Society*. London.

Huttenback, R.A. (1916) *Racism and Empire: White Settlers and Coloured Immigrants in the British Self-Governing Colonies, 1830–1910*. Ithaca, NY.

Jones, C. (1977) *Immigration and Social Policy in Britain*. London.

Jones, K. and Smith, A. (1970) *The Economic Impact of Commonwealth Immigration*. Cambridge.

Jones, M. (1956) *British Nationality Law*. London.

Kadish, S.H. and Kadish, R. (1979) *Discretion to Disobey*. Stanford.

Landa, M.J. (1911) *The Alien Problem and Its Remedy*. London.

Landis, J. (1936) *The Administrative Process*. New Haven, CT.

Layton-Henry, Z. (1984) *The Politics of Race in Britain*. London.

Legomsky, S. (1987) *Immigration and the Judiciary*. Oxford.

Legomsky, S. (1992) *Immigration Law and Policy*. New York.

Lester, A. and Bindman, G. (1972) *Race and Law*. London.

Lustgarten, L. (1978) *Legal Control of Racial Discrimination*. London.

Macdonald, I. (1983) *Immigration Law and Practice in the UK*. London.

Macdonald, I. and Blake, N. (1991) *Immigration Law and Practice*. 3rd edn. London.

Oppenheim, L.V. (1955) *International Law*. London.

Palley, C. (1991) *The United Kingdom and Human Rights*. London.

Parry, C. (1957) *Nationality and Citizenship Laws of the Commonwealth and Ireland*. London.

Peach, C. (1968) *West Indian Migration to Britain*. Oxford.

(1981) *The Pivot of the System: A Briefing Paper on Immigration Appeals*. London.

Plender, R. (1972) *International Migration Law*. Leiden.

Ralston, J.H. (1926) *The Law and Procedure of International Tribunals*. Stanford, CA.

Rawls, J. (1972) *A Theory of Justice*. Oxford.

Rex, J. and Tomlinson, S. (1979) *Colonial Immigrants in a British City*. London.

Robertson, G. (1989) *Freedom, the Individual and the Law*. Harmondsworth.

Rose, E.J.B. (1969) *Colour and Citizenship*. Oxford.

Ruggiero, G. de (1927) (trans. by R.G. Collingwood) *A History of European Liberalism*. Oxford.

Sabine, G.H. and Thorson, T.L. (1973) *A History of Political Theory*. Hinsdale, IL.

Schwerzenberger, G. (1949) *International Law*. London.

Sibley, N.W. and Elias, A. (1906) *The Aliens Act and the Right of Asylum*. London.

Smith, T.E. (1981) *Commonwealth Migration*. London.

Steel, D. (1969) *No Entry*. London.

Storey, H. (1983) *Immigrants and the Welfare State*. London.

Turpin, C. (1990) *British Government and the Constitution*. London.

Vincenzi, C. and Marrington, D. (1992) *Immigration Law: The Rules Explained*. London.

Walvin, J. (1984) *Passage to Britain*. London.

Weis, P. (1979) *Nationality and Statelessness in International Law*. Leiden.

ARTICLES

Asimow, M. (1983) Delegated Legislation. *Oxford Journal of Legal Studies* 3, pp. 258–61.

Baldwin, R. (1990) Why Rules Don't Work. *Modern Law Review* pp. 321–37.

Baldwin, R. and Hawkins, K. (1984) Discretionary Justice – Davis Reconsidered, *Public Law* pp. 570–79.

Baldwin, R. and Houghton, J. (1986) Circular Arguments: The Status and Legitimacy of Administrative Rules. *Public Law* p. 239.

Beatson, J. (1979) Legislative Control of Administrative Rule-Making: Lessons from the British Experience. *Cornell International Law Journal* 12, pp. 258–61.

Beatson, J. (1981) A British View of Vermont Yankee. *Tulane Law Review* 55, p. 435.

Ben-Tovim, G. and Gabriel, J. (1979) The Sociology of Race: Time to Change Course. *The Science Teacher* 8 (4), pp. 143–71.

Blake, C. (1983) *Immigration Appeals – The Need for Reform*, AGIN (unpublished).

Calavitta, K. (1989) The Contradictions of Immigration Lawmaking: The Immigration Reform and Control Act of 1986. *Law and Policy* 11(1), pp. 17–47.

Lord Campbell of Alloway (1985) Codes of Practice as an Alternative to Legislation. *Statute Law Review* 6, pp. 127–32.

Del Rey, A.J. and Fragomen, A.T. (1979) The Immigration Selection System: A Proposal for Reform. *San Diego Law Review* 17(1), pp. 1–36.

Diver, C.S. (1983) The Optimal Precision of Administrative Rules. *Yale Law Journal* 93, p. 65.

Drabble, R. and Lynes, T. (1989) The Social Fund: Discretion or Control? *Public Law* pp. 297–322.

Dummett, M. and Dummett, A. (1982) The Role of Government in Britain's Racial Crisis. In *Race in Britain* (ed. by C. Husband), pp. 97–127. London.

Duyssens, D. (1977) Migrant Workers from Third Countries in the European Community. *Common Market Law Review* 14, pp. 501–20.

Edmonds, J. and Behrens, R. (1981) Kippers, Kittens and Kipper-boxes: Conservative Populists and Race Relations. *Political Quarterly* 52, pp. 342–8.

Evans, A.C. (1982) European Citizenship. *Modern Law Review* 45, pp. 499–515.

Fragomen, A.T. and Del Rey, A.J. (1979) The Immigration Selection System: A Proposal for Reform. *San Diego Law Review* 17(1), pp. 1–36.

Freeman, M.D.A. and Spencer, S. (1979) Immigration Control, Black Workers and the Economy. *British Journal of Law and Society* 6, pp. 53–81.

Garrard, J.A. (1968) Parallels of Protest: English Reactions to Jewish and Commonwealth Immigration. *RACE* 9, pp. 47–64.

Gilbey, J.A. (1991) Deciding Who Gets In: Decision-making by Immigration Inspectors. *Law and Society Review* 25, pp. 571–99.

Hamelfarb, S. (1980) Consensus in Committee: The Cases of the Select Committee on Race Relations and Immigration. *Parliamentary Affairs* 33, pp. 54–78.

Hutton, J. (1986) Legal Education and the Law of Immigration and Nationality. In *Towards a Just Immigration Policy* (ed. by Ann Dummett), pp. 211–13, London.

Layton-Henry, Z. (1978) Race, Electoral Strategy, and the Major Parties. *Parliamentary Affairs* 31, pp. 268–81.

Layton-Henry, Z. (1979) The Report in Immigration. *Political Quarterly* 50, pp. 241–48.

Hepple, B.A. (1971) Aliens and Administrative Justice: The Dutschke Case. *Modern Law Review* 34, pp. 501–19.

Jenkins, J. (1984) The Middle-Class Vote. *New Statesman* 30 November 1984, p. 17.

Juss, S. (1986) Judicial Review and the Duty to Give Adequate Reasons. *Cambridge Law Journal*, November, p. 372.

Juss, S. (1988) Time for Parliament to Stop Playing the Numbers Game. *The Independent* 2 April 1988.

Juss, S. (1988) Family Life, the Courts and Section 1(5) of the Immigration Act 1971. *Family Law*, April, p. 145.

Juss, S. (1991) Practice and Procedure in Immigration Appeals. *Litigation* 11(2), pp. 70–4.

Juss, S. (1992) Rule-Making and the Immigration Rules. A Retreat from Law? *Statute Law Review* 13(2), pp. 211–26.

Juss, S. (1992) Public Policy and the Enforcement of Contracts of Employment. *Industrial Law Journal* 21(4), pp. 301–4.

Lauterpacht, H. (1945) Allegiance, Diplomatic Protection and Criminal Jurisdiction over Aliens. *Cambridge Law Journal* 9, pp. 330–46.

Leigh, S. (1983) Family Settlement Problems AGIN (unpublished).

McCrudden, C. (1988) Codes in a Cold Climate: Administrative Rule-Making by the Commission for Racial Equality. *Modern Law Review* 51, p. 409.

Marrington, D.K. (1987) Commitment and Contradiction in Immigration Law. *Legal Studies* 7, pp. 272–91.

Marshall, G. (1992) Ministerial Responsibility, the Home Office and Mr Baker. *Public Law* pp. 7–12.

Motomura, H. (1990) Immigration Law after a Century of Plenary Power: Constitutional Norms and Statutory Interpretation. *Yale Law Journal* 3, pp. 545–613.

Mullard, C. (1976) Racism in Britain: Management of Concepts,

1948–1975. *Case Studies in Human Rights and Fundamental Freedoms*. The Hague.

Norton, P. (1976) Intra-party Dissent in the House of Commons: A Case Study. The Immigration Rules 1972. *Parliamentary Affairs* 29, pp. 404–17.

Peiris, G.L. (1988) Judicial Review and Immigration Policy: Emerging Trends. *Legal Studies* 8, pp. 201–28.

Qureshi, S. (1988) Opening the Floodgates? Eligibility for Asylum in the USA and the UK. *Anglo-American Law Review* 17, pp. 83–107.

Rees, T. (1982) Immigration Policies in the UK. *Race in Britain* (ed. by C. Husband), pp. 75–95. London.

Roberts, M.A. (1980) A Specialized Statutory Immigration Court. *San Diego Law Review* 18(1), pp. 1–20.

Rose, H. (1973) The Politics of Immigration after the 1971 Act. *Political Quarterly* 44.

Rose, H. (1973) The Immigration Act 1971: A Case Study in the Work of Parliament. *Parliamentary Affairs* 26, pp. 69–91.

Scannell, R. (1992) Primary Purpose: The Shift in Judicial Sympathy. *Immigration and Nationality Law and Practice* 11, pp. 3–6.

Schuck, P. (1984) The Transformation of Immigration Law. *Columbia Law Review* 84, pp. 1–90.

Shapiro, D.S. (1965) The Choice of Rulemaking or Adjudication in the Development of Administrative Policy. *Harvard Law Review* 78, p. 921.

Storey, H. (1984) United Kingdom Immigration Control and the Welfare State. *Journal of Social and Welfare Law*, January, pp. 14–18.

Thornberry, C. (1963) Dr Soblen and the Alien Law of the United Kingdom. *International and Comparative Law Journal* 12, p. 414.

Vincenzi, C. (1985) Aliens and the Judicial Review of Immigration Law. *Public Law* pp. 93–114.

Vincenzi, C. (1992) Extra-statutory Ministerial Discretion in Immigration Law. *Public Law* pp. 300–21.

White, R. and Hampson, F.J. (1982) The British Nationality Act 1981. *Public Law* pp. 6–20.

Williams, G. (1950) The Correlation of Allegiance and Protection. *Cambridge Law Journal* 10, pp. 54–68.

REPORTS AND GOVERNMENT DOCUMENTS

(1843) *Report on the Laws Affecting Aliens*. HC 307.

(1869) *Royal Commission on the Laws of Nationalisation and Allegiance*. Cmnd 4109.

(1903) *Royal Commission on Alien Immigration*. Cmnd 1742.

(1906) *Immigration Regulations*. Cmnd 2879.

(1910) *Committee on Distressed Colonial and Indian Subjects*. Cmnd 5134.

(1920) *Aliens Order*. SI 448.

(1953) *Aliens Order*. SI 1671.

(1965) *Immigration from the Commonwealth*. Cmnd 2379.

(1967) *Report of the Committee on Immigration Appeals* (the Wilson Committee). Cmnd 3387.

(1969–70) *Report of the Select Committee on Race Relations and Immigration on Control of Commonwealth Immigration*. HC 17.

(1969–70) *Select Committee on Race Relations and Immigration* (Control of Commonwealth Citizens). HC 205-I, II.

(1970) *Statement of Changes in Immigration Rules for Control on Entry* (Commonwealth Citizens). Cmnd 4298.

(1970) *Statement of Changes in Immigration Rules for Control on Entry* (Non-Commonwealth Citizens). Cmnd 4296.

(1970) *Statement of Changes in Immigration Rules for After Entry* (Commonwealth Citizens). Cmnd 4295.

(1970) *Statement of Changes in Immigration Rules for Control After Entry* (Non-Commonwealth Citizens). Cmnd 4297.

(1973) *Statement of Immigration Rules for Control on Entry* (Commonwealth Citizens). HC 79.

(1973) *Statement of Immigrations Rules for Control on Entry* (Non-Commonwealth Citizens). HC 81.

(1973) *Statement of Immigration Rules for Control After Entry* (Commonwealth Citizens). HC 80.

(1973) *Statement of Immigration Rules for Control After Entry* (Non-Commonwealth Citizens). HC 82.

(1977) *Report of the Parliamentary Committee on the Feasibility and usefulness of a Register of Dependants*. Cmnd 6698.

(1977) *British Nationality Law: Discussion of Possible Changes*. Cmnd 6795.

(1977–78) *First Report of the Select Committee on Race Relations and Immigration*. HC 303, I and II.

(1979) *First Report of the Home Affairs Committee: Proposed New Immigration Rules and the European Convention on Human Rights*. HC 434.

(1980) *Statement of Changes in Immigration Rules*. HC 394.

(1980) *British Nationality Law: Outline of Proposed Legislation*. Cmnd 7987.

(1981) *Second Report of the Home Affairs Committee: Numbers and Legal Status of Future British Overseas Citizens without Other Citizenship*. HC 158.

(1982) *Proposals for Changes in the Immigration Rules*. Cmnd 8683.

(1982) *Revised Changes in the Immigration Rules*. HC 66.

(1982) *Fifth Report from the Home Affairs Committee: Immigration from the Indian Sub-Continent*. HC 90-I and II.

(1982–83) *British Nationality Fees*. HC 248.

(1983) *Statement of Changes in Immigration Rules*. HC 169.

(1984) *Immigration Appeals (Notices) Rules*. SI No. 2040.

(1984) *Immigration Appeals (Procedure) Rules*. SI No. 2041.

(1984–85) *The Immigration and Nationality Department of the Home Office*. HC 277.

(1985) *Report of a Formal Investigation: Immigration Control Procedures*. Commission for Racial Equality.

(1985) *Statement of Changes in Immigration Rules*. HC 293.

(1985) *Statement of Changes in Immigration Rules*. Cmnd 9539.

(1989) *Statement of Changes in Immigration Rules*. HC 388.

(1989–90) Fifth Report of the Home Affairs Committee: Administrative Delays in the Immigration and Nationality Department. HC 319.

(1990) *Statement of Changes in Immigration Rules*. HC 251. (As amended on 26 March 1991 by HC 320, 17 April 1991 by HC 356, 30 September 1991 by Cm 1672, 18 October 1991 by HC 670, 21 January 1992 by HC 175, 10 June 1992 by HC 49, and 5 November 1992 by HC 251.)

(1990–91) *Statement of Changes in Immigration Rules*. HC 670.

(1990–91) *Statement of Changes in Immigration Rules*. Cm 1672.

(1991–92) *Home Affairs Committee: Migration Control at External Borders of the European Community*. HC 215-I, II and III.

(1992) *Income: Pensions, Earnings and Savings in the Third Age*. Folkestone: Bailey Management Services.

(1992) *Employment: The Role of Work in the Third Age*. Folkestone: Bailey Management Services.

(1993) *Statement of Changes in Immigration Rules*. HC 725.

(1993) *Asylum Appeals (Procedure) Rules*. SI 1661.

(1993) *Immigration Appeals (Procedure) (Amendment) Rules*. SI 1662.

Index

189